BECOMING A PERSON
IN THE WHOLE CHRIST

Becoming a Person in the Whole Christ

by Edwin M. McMahon, S.J.
and Peter A. Campbell, S.J.

Sheed and Ward: New York

© *Sheed and Ward Inc., 1967*

Library of Congress Catalog Card Number 67–13768

Imprimi potest:
    John F. X. Connolly, S.J.
    September 30, 1966

Nihil obstat:
    Thomas J. Beary
    Censor Librorum

Imprimatur:
    † Robert F. Joyce
    Bishop of Burlington
    January 24, 1967

The Nihil obstat and Imprimatur are official declarations that a book or pamphlet is considered to be free of doctrinal or moral error. No implication is contained therein that those who have granted the Nihil obstat and Imprimatur agree with the contents, opinions or statements expressed.

Manufactured in the United States of America

*To the Alma College Faculty
and all those,
especially the Sisters we have taught,
whose lives in the Whole Christ
made it possible for us to write this book*

Foreword

WHEN ATTEMPTING synthetically to treat a subject as comprehensive as the one suggested by the title of this book, the writer is always faced with the dilemma of either being so global as to sound superficial or of entering into each idea with such thoroughness that the end-result is encyclopedic, and the average reader loses heart before he has even begun.

What we have therefore tried to do in the first part of this book is to take an over-all view of the important themes and ideas that we feel must be seen by the reader in their entirety and relationship to one another. Since this initial picture is not intended as an in-depth treatment, the reader will be left with many loose ends and unanswered questions as he finishes Part I.

In each of the remaining three parts of the book, we have tried to deepen the total picture by successively bringing back threads of the previous development and weaving them into a more integrated and clearly refined design. Hopefully, at each new return to the original themes, this manner of presentation will bring out a little more of the richness that is contained in them.

The purpose of this approach is to give the reader an opportunity to begin filling in the gaps with his own experience, to jump ahead and see further possible relationships, and to flesh out the initial outline with his own experiences in order to attempt a more personal synthesis. In a sense, therefore, we intend that the reader's personal reflections upon his own experience should be integrated with the ideas presented in this book. As we penetrate a bit deeper in each of our successively concentric returns, the reader should be able to synthesize more critically in terms of his own experience. He should, in other words, find that these new insights already have a personal "ground" of reflective thought for him.

This book is, then, not intended to be read for ideas alone. It should be reflected upon slowly, using the thoughts presented as a springboard to a further personal development, which hopefully will go far beyond what is contained in these pages. If this book serves as a catalyst to help each reader prayerfully to examine and re-evaluate what he feels is worthy of his efforts at renewal, then it will have been relevant to his growth in "becoming a person in the Whole Christ."

These pages are not meant to be read quickly in order to obtain some new capsule answers to personal problems or the lifetime task of growth. They are written for a kind of personal meditation, perhaps a section at a time, and they return to a new or old idea as the need for this spontaneously arises. This may seem strange to many readers who might be accustomed to having a traditional meditation book for such discursive prayer. But the authors feel that if this book is read merely at the intellectual level, as we are habituated to do with most idea books, and not "chewed over" and personalized with some thoughtful experimentation in terms of those non-intellectual ways of knowing and living that form the bulk of our daily life, then the reader will have missed the experience that these pages are intended to open for him.

Unfortunately, the printed word cannot adequately communicate or provide the kind of experiential setting that helps lead the reader in ways of "opening out" and listening with his whole "body-person" to the presence of the Whole Christ. This is more readily accomplished in the workshop-retreats the authors have given. Nevertheless, the reader who has some familiarity with what is discussed here, and who brings to his reading that capacity for listening which so characterizes any truly religious person, can, we believe, find something in the following pages that will provide a new intensity to his lifelong task of becoming a person in the Whole Christ.

This book will probably be misinterpreted, like any book that tries to convey personal meaning in abstract words. One of the built-in weaknesses of the printed word or the verbal symbol is that it can never fully convey to each reader the exact meaning that the author intended when he wrote it. Each of us associates many affective overtones with words because we came to recognize and learn them in concrete life-experiences. Therefore, when these same words are again brought before us, even though in an entirely different context from the one in which we learned them, we are often unable fully to comprehend the meaning of the speaker or writer because of our past associations with this word or phrase. At best, if our experience of a word has been only slightly colored by our past history, it is quite possible that we may then lose only the more subtle overtones and implications that the author intends to convey.

At a time when tensions mount because we are unable to remain indifferent to the forces of change, when we are compelled to take a stand because the issues at stake strike at the very heart of our personal lives, it is especially important for each reader of a book such as this to be alert and honest about what is *personally* brought to such a reading. As an example, it has been the authors' experience that the enthusiasm and outspokenness of many young people in the Church today has often alienated many older persons who do not share the same feelings. This has happened to such an extent that if in writing or speaking one uses the more existential and personalist-oriented language of the young, affective overtones may so color the receptivity of older people that they reject what might be quite acceptable and meaningful insights.

Words like *encounter, relevant, meaningful experience,* and even *charity* can be loaded expressions, depending on who uses them. Also, those who have not lived long enough with the words of a more traditional vocabulary (e.g., *mortification, detachment, indifference, silence*), can tend to "color them black" whenever they appear in conversation or in print. Frequently the young have not had time to discern the true reality underlying these terms, which only the experience of life itself can gradually bring to the surface of consciousness.

Throughout this book, our vocabulary will include many of

these old and new words, as well as a number of expressions that we have developed ourselves in order to communicate a verbal description of a personal experience of the presence of God. A Glossary has been added at the end of this Foreword to acquaint the reader with the specific meaning we attribute to some of the more important terms and phrases used.

A point we wish to stress is that any real renewal is under the guidance of the Spirit and takes place within the whole movement of an ever-deeper penetration into the mystery of Christ, which the tradition of the Church has always sought to reveal to man regardless of the limitations imposed by language and the modes of expression that are historically conditioned by time and culture and that are, of necessity, subject to change.

This is the lesson of history. What is relevant and helps bring us closer to the reality of Christ in our lives today must be sought and used, especially to help the young. This may mean breaking with many old forms, but even this must become a value. We have lived with centuries of relative stability in the essentials of Christian life as well as in many of the more nonessential customs, traditions, and pious practices that inevitably arise in religious groups and parish life. But now we are faced with the phenomenon of rapid external change not merely as a period of transition, but as a way of life in itself.

We must learn to structure change into our very lives and spirituality, not from the standpoint of change for change's sake, but because of the truth that man's very vocation to become a person in Christ is a dynamic relationship that he *grows into*. His very Christianity is, at root, a becoming.

Throughout the pages of this book we will occasionally refer to the Vatican Council's *Decree on the Appropriate Renewal of the Religious Life,* and many of our examples will be specifically directed to religious communities. We do not, however, intend that these reflections on personal growth in the Whole Christ should be restricted in their application to the priest, Sister, or Brother. Obviously, becoming a person in the Whole Christ is the task of every Christian. The life of Christ has made all things new and was meant to be shared by all. If our examples stress the religious life, it is because this is the source of much of the authors' own personal experience of Christian life, and it will inevitably color what we say.

There is one final pre-note that we must make. Throughout the following pages, our emphasis will primarily be upon the faith-experience of God's presence within our interpersonal relationships. We have not attempted to discuss the question of the Eucharistic presence in any great detail. Some may feel that this leaves a gap in our presentation, since they may be accustomed to think of the presence of Christ primarily in terms of the Eucharist. However, we must always remember that, in the existential order, we cannot consider the Eucharistic presence *apart from* the believing Christian community. *We cannot live with the Eucharist in isolation.* In our life of worship it is the "Eucharist-in-the-believing-community" that is the total sign of God's presence. This does not in any way detract from the great mystery of the true, real, and substantial presence of Christ in the Eucharist. It merely points out that the Eucharistic Celebration is always performed by an official minister *within* the ecclesial community, and that the faith, hope, and charity of the Church is an integral part of the "total sign" of the Eucharistic Presence. The faith-response of the community gathered in worship does not "effect" the presence of Christ in the Eucharist. This is done by the will of Christ acting through His ordained minister. But if we are to open ourselves in faith to the mystery that is at the heart of our cultic celebration, we must be aware of the dimension that our participation in the *community* of Christ's *agape* effects in us. It is this aspect of Christ's presence that must be explored in greater depth, and this, indeed, forms the subject matter of this book. We always bring our daily experience to the Eucharistic Celebration, which is really a celebration of life—His life growing within us. We, together with our brothers and sisters in the Lord, *are His Body,* and His Eucharistic Presence continually effects our growing unity with one another and our deeper identification with Him as we share in the life of His Spirit and are united with the Father.

We wish to thank all those who have helped us with their

prayerful encouragement and to express our gratitude to Mrs. Olga Powers and Mrs. Lucille Cano for the care they exercised in typing our final manuscript.

Alma College
Los Gatos, California
June, 1966

Contents

Glossary

AGAPE: A New Testament word describing the early Christian community's experience of the divine self-gift of God's own life of total, selfless, personal love; a love that continues to be incarnated within the Christian community today through the Whole Christ in the Spirit.

PERSON: From the outset the reader should understand our use of the word person. We mean a human being capable of leading a basically "other-centered" life with constancy, through listening and responding selflessly to the real needs of others. A fuller Christian development of this word will gradually evolve in the text.

BODY-PERSON: We use this hyphenated expression to emphasize the unity of man as incarnate-spirit.

SACRAMENTAL: We do not restrict the meaning of this word to the administration of the seven sacraments or to the use of the "sacramentals." A more extensive development of our understanding of this term will follow in the text.

THE WHOLE CHRIST: A phrase used to describe the continuing body-personal union of the risen, glorified Lord with His members into One Being.

PART I

THREE

1. Interpersonal Life and the Presence of God

MANY BOOKS have recently been written on the psychology of religious life and the psychological problems that can arise within religious communities. Excellent though most of these works are, we do not intend this book to be another of the same genre, because we feel that there is now a need to attempt going one step further. The first dim lines of an emerging synthesis are gradually beginning to appear in the complex data pouring in from theologians, Scripture scholars, psychologists, and sociologists. The area that urgently demands our united attention and research is an exploration of the precise relationship existing between the social and interpersonal dynamics of human self-realization and God's self-communication to man in his growth as a human person. Father E. Schillebeeckx, O.P., has succinctly stated the problem:

It is symptomatic that in the Western world, in which the Church has been rooted for centuries, the mass of the people no longer see or hear its witness. It is so easy simply to pass Christianity by. Hence in one way or another the witness, the telling visibility of the grace of Christ, is kept hidden. Yet it cannot be said that the level of the Church's holiness has fallen. There are, therefore, only two possible explanations: Either human encounter is no longer made use of as the effective sacrament of our love of God, and Christians sanctify themselves in their own little corner without having any contact with the rest of the world, or where new methods of approach in apostolic work have re-established a living contact with men, this human encounter is not sufficiently an interpretation of an inward encounter with God, a sacrament of divine love, but merely a new kind of convert propaganda.[1]

Today there is much confusion among Christians about the manner of God's presence in the world, particularly within the mystery of interpersonal relationships. Possibly this is because an inherited tradition of implicit Gnosticism pervades the interpersonal relationships of Christians and renders their redemptive potential ineffective.

Interpersonal relationships are often looked upon as largely something of a proving ground or a testing program where we receive a passing or failing score that is our ticket to heaven. We frequently fail to see these relationships as a here-and-now participation in divine life that truly brings Christ's redemption into the existential present of human encounter.

Interpersonal communications, the visible experiential avenue expressing human needs, have too often been relegated to the profane and not recognized as a crucial avenue of divine revelation along with Holy Scripture, Tradition, and the sacramental life of the Church. We may pay intellectual lip service to the truth that interpersonal communication is a visible expression of the Body of Christ, but experiencing it within our lives is an entirely different story.

Moreover, we often respond to the needs of men from the standpoint of duty, of a vague humanitarianism, or, within a more Christian framework, as somehow related to Christ and His commandment to love the neighbor. These human needs are not recognized as effective material signs that contain the sanctifying potential of Christ Himself when they are seen and responded to in faith. When the needs of another person are not received in faith as the needs of the Whole Christ, the sacrament of encounter with God, then Christian life, which is largely a continuum of

[1] Edward Schillebeeckx, O.P., *Christ the Sacrament of Encounter with God*, New York, Sheed and Ward, 1963, p. 257.

levels of interpersonal communication, cannot be personally understood and lived out in our day-to-day life as a sacrament of the encounter with God.

Not only are the interpersonal needs of others sacramental in the sense that they are a potentially efficacious sign of Christ's presence, but our response to these needs (if it is truly effective, that is, selfless) is also sacramental. Our response is sacramental in the sense that it can effect the transformation of the needer. If this healing interpersonal encounter is seen by either giver, or receiver, or both through the eyes of faith, it can become a conscious encounter with Christ. The transformation then not only moves in the direction of personal wholeness, toward development of the capacity for self-gift, but it also becomes a transformation into Christ, into the holiness of *agape* (perfect selflessness). This mode of encounter with Christ can then become an increasingly free choice, a deeper existential commitment, and more humanly mature way of life for the Christian.

We do not understand the sign value of human experience, of human needs, and of the interpersonal communication that renders them visible in the shared experiential world of human dialogue. These signs are not comprehended as God's personal self-revelation in and through these same human actions, thought patterns, feelings, words, and gestures. What has been lost sight of in Christian asceticism is that "For all men, encounters with their fellow men are the sacrament of encounter with God."[2] These signs are ways of communicating and expressing relatedness. They are modes of interpersonal encounter. The psychological and theological dimensions of this inter-relatedness and communication must be developed and spelled out in a spirituality that is truly incarnational and open to growth in an interpersonal relationship with the Whole Christ.

This is particularly true today when man's needs in an affluent society have increasingly evolved to a level in which food, clothing, and shelter are not the only cravings within his developing self-consciousness of what it means to be fulfilled as a human

---

[2] *Ibid.*, p. 256.

person. The needs of men today have evolved to include much more subtle levels of psychic aspiration for personal fulfillment and realization. These are largely interpersonal needs whose visible expression cannot be contained or answered by abstractions, philosophical concepts, or naïve idealizations. They can be satisfied only in the concretely experienced and personally realized sacramental gift-communication of his fellow man—a gift which, in fact, has been caught up in God's own revelation and communication of Himself to man in and through Christ's humanity. This communication and revelation continue today within our life-chapter of Salvation History in and through the Whole Christ.

In the past, when answering the more obvious material needs of men, our response was often so absorbed in this demanding task that the deeper levels of interpersonal communication were not recognized. Consequently, they did not always receive our care and thoughtful reflection. Attention was focused on bandaging the wound and filling the empty stomach. Today, in every affluent society where sizable segments of the population have these physical needs largely cared for (despite obvious areas of poverty and inequality), we are, it seems, becoming more aware of our human, psychic needs. Thus, there has arisen a sensitivity to new dimensions of personal fulfillment characterized by the more subtle levels of interpersonal encounter, levels that are truly more spiritual and specifically human than biological and physiological needs.

The effective material signs of interpersonal relatedness that truly effect the transformation of man must be brought into the communication of the Good News, so that Christ's Continuing Incarnation may then be preached at those deeper levels of becoming a person. Thus men may find the Whole Christ, Christ totally other yet immanent as a living presence at the core of their struggle for human freedom and their evolution toward integration and self-realization. This presence must not only be a truth intellectually acknowledged by the Christian believer but also a psychologically realizable experience within the framework of man's human potential for knowledge. Yet, in order for that experience to be responded to in faith as the presence of the living God,

Emmanuel, we are always dependent upon the gratuitous gift of this same faith.

By uniting Christ's transcendence and incarnation within the unity of his own human person, the Christian would extend the power of *agape* into the lives of others through his interpersonal communication with them, diminishing the kind of "transcendental" presence that has done so much to make God seem irrelevant in modern man's experience. This tangential presence to the world of many Christians has largely grown out of a rather subtle escape, in the name of Christianity, from the incarnational experience by those who, nevertheless remain in the midst of the world. Under the religious pretext that "they are not of this world," they have, in fact, really removed themselves from being in the world. Or as Péguy would describe them, "because they loved no one, thought they loved God."

The Christian's own "worldly" experience of faith, his own deepening commitment to the Whole Christ within the process of his personal integration into the family of man, will gradually cause the false dichotomy between God and the world to disappear. God is truly "Other," but His presence to man is normally through matter, through the incarnational way of knowing that is natural to man. The absolute dichotomy between God and man is within the order of existence, within the fundamental difference between the Creator and the created. It is not within the order of the "presence" of the Creator *to* the created. Here God has chosen to speak with us in our own language, through the "common" in human life, most especially through man's daily interpersonal communion with his fellow man.

By thus uniting the transcendence and immanence of Christ within his own personal presence to all of reality, the Christian's interpersonal communication becomes the effective material sign, the sacramental presence of the Lord Jesus whose resurrected and glorified presence to the Father continues to reveal itself to men through both the *agape* actions and the expressed needs of human interpersonal relationships.

Both the psychological and the theological literature up to this point has recognized that there is somehow a connection between man's growth in interpersonal relationships through life-experience and his capacity to relate to God. The interconnection, however, has always been developed with a kind of basic split between human life-experience here below and God "out there."

For example, if my relationship with my human father was not a warm and accepting relationship, then I find it difficult to discover and relate to God the Father as warm and accepting. I transfer the human experience to my relations with an unexperienced God. Ultimately, I project my experiences with an earthly father onto God, and end by relating to Him as I do to my own parent. This type of analysis is good insofar as it gives me some insight into the psychological mechanisms which come into play when I hear God described as "Father," but it tells me nothing about the possibility of discovering God in the interpersonal relationship with both my human father as well as other members of the family of man.

What we hope to discuss in this book is an incarnational insight based on an understanding of God's self-communication to man in and through the Incarnation, in and through the person of the Whole Christ. Our capacity to enter into interpersonal life with the Whole Christ makes it possible for us to enter into the experience of a personal dialogue with God the Father and the Spirit. The Whole Christ involves the human, because the members of the Body of Christ are joined and made one with Him. This united Being is the Whole Christ. It is unnecessary either to speak of or develop our relationship with the members of Christ as somehow separated from or simply analogously related to the person of Christ.

In what sense has the former psychological literature not integrated human interpersonal relationships and the divine-human interpersonal relationship as anything other than analogously joined? Christian authors who have had clinical experience in psychology have glimpsed an insight showing a parallel between man's relationship to God and man's relationship to man. They have discovered that, for example, the person who has had an unfortunate background and fragmented early childhood manifested many of these same symptoms in his ideas about God and his personal relationship with Him. Naturally the authors drew the interconnection between the two, most probably from clinical data more than from anything else. Possibly the Catholic psychologists then went further. After having studied the data of psychology concerning man's emotional maturity and his ability to integrate into society, they took the religious life or the priesthood, primarily in terms of its social functions and effectiveness in apostolic service, and developed the cause-and-effect relationship between the two. The person who was not able to give himself, unable to integrate himself, could not live peacefully and efficiently in a religious community with other people. This conclusion was a rather extrinsic yet nevertheless necessary development of the truth of man's dependence upon psychic growth for his adjustment in the priesthood or religious community. But the material written by some authors dealing with the question of emotional maturity for the religious is fundamentally developed in terms of the emotional maturity of *any* human being. These authors have not really plumbed the depths of the unity that is contained in becoming a mature *Christian* person.

Some recent theologians have begun to develop a deeper and more unified view; namely, that a mature Christian person must be described as one who is selfless and integrated socially precisely because of his conscious awareness in faith of the Trinitarian presence—Three Divine Persons in his interpersonal life. However, this still does not provide us with anything more than a statement of fact, whereas what we are dealing with is an evolving life-experience, a dynamic vocation to be realized in each person's own unique historical growth. It is precisely this growth process, this relatedness that must be explored. What we will reflect on in this book is the relationship between human growth and growth in Christ, and our experientially heightened consciousness of this dynamic process. Hopefully, this twofold development will point toward the unity that is our "becoming a person in the Whole Christ."

We have first discussed the distinction between what we are doing and what has been found in previous psychological literature. The theological point that we wish to make, following contemporary theologians who have more fully developed the meaning of *agape* and of the Whole Christ in their biblical research, is that when we say our encounter with mankind *is* our encounter with the Whole Christ, or that in seeing man we behold Christ as somehow identified with our neighbor, we are speaking of a relationship, of a dialogue, of a communication. This communication involves the mystery of Christ somehow present in my neighbor, myself, and the relatedness between the two. This divine presence is effected on the human, horizontal level and is made visible to me in the physical, concrete, material signs of myself as related at the body-person level of existence. My dialogue is in words. My communication is through expression, touch, sound, and gesture.

We must first explore the fact of the relationship, but for an ascetical theology and spirituality that can be lived, the relationship must also be examined from the standpoint of increased awareness of what it is to be a "becoming person." With this heightened sensitivity as a background, we must then seek through Scripture the reality of the divine presence that is "contained" within the "becoming process." "Becoming a person" is, in fact, "becoming a person in the Whole Christ."

The very title of our book provides a clue to what we are attempting to describe. *Becoming a Person in the Whole Christ* tries not to restrict the mystery of God's incarnational communication. It does not separate the transcendent divine from the human Incarnation in which we meet and become aware of It. Our stress is that in the very relatedness with one another wherein we receive our self-identity through the gift of selfless love, through responding to one another's needs through self-sacrificing generosity, we discover an experience of transcendence-incarnated and discover ourselves in the Whole Christ.

We are building on the new insights of Scripture studies in order to develop a deeper understanding of Revelation and the manner in which God communicates Himself to man. At the same time we are examining man's increased sensitivity to his own nature, to what it means to be a man, to be human. We are trying to show that these two approaches converge in human, interpersonal growth. Man is saved by becoming more a man and by sustaining and developing his truly human potential. Moreover, God does not communicate and give Himself to mankind apart from the values to which twentieth-century man is growing ever more sensitive. These two approaches, the psychological and the theological, converge precisely at the point where man fulfills his vocation to become human through living out and accepting his call to grow in the capacity for interpersonal life. Only in this way can God become relevant in what means most to men of today. We must be able to discover the very values that we seek in freedom, creativity, interpersonal life, union, and world brotherhood as values that are found precisely in Christ.

When modern man opens himself to God through Christ, he will really be able to achieve the very goals that he yearns for and is most sensitive to. This makes his relation to God extremely relevant, since it is at the heart of growth into what today are seen as desirable secular and humanistic advantages. However, men cannot realize these genuinely human values apart from God.

Scripture studies are making it clear that our union with God is an interpersonal relationship within our relatedness to one another in the Whole Christ. God's own divine life, which is the life of the Trinity, is shared with us, given in the person of the Holy Spirit who is mediated to us through the Bodily expressions of need and love in the Whole Christ. When these sensitivities have been explored and brought to consciousness, through the Church's ever-deepening penetration of the mystery of God's divine self-revelation, then, with a corresponding sensitivity to what it means to become a man developing within the humanistic sciences, we begin to see the convergence of these two approaches. They point in the direction of "personal relationship" as being at the center of our conscious response to and discovery of God. The capacity for human relatedness and becoming a person is at the core of Christian life. Our fundamental relationship to God is in the area of our interpersonal life and that area is an intrinsic part of becoming fully human.

We have always had the problem of discovering the invisible God within our life experience in the things we can touch, taste, and smell, in the things that reveal themselves, that brush against and come into contact with us. This is why the invisible God had to be imaged, why the Word had to become flesh in the person of Christ.

The Word is now fleshed in the Church, the People of God, the Body of the Whole Christ. In other words, there is only one Person, Christ, but we discover Him as the Whole Christ. We cannot discover the transcendent Lord apart from His embodiment to us which is the People of God, the Church, and we must remember that the Council Fathers at Vatican II have extended our understanding of the "Church" beyond some of the more familiar borders with which we have been accustomed. While saying that the Church of Christ *subsists* in the Catholic Church, they have also added that there are numerous elements of both truth and sanctification outside of her visible structure which are gifts belonging to the Church of Christ. It is thus only within the living, loving, needing context of the family of man as the People of God that we can truly discover Christ.

Whenever we speak of Christ as transcendent and immanent, the very words lend themselves to misinterpretation where our relatedness to Christ is concerned. We run the ascetical risk of attempting *first* to establish a relationship with the transcendent Christ and only then going out to other people. I withdraw in order to "establish" a relationship rather than to deepen one that was already a part of my life, even though I may have been only dimly aware of it.

Our point is that we cannot help people to discover Christ by separating them from the Body of Christ, separating them from the needs of Christ, from the transcendent, risen, glorified Lord as He presents Himself to human beings in and through His Body. We cannot develop a relationship with the transcendent Lord first and *then* work it out in terms of our love of neighbor. We cannot discover the invisible God apart from His visible embodiment to us. The transcendent Lord in this economy of salvation as He reveals God to us is the Lord Jesus, the Christ who is here present, who is the Second Person and who identifies Himself with the members of His Body. "Truly, I say to you, as you did it to one

of the least of these my brethren, you did it to me" (Mt. 25:40*).
The transcendent Lord is revealed to us precisely as immanent. It
is our lived experience in faith with the Whole Christ that fuses
His transcendence and immanence into the unity of a single Person who is both God and man for us.

SEARCHING FOR IDENTITY WITHIN THE RELIGIOUS COMMUNITY

The Second Vatican Council explicitly discusses the question
of religious orders and congregations in two major documents.
Chapter VI of the *Dogmatic Constitution on the Church* treats
the religious life and evangelical counsels as one manifestation
among many of the universal call to holiness that is addressed to
the People of God. Religious dedicate themselves through their
vows to a life of self-sacrificing love and service to the Body of
Christ, seeking to reveal Him through the selfless love and public
commitment that is manifested in their apostolically active or contemplative way of life. The *Decree on the Appropriate Renewal
of the Religious Life* lays down general norms for the many
religious families that are attempting to bring themselves, their
particular spirit, and their apostolic work into greater harmony
with the contemporary needs of the Body of Christ.

Renewal within religious communities of the Roman Catholic
Church has reached a point where quite a few members are experiencing what might be called an identity crisis. Many religious
have come to realize that the present forms of communal existence
and particularized apostolic work are not, in themselves, enough
to give that radical source of identification and meaningful self-
concept that a human being requires, if he or she is to pursue this
way of life fruitfully.

By fruitful we mean the *effective* witness to the theological truth
of their vocation as a special gift of God. For this witness to be

* RSV: *The Holy Bible, Revised Standard Version* (New York, Nelson,
1953). Copyright 1946 and 1952 by the Division of Christian Education of
the National Council of the Churches of Christ in the U.S.A. and used
by permission.

effective it must include the human efficiency that a mature and integrated self-identity would bring to an apostolic service of the People of God. It should also give evidence that this way of life is humanly fulfilling in its ability to foster support, and deepen the personal vitality, creativity, freedom, and openness to all reality of its members, as well as increasing their ability to assume individual and corporate responsibility.

But even when their work is done out of love for Christ and a genuine desire to answer the needs of the Church, many religious still do not feel that they have really found themselves or that they know how, in the midst of their activity, to open themselves to a deep, satisfying personal relationship with Christ. Unable to find identity and fulfillment in their work, large numbers of religious have left their communities and returned to secular life. Vocations to these same communities have everywhere fallen off to such a degree that it is now a cause of major concern within the Church. A deeper reflection on the meaning of religious community life and its capacity to influence the individual's personal identity and self-concept is necessary. We must explore the relationship between personal human growth in the religious community and this identity crisis.

The meaning of Christian community witness, through peace and union in Christ, is all-important in any discussion of religious life. A community held together in its apostolic activity by the force of a Rule and custom alone becomes an inauthentic sign of what it professes to be. Religious are meant to be joined together by the living *agape* of Christ. When this is lacking owing to the inability of the individual members truly to discover and become sensitive to the Whole Christ, then the primary cohesive bond becomes the Rule of the Institute. People instinctively know when they are dealing with a religious group united primarily by a Rule. They experience this type of corporate unity in many secular organizations that have united for a common cause, and they see no major difference between a religious community and any group of men in pursuit of a common goal. But when they experience a community whose deepest cohesive bond is that of a selfless love, inexplicable on the basis of human resources alone in its transforming power and effects, they then immediately recognize that the power of union at work here is not man-made.

Men have tried for centuries to build this type of community and inevitably have had to fall back on the threat of sanction as the ultimate force to secure union. Even an organization like the United Nations cannot always bring its individual members to transcend their own selfish interests. Corporate action is invariably that which serves the best interests of the majority or of the powerful. When the primary force of union in a religious community is the Rule and not Christ's *agape*, then for all practical purposes of witness we are dealing with a basically secular reality. Law can never be anything more than an external force for union. For this reason the Old Law was incomplete and had to be supplanted through the interiorization of the law that took place in Jesus of Nazareth, the obedient Son of His eternal Father. A community of law alone cannot reflect the true character of salvation in the person of Jesus Christ. St. Paul enunciates this truth with brilliant clarity when he writes to the Galatians that ". . . if justification were through the law, then Christ died to no purpose" (2:21,RSV). If external observance alone could effect man's salvation, there was no need for Calvary. Consequently, the witness of a religious community must somehow reflect a life in the *agape* of Jesus Christ. As an external force, the law is incapable of generating this new life. Of itself, observance of the law can witness to the efforts and hidden motivations of the human community without necessarily revealing anything about the presence of God. It is only the experience of *agape*, not the religious habit, or Rules, or even external apostolates that is ultimately the effective sacramental sign of the presence of God. Our observance of the law is an effective sign only when the underlying motive is *agape*.

A community of love that lives in peace and union thus bears witness to the presence within of a force which transcends the capabilities of its members. It is only by being joined to the divine power of selfless love in Christ that religious can live together on such a close basis, selflessly dedicating themselves to the service of mankind. Men instinctively recognize that there is a great mystery here, and to the extent that they open themselves to it (that is, to the *musterion* of Christ's Continuing Incarnation in the Spirit), they too become transformed, if c ˙l˙ fc˙ a moment, by the power of divine love and life which ˷ pre˷ ˙nt. What is it that makes the difference between the communi y of Rule and the community of *agape,* since even the ˸   n˷ eds regulations for effective action? How does the commur ˷y of ˺hristian *agape* become truly sacramental in its capacity to be an effective sign of the presence of Christ's love?

We believe that this can happen only when the members are actually growing in their discovery of their personal identity in the person of the Whole Christ. They must deepen their sensitivity to the presence of Christ's love which lies at the heart of their capacity to express human love for one another, before they can witness as *effective* sacramental signs of the presence of God's love. But this sensitivity to the presence of divine love in human, selfless love, this personal realization of the Incarnation, can be experienced effectively for each religious only when in faith he is able to develop his human capacity to meet, love, and be saved by his salvific encounter with the Body of the Whole Christ.

The understanding of Christ as a corporate personality is crucial if we are to open our entire selves in a love relationship with the person of the Whole Christ. This essential theological truth will be developed more fully in Part II. St. Paul gives us the scriptural basis for this type of a relationship to Christ when he describes the work of the ministry as ". . . building up the body of Christ, until we all become one in faith and in the knowledge of the Son of God, and form that perfect man who is Christ come to full stature" (Eph. 4:12-13*).

The profound mystery of human love in Christ is the mystery of the union of Christ and His Church. As Christians and religious, we dedicate our lives to living, realizing, and experiencing this mystery publicly in our humanity and our life of love. We must find our radical identity not in terms of a successful apostolate nor in terms of the exclusive love of one spouse, which when

* C: *The Holy Bible.* Confraternity Edition. Copyright 1962 The Confraternity of Christian Doctrine.

lived in faith by the Christian married couple *is* their most profound experience of Christ, but by discovering the transcendent Christ in the Body He presents to us, the People of God. We must come to realize that the Body through which Christ loves and manifests His needs to us is the Body of the Church, the People of God in our immediate life. Our identity is found in terms of these people whose needs and love are the visible manifestation of Christ to us. Insofar as we religious seek self-identity at a more external or peripheral level of existence, we are hamstrung by irreconcilable conflicts.

The religious community then, must stand as a continuous witness to the effects of *agape* in our lives. It should be a source of the rich, warm humanity and self-identity which grows in each of us as we live together in Christ and an effective witness to the very presence of Christ within our lives. This is possible, however, only if we are joined in *agape* and not exclusively by the Rule of our Institute.

2. The Renewal of Religious Life

THE SECOND VATICAN COUNCIL recognized that there is a distinction between the adaptation of external methods and Rules and the renewal without which adaptation is an empty exercise. The Council defined adaptation as "an adjustment of the community to the changed conditions of the times,"[1] and then went on to speak of renewal as a continuous return to the source of all Christian life and a return to the original inspiration behind a given community.

The *Dogmatic Constitution on the Church* points out that the life of charity expressed through some specialized service to the Body of Christ is the purpose of religious life. The "original inspiration" that guided the founder of an approved religious Institute was always determined by the historical conditions and needs of the Church at the time. The particular expression of the life of charity proper to each religious family will therefore naturally differ from one group to the next. Each Congregation and Order will have its own "flavor" of service; but while this may be recognizable as a family mark, it should by no means be the primary source of self-identity for its members.

It is in a "continuous return to the sources of all Christian life," and especially in finding and personally living out our self-identity in and with the person of the Whole Christ, that we will be able so to renew our religious life that it will become an effective sign

[1] *The Documents of Vatican II*, p. 468.

20

to men of the presence of God's love. The Council was so conscious that adaptation of methods and Rules without this growing capacity for personal union with Christ was vain and empty that, in its statement of the general principles for accommodated renewal, it noted the following:

> Since the religious life is intended above all else to lead those who embrace it to an imitation of Christ and to union with God through the profession of the evangelical counsels, the fact must be honestly faced that even the most desirable changes made on behalf of contemporary needs will fail of their purpose unless a renewal of spirit gives life to them. Indeed such an interior renewal must always be accorded the leading role even in the promotion of exterior works.[2]

This inner renewal and union with God must be effected through an increased, conscious faith-awareness, together with sensitivity to the presence of Christ's own life and love at the heart of our struggling attempts at selfless human love. As we experience the capacity both to receive and to mediate selfless love, and consciously find our identity in terms of this activity, we gradually develop the ability to discover our identity as truly rooted in the Whole Christ. St. Paul caught the full significance of this experience throughout his Epistles where he so often used "in Christ" and "in *agape*" as synonymous expressions.

As a Christian I must understand and live out my interpersonal, human development as growth in the Whole Christ; and, without in any way being able to force God's self-gift, develop my human capacity to receive and mediate God's *agape* through the growing capacity to love selflessly and be loved. I will then mature in my ability to find and identify myself continually in the Whole Christ, no matter what the external circumstances of my life may bring.

We feel that it is worth studying this problem of self-identity within the religious community, not only because its resolution results in greater apostolic effectiveness but also because the very

[2] *Ibid.*, p. 469.

purpose of religious life in the Church demands it. If this problem is not clearly stated and practical attempts made to resolve it, religious communities will become little more than convenient sources of celibate manpower capable of maintaining the institutionalized apostolates of the Roman Catholic Church. If they are to be no more than this, there is little need for individual religious to go through the added effort of attempting to live a common life together. The dimension of community life adds nothing to their capacity to fill a position in school, hospital, church, or mission. However, the Second Vatican Council and many centuries of religious life bear witness to the fact that, in its common life, the religious community presents a far more profound testimony to the world than that of mere corporate efficiency.

If this witness, at the present moment in Salvation History, has lost something of its luster, it is a challenge to the religious men and women of today to show their response to the unique expression of His self-communication to them by trusting in Him enough to risk the arduous re-examination that lies ahead. Only a deep faith and openness to Christ as He truly exists today and is present in His entire Body will make us open to the many sacrifices and painful realities that must honestly be faced. Change is often painful. But change is also a sign of life, and it is at the root of any genuine growth. Our call from God is a call to growth in the discovery, love, and gift of ourselves to Him in and through the Whole Christ.

There is only one person who grows in this process and that is ourselves. God does not mature and gradually become more God. What we must honestly examine is our growth, together with all that it entails, in response to God's call to become a person in Christ. Since it is we, as human beings, who do the maturing, we must reflect on the relationship between our growth in human personhood (that is, our capacity for self-gift in selfless love) and our growth in the Whole Christ.

Perhaps because of the constant demands of our specialized apostolates, we religious have not been able to give full attention to the precise area of our effective witness. In many instances we have been too busy or too exhausted to critically evaluate the methods we use in preparing ourselves to develop the aptitude to receive and mediate God's love. The need for continued effectiveness in our specialized apostolates immediately forces us to reexamine our methods of preparation when we find that we are becoming outdated. Failure to do this lays us open to the charge of incompetence and growing irrelevance. But frequently we fail to apply this same rule to developing and sustaining our capability as effective witnesses to the presence of Christ.

The constant need we have throughout our lives for the ability to witness to *agape* can be submerged and lost in the struggle to fill positions in the institutional apostolates. For example, the school can continue because someone is teaching the class, even though the sacramental sign-value of the institution or many of its individual teachers are not an effective witness. But the primary question remains. Why are we there as religious? If it is to do something more than teach a geometry class, we must critically evaluate how we are going about achieving this "something more."

Perhaps the answer lies not so much in the specialized preparation for particular institutionalized forms of the apostolate, but rather in the development of the human capacity to be and experience living as a sacramental, effective sign of the presence of God's love, *agape*. This deeper value must be lived as the source of one's self-identity within the context of apostolic action. The religious community, as a community whose institutional structure is dedicated to the fostering of *agape,* should enable men and women to open themselves more and more to God's life and develop their human capacity to mediate His love. The witness of the religious life should be the witness of a community of *agape,* which transforms its members so that they may love with God's life in a more deeply human way.

The problem that all religious communities face, with both their young and their old members, is how to provide an environment that will enable the religious to develop and maintain the capacity for ever-deepening sensitivity to the presence of Christ in their lives. The traditional procedures that have been used to achieve this end are perhaps most clearly seen in the period of novitiate formation. Here the groundwork is laid, and whatever comes afterward is usually a development from these earlier methods.

It should be noted in passing that there have been many successes and not a few failures associated with traditional ascetical practices, but the successes must not deter us from a critical evaluation of methods which, with the passage of time, may become actual hindrances to the experience of union with Christ.

Contemporary authors have pointed out that religious communities in some sense stand in the forefront of human evolution. Their purpose is to foster development within the psyche of man at the very heart of his personal life where he relates to God. This is the point at which modern man is in a state of profound evolution. Technology represents a projection of man into matter, which develops according to its own laws as an imitation of what is happening within man. As man seeks for greater personal union with his fellow man, his technology reflects this in the transcendence of physical barriers through the marvels of the speed of transportation and the swiftness of communication.

The religious community, as a community of *agape,* dedicates itself to the deepest of all possible unions among men, a union with one another in the Whole Christ. While the existence and experience of this union are a total gift, man can, nonetheless, prepare himself to receive it without in any way coercing or forcing God. There are certain laws of development in becoming a person in the Whole Christ, and the truth that is becoming more clear with each advancing step of man's social evolution is that in the normal course of events God does *not* step outside of these laws of human growth, which He has given man, in order further to communicate to him a share in His divine life.

Today, as we said before, renewal within religious communities in the Roman Catholic Church has reached a point where many members are experiencing what we might call an identity crisis. We believe that the root of this problem lies in the failure to see the radical unity that the Whole Christ brings to our human growth as persons and our self-identity in Christ. What we are saying, is that our growing identity, which modern psychology has shown is conferred on us by the selfless love of others, is not merely a "structural" identity of man's own making which he achieves through applying various ascetical formulas. It is, in fact, an identity through, with, and in the Whole Christ.

THE GIFT OF SUPERNATURE "WITHIN" NATURE

Possibly one reason why we have been slow to join together man's natural growth as a human person with God's self-communication to us, is because of our firm resolve to preserve the absolutely gratuitous character of the supernatural order. The gift of God's life is certainly outside of nature and what we call the natural growth process. It is in no way intrinsically dependent upon it. The truth we wish to make clear, however, is that God's gratuitous gift of divine life is normally given *through the natural growth process*. This is a point on which there has been much confusion.

God has not chosen to bypass human development, especially interpersonal growth in selflessness and the capacity to give oneself to others, as His ordinary way of self-gift. God does not need to step outside of what He has created in order to continue sharing Himself with us. It is not necessary for Him to create another "way to holiness" apart from man's social nature and his God-given vocation to become a person.

In trying to stress that divine Revelation is in no way owed to man's created nature, we have tended to look on God's self-communication to man as something *apart* from human growth. When we say man does not have a natural right to share in divine life, we tend automatically to think that this absolutely gratuitous divine gift is independent of the dynamics of social maturation.

The "grace that perfects nature" has too often been looked upon as something given outside of man's growth toward interpersonal maturity and integration—a kind of heavenly skyhook that lifted man out of his mundane struggle for human self-realization. The point to be made clear is that *apart from* and *not owed to* or *due to* are by no means identical. God can freely give Himself to man as gift, but this self-gift can be, and in fact is, in and through the Incarnation, neither separate from nor outside of the laws of personal growth. Nothing of the gratuity of God's self-communication is destroyed when we say that man, struggling to develop the capacity for "other-centeredness" in selfless love, is the principal recipient of that very gift; and further, that it is given to him within and as a part of what man is by the very fact that God created him as social.

The saving will of the Father, the divine *Charis,* has been irrevocably united to man's nature and its laws of personal growth in the divine person of Jesus. The gratuitous gift is given to man in and through the humanity of Christ, whose redemptive intention and Spirit of Love still continue to reconcile men to the Father in and through His earthly visible Body. The self-communication of Divine life continues to be given to man within his own nature, a nature whose laws are not violated and whose freedom is not destroyed, but whose natural endowments can become the visible, concrete signs of God's invitation to share in His own divine nature in and through these sacramental signs of His presence to man.

The whole process of growth in the capacity for personal life should be explored by Christian psychologists and theologians as the way in which God's gift of divine life is manifested in the order of human existence. Man's discovery of his self-identity as a human person through the gift of selfless love from another should be viewed as the way in which he is, according to the laws of his nature, in communion with the Whole Christ.

Because of the Incarnation, all of nature has been caught up and contained in Christ, so that when we are loved selflessly, we are already being perfected in the basic relationship with the Whole Christ that gives us our radical self-identity. This was the vision that inspired St. Paul to exhort the Colossians to " . . . put on *agape* which binds everything together in perfect harmony. And let the peace of Christ rule in your hearts, to which indeed you were called in the one body" (3:14–15,RSV). The true peace of the Lord is found in the capacity to identify ourselves with Him as He, in reality, actually exists during our life in His Body.

We have often tended to look upon a person's increasing capac-

ity for selfless love as a purely natural phenomenon, whereas
in reality this very human growth process is supernatural precisely because it is the free gift of God. Man cannot develop the
capacity for selfless love by himself in a Pelagian manner. It is
always a gift from another, and insofar as the lover has the
capacity to love selflessly, it has been a prior gift to him. We
are at all times in the domain of total gratuitous gift when we
experience genuine selfless love, and this agape-life *is* the realm
of the supernatural.

There are no periods of chronological growth or times or
places that are not caught up and contained within the Whole
Christ. The individual is always free to reject His gift, but all of
created reality, whether the individual rejects it or not, is onto-
logically contained in a graced state of nature: ". . . for in him all
things were created, in heaven and on earth, visible and invisible
. . . all things were created through him and for him. He is before
all things, and in him all things hold together. He is the head of
the body, the church; he is the beginning, the first-born from the
dead, that in everything he might be preeminent. For in him all
the fullness of God was pleased to dwell, and through him to
reconcile to himself all things, whether on earth or in heaven,
making peace by the blood of his cross" (Col. 1:16-20,RSV).

Religious men and women, whose lives are dedicated to the
development of their human capacity to incarnate the gift of
God's selfless-love within them, must be helped to realize that
their personal identity, grounded in their experience of selfless
love from another, is found in their experience of relatedness
with the Whole Christ. By not identifying merely with the institution and externals of religious life, the resulting self-concept,
fundamentally a missionary concept, is not isolated.

We grow in our capacity for interpersonal life because our
self-identity is with the only One who can ultimately give us
this gift. We are rooted in a level of existence that perdures
through change, making possible the adaptation called for by
Vatican II, and we are securely grounded in the only possible
source of strength for an effective renewal, the very power of
God's presence, Trinitarian love-life, *agape*.

The world can experience the presence of a transcendent God

in its midst only insofar as this transcendence is enfleshed, incarnated, somehow made visible. In his First Epistle, St. John makes it clear that the experiential embodiment of transcendence is the experience of *agape*. He stuns us with the simplicity of his statement that "God is *Agape*" (4:8,RSV).

It is selfless love that enables people to mature as persons, that is, in their capacity for self-sacrificing love, and to grow in their sensitivity to the experience of the Whole Christ once the revealed word of this reality has been preached to them. *Agape* makes interpersonal life possible at ever-deeper levels. *Agape* is at the heart of human growth and integration, and it is at this point that the person of Christ may be found and revealed within our experience. It is here that God communicates Himself most powerfully through man's nature. We can discover God in our "becoming" as human persons. As we struggle in faith with this task of personal development, we will find God through our openness to His presence at the focal point of this dynamic process—this growth becomes our prayer and contemplation.

With this kind of a faith-response, it is really God who effects our integration and makes personal, human maturation possible. By this we do not principally stress physical or biological growth, although this is not excluded. We are speaking more of the developing capacity for self-gift, of the identity that is deeper than peripheral, of the interpersonal life that man is created to enjoy, and ultimately of his interpersonal life with and in the Whole Christ. This latter is a free gift to man, effected and communicated through the sacramentality of his personal growth process and vocation of relatedness to other men.

"PRAYING ALWAYS" IN PERSONAL LIVING

When this type of awareness becomes an integral part of our daily life, then, perhaps for the first time, many of us can really become contemplatives in action, in the sense of being conscious of the presence of the Whole Christ in the activity of living out our vocation to become human persons. We can become contemplatives in our whole personal growth process. Our prayer will then not be limited to certain times, places, circumstances, religious traditions, or practices. Our encounter with God will be open-ended. We will be more aware of the gift of God in all of reality, in the Whole Christ, and in our human growth. In all of our relatedness to reality there will be this sacramental consciousness, this awareness of God's self-communication to us, especially within our interpersonal relationships. This, it seems to us, is the true meaning of that "contemplation in action" so strongly reflected in the thought of St. Ignatius of Loyola—to become conscious of the presence and self-communication of God in the midst of our interpersonal activity. The daily experiences of love, fear, anger, joy, and threat gradually come to be recognized as our "lived reactions" to the Body of the Whole Christ.

Areas in which it would seem that we could well afford to become more alive to God's presence and communication to us might be, for example, in the consciousness of our own bodies and their various emotional and physiological changes, drives, appetites, and needs. When we live a life of sensitive, conscious relatedness as body-persons to the Whole Christ, we can become close to ourselves as we really are. We do not have to look on our bodies and their biological and physiological needs as somehow separated from a growing awareness of closeness and presence to God's self-communication. In most instances our reactions of fear, anger, hatred, joy, love, and boredom arise from dealings with our neighbor. Our most vividly felt human reactions are nearly always caused by relationships with other people. When living a conscious awareness that our reactions are really reactions to the Body of Christ, and at the time that we are angered or threatened or otherwise filled with socially unacceptable, un-Christian feelings, we need not withdraw into isolation to fight the battle with our emotions in fear-ridden solitude. When we exist in conscious relationship to the Whole Christ, we have the capacity to see our bodily needs *as related*. Because we live relatedness, we can risk attempting to open ourselves to the other sources of love and need in His Body that call us out of preoccupation with ourselves and heal us as body-persons. We do not become conscious of our emotions in a kind of morbid isolation. Nor do we become trapped in the fruitless effort to deal with our un-Christian feelings by means of intellectual rationalizations or psychological repressions. There is no picking away at oneself in the loneliness of one's heart. We always experience ourselves in fear or in joy *as related* and caught up in the Whole Christ. We deal with our feelings in a total body-person relationship with the Whole Christ, which is capable of preventing us from slipping into a solitary struggle within ourselves. By living with our feelings in this "related" manner, we gradually discover and become more aware of ourselves. We begin to recognize how, in our capacity to live an other-centered life, we are really living in virtue of a gift from another. We become more aware of the radical sources of our selfishness and selflessness.

We find that we grow in our personal life because we are loved, because we are being given the gift of our *personal* existence as sensitive biological, physiological, psychic individuals. We begin to realize that all the new depths and richness that we discover welling up within us do not come from within ourselves alone, but rather come because we are being created by our personal relatedness. As men and women who are loving and being loved, we are being created. This is our experience of God's self-communication in and through the Whole Christ.

This task of deepening our capacity for personal union, which is not just a kind of physical presence to one another or merely a growing aptitude for mutuality—this whole process with all of its problems in constancy, its pitfalls and joys, must become the conscious subject matter of our life in God. It should often be our prayer and meditation.

As we go through life coming up against people who annoy us, threaten us, cause us pain and inflict evil upon us, people who greatly appeal to us or with whom we deeply desire to share ourselves—in all of this we are called upon to develop a deeper capacity for contemplation and a more constant capability for self-gift. All these "human moments" now become *our relationship* with the Whole Christ.

Too often in our dealings with others we merely *feel* a repulsion or a strong attraction. We are unaccustomed to becoming consciously close to our feelings and sensitive to them as a meditation and prayer in itself, because we have frequently failed to see that being threatened, loved, desiring, and so forth, speaks to us about our here-and-now relationship with the Whole Christ. This type of spirituality is little understood and has not been stressed in the Church up to the present time. In faith we have believed that what we do for our neighbor is somehow related to Christ simply because He said so, and we accept what Revelation teaches. But the whole process of opening ourselves to human interpersonal relationships has not been understood as, in fact, the opening and developing of our interpersonal life with the Whole Christ.

During this time of renewal within the Church, all Christians, but most especially religious, could ground their identity with greater theological depth and closer conformity to the God-given laws of human growth if they more clearly understood the profound religious implications of the Whole Christ.

PROBLEMS OF IDENTIFYING WITH THE PERSON OF CHRIST

Perhaps the identity crisis that many experience today has resulted partly from our need to identify ourselves with a person, a kind of one numerical person within our human experience.

This may have led us to identify predominantly with our picture of the historical Christ of the Gospel narrative. Such a tendency could have been accentuated by the kind of contemplations on Scripture that put us back in Galilee, watching Christ walk on the lake shore or preaching to the multitudes. This could dispose us to focus our spiritual life around *our own image* of the historical Christ. When faced with the reality of the Ascension and references to Christ as the transcendent, risen Lord in power, we might have tended to place Christ somewhere apart from mankind, except for His visible presence in the Eucharist and cultic sacramental acts of the Church. We believe that Christ loves mankind and came to save us, and we take it on faith that there is some kind of an identification of love between Himself and our neighbor. But experientially putting the one person of Christ together with His many members is a bit difficult.

For our own personal life, we need a tangible relationship with some concrete individual. It is only natural that many would be disposed to identify largely with the transcendent Christ. Our relationship to our fellow men perhaps then became something like the following illustration. Let us say that I know my mother loves my brothers and sisters. If I love my mother but do not care too much for my brothers and sisters, I will love them for her sake, because I love her and realize that there is a relationship of love between her and them. But the point is that I do not *identify* myself with them *in love*. I do not find my self-identity in terms of my *relationship* with them. I receive my identity from my mother, whose love I have experienced apart from my relationship to my brothers and sisters. My brothers and sisters mean something to me largely because my mother loves them.

Our tendency is to see the people around us as related to the transcendent, risen Lord whom we love. We love them *because He* loves them. All of which, of course, is true. We miss, however, the significance of Matthew's statement: ". . . as often as you did this to one of these the least of my brethren, *you did it to me"* (25:40,RSV). What is not clearly understood is that the transcendent Christ, taken in isolation, is not the whole reality of the One with whom I am to identify myself. He is the person with whom I am to identify, but we cannot come into communion with the transcendent Lord apart from the Body that He presents to us. Thus, the Person whom we meet is the Whole Christ. To identify ourselves with just the members or with just the transcendent Head in isolation from His Body, the People of God, is not to identify with the reality that is the person of Christ. We must become conscious of our identification and interpersonal life with Christ *as He truly is today,* the Whole Christ, head and members together, one reality. St. John puts the two together beautifully in his First Epistle: "If any one says, 'I love God,' and hates his brother, he is a liar" (4:20,RSV). We cannot divorce our love of

God from the very Body through which He loves and reveals Himself to us.

Our personal life is not something given at birth, but rather is a task set for each man, a vocation to be lived out. We grow into it, gradually becoming lovable because we are loved. The whole dynamic process must therefore become an intimate part of our prayer life. It is our growing identification with and capacity for entering into a relationship with Christ as He truly is. Any man or woman who seeks the Lord apart from becoming a person in His Body runs the risk of a theologically unsound process of identification with Christ.

To consider prayer, ascetical theology, or religious formation apart from the growth process of human interpersonal life as we open ourselves to give and receive selfless love is, in fact, to isolate it from the way God seeks to communicate with man in the order of salvation that He has established—the Incarnation.

We have too often made interpersonal life into a profane reality. Man cannot truly be helped to pray until he learns how to discover and be open to God's self-communication in *all* of reality. In the daily struggle each of us must go through to become a person capable of loving his fellow man, we are called to discover the dynamic reality of the transcendent Lord incarnated at the heart of our interpersonal life with others.

PART II

3. Jesus, Spoken in the Language of Man

REFLECTIONS ON THE PAGES THAT
FOLLOW

IN THE CHAPTERS that follow, there is certainly nothing comprehensive, let alone definitive, in the theological, philosophical, and psychological truths that are presented. Recent years have brought a great mass of newly developing thought in each of these areas, together with the necessary scholarly research into their deeper levels of meaning.

The present work, however, is not written for the specialist. It does not pretend to treat any of its truths or hypotheses in a manner that would adequately expose the present level of scholarly development. The authors nevertheless believe that the time has come to take on the task of delineating the bold lines of a vision that is emerging. Of course, it is only because of the tireless and accurate scholarship of many men, in what would at first appear to be widely divergent fields, that such a synthesis can even be attempted.

Published works in each of the disciplines we draw from have become so vast that the ordinary person cannot hope to read widely and deeply enough in all of them. Moreover, even when this is attempted, the sheer weight of material tends to cloud the necessary synthesis and to diffuse the converging elements that should be assimilated into some kind of a comprehensible unity, if they are to result in a practical deepening of everyday religious life.

If each theological, philosophical, and psychological truth dealt with in this book were examined and explored with the depth and breadth that its present level of scholarship has both attained and demands, then the very purpose of this writing would have been frustrated. For what is needed today is a more synthetic view, a descriptive reflection on the convergences.

If ever there was a time when the Church needed to listen to what the Spirit was revealing, it is now. In all the explorations that touch on man's understanding of himself, of his relationship to his fellow man, and of his direction toward God, the Spirit is now revealing and teaching. For the family of man has reached a point of sensitivity to what it means to be a human person that cries out for a corresponding new development of sensitivity to God's presence in interpersonal growth, in freedom, and in human self-realization. In the words of Christopher Fry:

> "Dark and cold we may be, but this
> Is no winter now. The frozen misery
> Of centuries breaks, cracks, begins to move;
> The thunder is the thunder of the flows,
> The thaw, the flood, the upstart Spring.
> Thank God our time is now when wrong
> Comes up to face us everywhere,
> Never to leave us till we take
> The longest stride of soul men ever took.
> Affairs are now soul size.
> The enterprise
> Is exploration into God."[1]

Today it is certainly a truism to say once again to many religious that "holiness is wholeness," as profound as that statement remains. This book, therefore, is written for those religious who have already come to accept this truth but who are searching for an identity truly rooted in Christ as He is present in their world of personal growth. It is written for those who are searching into

[1] Christopher Fry, *A Sleep of Prisoners*, New York, Oxford University Press, 1951, p. 47.

the experienced relationship between wholeness and holiness, because they realize that wholeness is achieved only through interpersonal relatedness, and holiness is relatedness to the Whole Christ.

What therefore follows in the next three parts of this book is not the comprehensive, scholarly, in-depth treatment of any theological, psychological or philosophical truth. Rather it is an attempt to reveal in the authors' own words what we have found to be a meaningful—and we believe accurate—interpretation of the powerful, converging insights that can bring to the religious life new integrity, relevance, and richness.

MODERN MAN SEEKS THE INVISIBLE GOD

Man's search for God has assumed many shapes during his tenure on earth, and we can learn much from these efforts, together with their failures and successes. While a historical study of the way that man has sought to discover God is academically interesting, twentieth-century man's doubts and certitude about the existence of God are not academic subjects. His convictions and uncertainties are deeply rooted within the center of his personal life, at the heart of what it means to be human. When exploring such a delicate area, man cannot assume the aloof objectivity and impartiality that are his while analyzing the material world. He cannot pass his own unique, personal life beneath a microscope and then view it as a detached observer.

Perhaps we might make an attempt to restate the problem that many have when they are confronted with the question of a Supreme Being. The existence of God *could* really be described as an academic question. The most detached observer can freely participate in this sort of a discussion without any great admixture of personal feeling. So possibly the existence of God is not really the heart of the problem. We might phrase it another way and suggest that the personal element enters in when man opens himself to the question of doubt or certitude about the existence of "God-with-us."

We instinctively recognize that if God is not personally present as a vital force in our life, then He does not really exist "for us," "for me." It is this element of "for us," "for me" that the ancient Hebrews tried to describe in the word *Emmanuel,* God-with-us. This is the true question that touches on our personal problems about the existence of God. If God is to be "for me," I must be able to find Him in my life. If the Bible is to mean anything, it must open me to the discovery of God within my own experience.

Although Scripture may reveal the intimate union between God and man that has been effected through the Incarnation, there is a great difference between our *knowledge* of this union and the actual *experience* of the personal relationship. These two are not identical, and one of the major efforts to which religious education in the twentieth century must bend all its resources is toward the creation of an environment within which "realization," and not just abstract knowledge of Revelation, can take place within personal life.

Numerous difficulties face man in the attempt to realize his communion with God. God is revealed as being both transcendent (personally complete within Himself alone, apart from His creation) as well as salvific self-gift to mankind; while man initially experiences himself as wanting to be totally for himself, to be autonomous, to be, in fact, God. The paradox is that he wants to imitate God as "autonomous," but not God as "self-gift to another." Man wants to be the center of his own existence and live in such a way that he is not self-gift to the other but is, in a sense, self-gift to himself. Only God, who is a Trinity of Persons within Himself, can live in this way. When man attempts it, he becomes ensnared in the web of his own egotism and narcissism. Man cannot be an autonomous person, whereas God can be existentially autonomous in His personal life because He is a Trinity of Persons within Himself.

God also reveals Himself to mankind as being totally other than self-centered in His relationship with man. He is the faithful Yahweh who seeks His spouse, Israel, in the midst of her infidelity. He is total self-sacrificing love, always forgiving, always pursuing

His errant lover. Christ on the cross is the ultimate incarnation of this love. God thus reveals Himself as the exact opposite of what man experiences as the selfish pull inward that he feels within himself. St. Paul describes the dilemma that man feels in the face of this tension: "I can will what is right, but I cannot do it. For I do not do the good I want, but the evil I do not want is what I do. Now if I do what I do not want, it is no longer I that do it, but sin which dwells within me. So I find it to be a law that when I want to do right, evil lies close at hand" (Rom. 7:18–21,RSV). Paul thus contrasts the law of selfishness within his own members with the law of God that tells him that he is made for other-centeredness and selfless love.

Yet even while he is conscious of his pull to self-centeredness, man instinctively recognizes that he is not complete without the other and without God. His very attempts at self-centered aggrandizement show his radical poverty. He cannot identify himself as man in isolation. He needs other people and especially the capacity to open himself to that gift of love from another which ultimately enables him to transcend his own self-centeredness.

If man remains open to this love in the midst of his selfish thirst for fulfillment, he gradually begins to discover in others and, little by little even within himself, the capacity to transcend his self-centered way of life. He can begin to lead a fulfilling existence based on the gift of self. He begins really to discover himself, his radical deep self, not only in terms of the gift of others to him but most especially in terms of his own growing capacity for other-centered love. Reflecting on himself, he becomes aware of the fact that he is growing in the capacity to be able to transcend that aspect of himself that creates the problem of trying to relate to God. Man has and can develop this capacity, however, only when it is freely given to him as a gift.

Man also experiences difficulty in realizing and experiencing a personal relationship with God because of God's spirituality and man's materiality. Revelation shows that God is not limited to the material and created, whereas man is bounded in his corporeal existence by space and time.

The only way in which man can "be-in-relation" and transcend his isolation is by being in communion with another through the efficacious sign of himself in matter. He can *reveal* the *mystery* of himself only through an act of *incarnation*. He can come into communion and *covenant* with another only when he knows how to communicate fully through the language that is properly his as a man. *Mystery, revelation, incarnation, covenant:* this is the incarnational language of man through which he must naturally speak and become, as a person, and through which God, as divine person, has chosen to speak to man. In God's plan this is the ordinary way in which man as incarnate spirit is able to relate to the divine.

God is also revealed as the invisible one. We frequently feel that He has no real part in our tangible human contacts and relationships because He is not limited to space and time. By His nature He is not restricted to visible, verbal, sacramental, signs of communication through matter. Since God does not communicate with us in exactly the same manner as another man with his sensible, individual, corporeal presence, there is a certain obscurity and confusion in our attempt to develop a personal relationship with Him. As we mentioned before, this does not mean that we cannot *know* about the existence of God and His decision to reveal Himself to man through corporeal signs. But knowledge of the existence of God and the development of a personal relationship with Him are quite different.

Thus God is the totally Other, the totally outside myself. He is neither limited to matter nor exclusively identified with my experience of my own body-person or that of another created human being. How then is it possible for me to develop a personal relationship with God? How is He to be relevant and intimate to me as a part of my life and growth as a human person? How is God relevant to twentieth-century man in the values that he prizes and strives to make a part of his life?

People today are so conscious of the personal values in freedom, self-realization, fulfillment, interpersonal relatedness, and communication. How is God a part of all this? How is He related to the tendency toward world brotherhood and lasting peace through union and federation? Is His presence reflected in our dawning awareness of being related to all men and in our growing capacity to be able to show genuine concern for others? These latter values are especially visible today in the contemporary phenomenon of so many young people giving themselves to others through the Peace Corps and similar basically altruistic organizations.

Twentieth-century man must live out his life during an age of great specialization and deep penetration of the laws of the universe. It is a time of exploration into the cosmos. It is also an age where the need for specialization and concentration on very narrow areas of research has created a very real danger that the individual may close himself off to much of reality as he deepens the area of his competence. He can easily become insensitive to those aspects of interpersonal life that are largely spiritual, not governed by the laws of natural science, and incapable of being subjected to the kind of verification with which the scientist must work. Man's very technology and search for truth can end by destroying his vocation to become a person. Thus, twentieth-century man has great need for God, since He alone is ultimately the source of his interpersonal growth. God is the One who enables him to become and remain a man while fully engaging himself in the exploration of the truths of nature.

A scientist, for example, who values his commitment to some particular area of truth, and who recognizes the discipline and total gift of himself demanded by the specialization involved in this effort, faces a serious tension and conflict in his life. How does he remain open to other values, especially those that lie outside the scope of his highly specialized technical world? He can so easily become dulled to the more subtle values of interpersonal life. How can he risk plunging deeply into a definite area of research and still maintain the necessary openness, especially to other persons, in order that his pursuit of truth will not enslave and in the end dehumanize him? This is a problem that today manifests itself even in family life. How are couples to sustain a rich interpersonal union that can foster peace, harmony, and personal growth within their family when they are faced with the constant demands of a technological society? Simple leisure is not the answer.

Much the same problem exists within religious communities as they adapt to the dynamic growth of the twentieth century. They too reflect the need of specialization in their staggering commitments to highly developed forms of the apostolate. Faced with continued evolution in this direction, the Vatican Council urged religious to undertake renewal through a continuous return to the radical sources of personal growth. Religious are thus faced with fundamentally the same problem of rediscovering God's relevance as their contemporaries.

God must become relevant to man as the One who sustains him both in his commitment to truth and in his growth as a person. This latter is the inner source that alone, over a lifetime, can sustain his creativity in searching out the mysteries of nature. It is his very capacity for self-gift that makes it possible for man to explore the mysteries of the universe around him. His ability really to give himself to a mystery, to be so possessed by truth that it grasps and literally orbits him into space, is what enables man to sustain the drive and energy required by his effort. If his personal life falls apart or he is dehumanized by the search, it will soon affect his very creativity and capacity to go deeper into the mysteries that he explores. In other words, he must be able to continue becoming a man while exploring the world. How then is God a part of man's need to commit himself even to unraveling the secrets of the universe and refashioning them through science and art?

God must constantly renew all men as they struggle with the innate tendency to selfish isolation that thwarts their re-creation of the human universe and created matter. Growth is always renewal, and man requires continual re-creation through a vital relationship with God while re-fashioning God's creation the better to support his own personal life. Ultimately this is why God is so important. Only the Divine Persons can keep man from destroying himself in his search for truth.

As Christianity and the Church face the difficult effort of religious renewal, how is God intimately a part of this necessary revitalization? How can we find and identify with Him, making Him real in our religious commitment and growth as religious persons? In what way is God part of the experience that we have already described as a consciousness of turning inward toward isolation rather than outward in self-gift?

LEARNING THE LANGUAGE OF GOD

Since we constantly struggle to meet God and to find Him as God-for-us, Emmanuel, why are we so reluctant to search for Him in our personal experience? Why do we hesitate at the thought of a personal awareness of God that is more than intellectual? Perhaps we may be slow to discuss an experience of God's immanence in our life because we have lived with ourselves, with the experience of ourselves as body-persons, *apart* from the Whole Christ for so long that we cannot incarnate the Incarnation in our interpersonal relatedness to God. We have been unable to appreciate the Incarnation as anything more than a past event whose personal relevance for us is now purely historical.

In our life with one another, we know when we are thrilled and when sad; for the most part we know when we have done well at some task or when we have deeply hurt each other. We are conscious over the years of a certain growth or lack of growth in our ability to be open and listen to others. More important, if we have been fortunate enough to be selflessly loved and to return a self-sacrificing love, we realize how the effects of this union have made us into a "new creation."

Nevertheless, even though we have been told, even though we intellectually consent, even though our feelings may move us to suspect it, we are still reluctant to believe that God's language to us is no different than that of our neighbors. We simply try to hedge around taking God at His Word. We cannot bring ourselves to accept the Word Incarnate at those deeper levels of our body-person existence that instinctively hold us back from opening to the radical transformation that would inevitably take place if we allowed ourselves to listen to the Continuing Incarnation that is happening within man today. For God has chosen to speak to us in our own tongue—a language of fleshly realities, of sounds and feelings, smiles and tears; a language couched in human terms that touches and changes our whole being when we allow ourselves to be open to it and to dialogue on this human level of encounter.

If the religious life, and Christianity for that matter, is to be at all relevant, it must discover an "earthly spirituality" that enables modern man to become sensitive enough to his own human growth so that he can discern the language of God in the flesh-and-blood realities of his daily life. In the search for the presence of Christ, nothing human can be exempted. Everything has some importance: whether it is the thrill of first love, the joy of mature friendship, the sheer exuberance of bodily control in athletics, the aching loneliness at the death of a loved one, or the wonder of discovery in study and science.

The purpose of religious life is to help develop the experience of an incarnational spirituality that is more than theory alone. The theology of transcendent realities has meaning for man only when it is spoken in his own language. He does not worship a God "out there" but rather a transcendent God *within* who has not evolved as man has, and who, while remaining totally other in His uncreated existence, is nonetheless both the heart and goal of human growth through His presence in human history. An incarnational spirituality involves man in the discovery and development of a sensitivity to the presence of Christ, the Whole Christ, in all of reality.

But first I must become aware of the possibility of hearing the language of God at the heart of my human growth struggle before I can risk attempting to find Him there. The search is painful, because attentive listening often reveals aspects of my inner life that I would rather not acknowledge.

The sooner I recognize that the language of incarnation is the language of Christ, the sooner I will be able to risk in faith "getting close to myself" so as to discern and grow in an awareness of God's self-revelation in the reality that is "me." It is the "faith-experience" of my growing capacity to listen to and accept myself as I am, precisely because He is accepting me as I am, that allows me to risk being myself with Him. I can venture to be with Him as I really am, not just as I feel I *should* be. There is no need fruitlessly to try willing away my un-Christian feelings toward my neighbor in order to be present to Him. It is unnecessary first to root out my feelings—as though presence to the Lord were impossible when in this state of mind. I can risk being alive to myself as I really am in every encounter with reality because I know that I can be this way *with Him*. Ultimately His presence is what will heal my inner division when I can be open and consciously present to Him in faith, *as I authentically am* here and now.

This is not just an intellectual encounter, but a whole body-person awareness, a "reflective body-person presence" to Him within all the relationships that make up my daily existence. I can risk truly being present to myself, a kind of growing in "closeness to myself" as I live out each day's encounter with reality, because I do not experience myself as isolated, as separated from God's intimate gift of Himself to me in my own way of communication as incarnate-spirit—the language of human self-realization, interpersonal relatedness, and gradual integration.

This "faith-experience" of which we have just spoken is an integral part of our actually living (in the full human sense of that word) our day-to-day faith-response to the Whole Christ, what we have sometimes called "a life of faith." When this reflective body-person experience is missing in our personal belief and commitment to Christ, when our "obedience of faith" (Rom. 16:26,RSV) is not that daily renewed self-gift "by which man entrusts his whole self freely to God,"[2] then there is a temptation to substitute the Rule, a particular way of life, our own special interests and work in the community, or something else in place of the Whole Christ.

Faith is always commitment to a person, not to an abstraction, an ethic, a truth, or a way of life. But the personal presence of Christ to me is His bodily presence, the People of God. Therefore,

[2] Walter M. Abbot, S.J., General Editor, *The Documents of Vatican II*, New York, Guild Press, 1966, p. 113.

faith involves believing in one another, i.e., in Christ's Body as
the sacrament of God's self-communicating presence to me within
my experience. Christian faith means committing myself to God's
self-gift through the Body of Christ, through the visible interpersonal signs of His Body, no matter how obscure they may
be because of human frailty and self-centeredness.

Those extraordinary signs of divine presence, the miracles
with which Jesus caught the attention of the Jews so that they
might respond to Him in faith, are not the interpersonal signs
of our ordinary way of coming to believe in Christ today. Yet
we also have signs and must also come to believe. Our signs,
however, are seldom of such obvious divine origin. They are not
so easily interpreted as being out of the ordinary. Nevertheless,
we must learn to listen in faith to our whole selves, our bodies,
our feelings, our fears and joys as genuine, sacramentally effective signs of Christ's presence.

Seldom have we learned to listen to ourselves as human beings
together with all that this entails in our growth and relatedness, our
needs and secret yearnings; and to discover, hidden within, the
ever-deepening presence of the risen and glorified Lord. It is a
personal presence whose intimate involvement with me calls out
a faith-response, dynamic and filled with joy in the freedom of
my "faith-commitment" to human growth as becoming a person
in the Whole Christ. My own personal weaknesses, faults, and
self-centeredness, as well as my selfishness and inward pull to
isolation from others, can then be seen and responded to in faith
as the "needs" of the Whole Christ. Unless we keep our faith
alive on the horizontal level among one another in His Body, we
grossly deceive ourselves about our faith in Christ. He asks us
to believe in Him *as He really exists* today, even though that
divine presence appears hidden or is not manifested in an extraordinary way. This is the essence of an authentic faith in
Christ for us; and without this genuine, deeply personal involvement with His Body, we can easily use the Jesus of history "back
there" or the risen Lord "out there" as ground for an unreal faith
experience of Christ. We can end by creating our own God in
order to bypass the pain and sacrifice involved in a daily life of

very "worldly" faith in the Continuing Incarnation of Christ within the family of man.

CONDITIONED REFLEXES AND INTERIORITY IN HUMAN BECOMING

We must take certain risks in the formation of religious. We can no longer be content with a type of protective training that emphasizes a negative mentality, because in this process we pay too high a price in the loss of positive and apostolically necessary human values. We frequently damage far too many of our young people by forming them along the lines of conditioned reflexes that cause them to react to their emotions, sexual feelings, and temptations with an irrational response of guilt and repulsion. Such conditioned reflexes (largely inculcated through a tone of voice or attitude, but most especially as the result of our own lack of integration and irrational behavior when these same threatening emotions, feelings, and temptations are brought to our attention) develop in our young people an ascetical foundation built upon unconscious feelings, rather than on the solid, conscious awareness of reality as it is. Not only does this prevent the conscious control of one's emotional and appetitive responses (for they now lie hidden in repressed corners of the unconscious), but it also prevents the development of a mature spiritual life. True contrition is impossible, gradual growth in responsibility is out of the question, and all that remains is an increasing anxiety to protect oneself from the many threats of the unknown.

We must develop within our body-consciousness, especially regarding our sexuality, a deep built-in motivation, an instinctive sense of what is the "right way to feel" for a mature human being. This can be accomplished neither through fear nor conditioned reflexes, which provide built-in safeguards only in the form of conditioned repulsion or disgust. This sensitive human growth cannot be achieved through a somewhat naive common sense type of instruction, or from the pressures of correct social behavior, or even from a lengthy study of the laws of the Church, the laws of nature, or Christian morality as it is taught today.

We must rather take on a risky and very delicate task. Ideally it should begin from the earliest years. Even if this has been neglected, we should not let it discourage us from beginning somewhere.

What we are saying is that we must risk involving our young people with reality as it is. We must open them to life, not close them from it. We must teach them how to listen not only to themselves but to the Holy Spirit in all the marvelous works of creation around them. However, this lays both them and us open to many moments of sorrow, suffering, and exploitation, because we are aiming to form a human being sensitive, according to his individual capacity, to all kinds of goodness and beauty—and therefore to all kinds of evil and ugliness.

This personal formation runs the constant risk of failure because, based as it is on a sound Christian anthropology, it seeks to minimize those unconscious mechanisms of defense, automatic safeguards, and legal walls of protection that the immature seek out in order to avoid the pain of growth and the threat of mature faith. It stresses primarily the safeguard of the person's own deeply rooted human desire and thirst for goodness given by the Spirit in the Whole Christ, especially that thirst as expressed in an attitude of love and reverence, of awe and wonder at the ever-present reality of God in all creation. It is an attitude of care and gentleness with the things of nature, with animals, with one's body and the bodies of others; an attitude of quiet joy because of the creative potentiality that religious discover within themselves as they work with their hands, their minds, and their hearts. This they see and begin to admire not only in themselves but also in other persons. They learn to love the beauty of order and design, of color, and the nuances of shade and pattern all around them. They come to marvel, with each new discovery, at the complexity and intricacy of nature's laws and habits. And so in all that they confront, they learn to discover and experience the creative, loving presence of God and to develop an innate sense of restraint and discipline in the presence of the vast array of gifts poured out on them each moment of their lives. In using these gifts, their all-pervading mode of action is "not to spoil" but to love, to love that in which God is freely allowing them to share, and in return, to use their humanity in bringing all back to God.

This is the kind of human formation that recognizes and appreciates man's nature as created to receive in *openness* God in all of reality. It manifests esteem for man's capacity freely to respond in a human way and to be conscious of this response as his relationship to God.

JESUS—SPOKEN IN THE LANGUAGE OF MAN

Through our correct understanding of man's nature as incarnate-spirit, we begin to glimpse part of an answer to the fundamental problem of relating to God. We might phrase the problem as follows: How does man as body-person develop an interpersonal relationship with a nonbody-person? Is it merely a spiritual communion? If this is the case, how does man's earthly dimension, which makes him *incarnate*-spirit and is his way of knowing and communicating, find fulfillment? How can man as body-person truly enter into any relationship that he cannot recognize and be conscious of as interpersonal according to his incarnate way of being.

The very relationship, the "between," as Martin Buber would phrase it, may indeed be non-material. But in order for man to grasp its relevance for himself and to become aware of its unique direction toward him personally, this relationship must find some visible, concrete, material expression. True personal encounter for man must be mediated through those acts that affect him in a perceptible way according to his bodily presence in the world. If we try to develop a relationship with God by going outside "our way of knowing," we run the great risk of creating an idol of our own making, an idol of the imagination or of some finite created reality. We will return to this point shortly. How then, in the midst of our incarnate existence, do we find the God who is really God?

We have just described something of the perplexity that man

has always faced in his attempt to develop a relationship with God. Into this confusion, however, the Father has communicated Himself in the person of Jesus of Nazareth, the Word become flesh, the image of the invisible God. His historical presence was the sacrament of encounter with the invisible God, the efficacious, visible sign of God's presence among men. Jesus joined the invisible divine nature with the visible human nature in His concrete person.

God revealed Himself to the Chosen People according to *"their way of knowing and receiving,"* in the person of Jesus of Nazareth. Jesus was sent by the Father in order to communicate God in the Chosen People's language. Their nature was created as ours, to receive the spiritual, and therefore divine life, in and through the material, namely, the human nature of Christ. It is in the person of Jesus that we have the mysterious union between the two levels of existence.

The Incarnation forms the background for any discussion of communion between man and God. As a terrestrial being, man's language is inevitably incarnational. To communicate is to incarnate. Man can reveal the unique mystery that is himself only when he fleshes this revelation in a word, a smile, or a gesture. Hopkins' poetry, the tears of a child, the music of Beethoven— all these are the incarnational language of man's self-revelation.

The Epistle to the Hebrews carries this language of incarnational communication to the divine level when it notes how the Father has spoken to us in the Son. Jesus Christ is the fleshed Word of the Father, the Word made flesh that can be heard by man, the everlasting sign that the Father has chosen to be in communion with us, to make Himself known in our language.

Jesus embodies this very unity of the spiritual and the material, the limited and the unlimited, the divine and the created. He combines the self-gift of God together with our inward pull to isolation. By becoming man, He assumed the full weight of man's isolation, our heritage as sons of Adam. But because of His constant desire to be other-centered and to do the will of His Father, Jesus never ratified His human tendency to isolation as a way of self-fulfillment. "For we have not a high priest who is unable to sympathize with our weaknesses, but one who in every respect has been tempted as we are, yet without sinning" (Heb. 4:15, RSV).

The difficulty man faces in his attempt to communicate with God is twofold: first, he frequently lacks an understanding of his very nature as created in openness to receive God; and secondly, he is often not sure of the meaning of divine revelation in Christ. As incarnate-spirit, man is so created that he can receive God should His Creator choose to reveal Himself in a special way. But man's reception of God's communication, in the normal course of events, is in and through the human way of knowing. This is the language of Incarnation, of sacrament, of material signs efficaciously revealing the spiritual mystery. As incarnate-spirit, man knows sacramentally.

Jesus' very being is sacramental. He is a material sign of a spiritual reality, but in Jesus the sign is efficacious. It actually causes the person who comes into a faith-encounter with the material sign, the human nature of the Divine Person, to be transformed into an adopted son of God.

The person who really "hears" divine revelation pierces the human language in which it is couched in order to be touched by its efficacious significance as God's Self-revelation. The man who has "ears to hear" does not stop short with the human word. He is open to receive and be transformed by the sacramental presence of the Divine Word efficaciously mediated to him in his own human language. In the normal course of events, God speaks to men without stepping outside the order of man's created nature. The incarnation of Jesus was the bridge, the sacramental reality, the material sign of God's saving presence among men. Through Jesus, man had a concrete, visible experience of God-with-him, Emmanuel. Man could enter into interpersonal relationship with Him and thus identify himself with Christ in love, faith, and mutual friendship.

4. The Continuing Incarnation

THE ASCENSION presented the disciples of Jesus with a new problem. The body-person of Jesus of Nazareth was no longer with them. The visible, sacramental sign of Incarnation and communication was gone. It was as though the spoken Word had become stilled. No sound could be heard, no sign could be perceived. The disciples could no longer be related to God because the sacramental sign of His presence, the body-person of the glorified Lord, had ascended to His Father.

How were His disciples to continue their intimate personal friendship with Christ? For a time they had encountered the Father and heard Him speak and felt His love in the warmth of Christ's presence. "Philip . . . he who has seen me, has seen the Father" (John 14:9,RSV). Now this was ended.

Yet there lingered on the mysterious words of Jesus spoken at the Last Supper: "I will not leave you desolate. I will come to you" (John 14:18,RSV). "It is to your advantage that I go away, for if I do not go away the Counselor will not come to you; but if I go, I will send him to you" (John 16:7,RSV).

If God's gift was to perdure and Christ's intention to redeem mankind through our own incarnational way of knowing and being was for all times and all men, how was this to continue if it was limited to some thirty years? The whole point of Christ's life would be absurd if it ended with His ascension. The letter to the Hebrews begins by telling us that: "In many and various ways God spoke of old to our fathers by the prophets; but in these last days he has spoken to us by a Son" (Heb. 1:1–2,RSV). We now live in the "last days," and the perduring mystery of God's communication during this time is the mystery of the People of God as the Body of Christ the Son, the mystery of the Whole Christ. It would be almost a contradiction for God to incarnate Himself in order to communicate with man, and then limit His dialogue to thirty years or to one group of people. The mystery of God's self-communication is not restricted to a passing moment in history or to a single race of people. The intention of God continues throughout Salvation History. The visible presence of Christ remains. The salvific will of God, His grace and the universal gift of Himself, is to flow throughout all human history in a way that man can perceive.

For so many, the Incarnation is but a static moment in time. It is a point in history, *the* point, perhaps, but nonetheless only a fleeting moment that happens and then is gone. It is the Epiphany of God, the sudden bursting forth in history and time of the Word made flesh.

But the incarnation of Christ continues, and man's language of incarnation is *continual.* Those who are growing in love are caught up in a dialogue of ever-deepening communication and revelation of that unique mystery which is themselves, and it is a dialogue always expressed through the body. As incarnate-spirit, man must share himself with other men. He matures personally only through communicating as a body-person with others, thereby fulfilling his social nature. It is because men have a history, and because to *be* a man is to *become* a man, that we must continually be incarnating.

Man, as we pointed out, must reveal and discover himself together with others in dialogue because he is a body-person. He is "body-person in the process of becoming!" He grows by communicating and sharing his life as incarnate-spirit with others. This is the way of knowing and growing that is in accord with our social nature. God has not stepped outside of this language of continual incarnation when revealing Himself to us. He continues to express, communicate, and share Himself through visible signs in matter, and thus to create the union that fulfills our need for others.

Perhaps we can best understand the significance of the Continuing Incarnation of Christ within the family of man by using a term which Father Teilhard de Chardin posed as a corollary to "Epiphany." He referred to the divine "Diaphany" in the world. An example may give the best description of this new term. When a photographer is at work in his dark room printing a portrait, he takes a blank sheet of photographic paper and lays it beneath the enlarger, exposing the image of a face on its surface for a few seconds. After the exposure has been made, the light is turned off in the enlarger, but the paper remains as blank as it was before. There is no image upon it. Then the photographer dips this nascent print into a chemical bath and waits. For a few seconds nothing happens, but soon, slowly, almost miraculously the outlines of a face gradually begin to appear. First the very dark portions of the face and hair, then the highlights—eyes, shadows, the softness in color and texture of the cheek—gradually all begin to emerge. What was hidden becomes manifest. This is the meaning of "the Diaphany of God," the gradual appearance of the face of Christ within the heart of humanity. It is the birth of the Whole Christ. God's gift takes root and man gradually becomes aware of the mystery that lies hidden in his personal history.

The Epiphany of God occurred at the birth of Jesus of Nazareth when the Divine Word was fleshed in our humanity. The Diaphany of God is the continuing birth of the Whole Christ. The Epiphany of God is the first revelation to man of the body-person of Jesus; the Divine Diaphany is the growing revelation of the Body-Person of the Whole Christ, the People of God in union with their risen Lord. St. Paul spoke of this mystery in his letter to the Ephesians: "God has made known to us in all wisdom and insight the mystery of his will, according to his purpose which he set forth in Christ as a plan for the fullness of time, to unite all things in him, things in heaven and things on earth . . . and he has put all things under his feet and has made him the head over all things for the church, which is his body, the fullness of him who fills all in all" (1:9–22,RSV). The incarnation of Christ continues, but within the family of man.

The Diaphany of God is the birth of the Whole Christ, Head and members united in one Body, one Being. Father Teilhard de Chardin described it as our growing awareness and realization of the "Christification" of man. The Body becomes sensitive to the fact that it is a body, that it is united with one source of life that courses through it. It is Christ who struggles to be born in the family of man; but it is the Whole Christ, Jesus of Nazareth, who is the risen, glorified Lord and ruler of the entire Body. The Incarnation continues within the family of man as the Spirit of Christ gradually suffuses this Body with new life. Just as the physical body of Jesus of Nazareth grew to maturity during His life on earth, so too the new Body of the Whole Christ, a Body-in-the-Spirit, grows as well. This is not, however, just physical increase or quantitative enlargement. Growth is both physical and "personal." The Body increases physically to embrace the entire family of man, but the principal area of growth is in the deepening capacity for selfless interpersonal life and union.

What is the Christ-life that is beginning to pulsate through this Body? How is it transmitted? Where are the veins through which it is carried? Where are the cells? What are the vital organs? Where do I look to find Christ's blood, in the sense of His life? If a new reality is coming to be, where are the areas within which I must develop sensitivity in order to be aware of this life of the Whole Christ? I am conscious of the sources of physical life when I feel my heart beat or see someone bleed. I am aware of the life of the personality when I experience the joy of being with another, of sharing myself, or perhaps when I feel hurt. But what of the Christ-life of the Whole Christ? Where is it found? Where can I probe the Body, as it were, and feel the life forces at work? At what point can I place my ear against the side of humanity in order to hear the heartbeat of Christ-life?

The place where the Body grows is in the subtle area where persons meet and the Spirit is communicated. These meetings, these crossings of lives, these areas of the "between," as Martin Buber has called them, *are* the cells, the veins, the vital organs of the new creation when they are suffused with the life of the Spirit, *agape*.

The Christification of man is really the transformation of Adam into Christ. Adam is the head of the family of man. He was an individual who walked the face of the earth just as we do. But there is a sense in which Adam is a collectivity. To the Semitic mind he was a corporate personality. Although this is difficult for the Western mind to grasp, there is a true sense in which we are all "Adam." This is because we are all sons of Adam and share in his fault.

Adam's sin was to cut himself off from God. He sought self-fulfillment as a person in isolation from the source of all personal life. Adam, however, is both one and many, just as Christ, too, is one and many. We do not read St. Paul accurately unless we attempt to appreciate his understanding of corporate personality as applied to Christ. Just as Adam is the head of isolated man, so Christ is the Head of united man, of man in union with God. To the extent that we share in this union, we are of Christ, of the Whole Christ.

The story of Salvation History is the saga of the transformation of the Total Adam into the Whole Christ. This dynamic "Diaphany" takes place within the entire family of man, and at the same time it happens within each of us. The inner struggle that we each feel in our personal history is a reflection of the larger struggle that is going on within the entire family.

We feel the self-centeredness of Adam within us and at the same time experience the call to other-centered life. We recognize the sacrifice necessary to reach out to other persons. We experience the beginnings of Christ-life when we feel the transformation that the selfless love of another, *agape,* has wrought in us. Our experience increases when we in turn, because of this initial gift, can risk opening ourselves to attempt responding selflessly and with personal sacrifice to the needs of Christ's Body.

The Continuing Incarnation, the new birth of the Whole Christ, touches every aspect of our interpersonal existence. A new life within is struggling to be born in our every attempt to open out onto the world of others, to live as a person in a world of persons. This is our unique experience of Salvation History. It is our growing sensitivity to the reality of Adam's transformation into

Christ. It is a knowledge that comes with increased awareness of the presence of the Spirit. The Diaphany of God is our experience of the gradual Incarnation of the Whole Christ. We are caught up in the growth of the Body in which we are immersed as members.

Perhaps we can approach the meaning of the Continuing Incarnation from a different point of view. The angel asked Mary if she was willing to be the means of God's Epiphany in the world of man. Would she give birth to the Savior? Would Mary allow the Word of God to become incarnate in her womb so that the family of man might hear within its own flesh the language of God?

We patiently wait for a little child's first intelligible sign of recognition. The poet Virgil penned a profound line when writing, "Learn, oh little child, to know your mother with a smile." A word and a smile are such beautiful acts of incarnation and signs of communion. Mary was asked to be the *way* of the Incarnation of God's word. Would she allow the smile to reach the family of man through herself?

"Behold the handmaid of the Lord. Be it done to me according to your word" (Lk. 1:38,C). And in return we might imagine the Father responding: "You shall be a mother, you shall give physical life to the Word of God. This Word will become Flesh in you, and man will hear in the intimacy of his own language the Word of God."

What is the meaning of Mary's *fiat?* Is it not an attitude of openness to allow the Incarnation to happen? She was called upon to consent to the Epiphany of God. Mary freely allowed this in the birth of Jesus Christ. Our collective *fiat* must allow the Diaphany of God in the birth of the Whole Christ. The Epiphany depended upon Mary's openness, her *fiat,* her response, her joyful acceptance. The Diaphany of the Whole Christ depends upon our openness and sensitivity to the presence of the Spirit. If the Whole Christ is to be born in us and in the family of man, we too together with the Mother of the Church must say our *fiat.* If we are to communicate the Spirit, which is the Spirit of life that animates and builds the Body, we must remove the barriers to that openness to one another which is the "*fiat* atmosphere" within which the Spirit can communicate. In order to do this, there is need for growth in our natural capacity to live with one another on ever-deeper levels of interpersonal life.

Let us approach our understanding of the Continuing Incarnation from one final vantage point, that of the evolution of the family of man. For the moment let us contemplate the surface of our planet and be impressed with the vast cities, teeming populations and multiple treaties and political organizations which are growing among the nations. The globe is being girdled by lines of communication that bind us together in one common awareness. When President Kennedy died there was a throbbing ache in the heart of the entire world.

But what does our genius in technology, bridge-building, and mastery of swift communications tell us about the interior of man? We must learn to look at the wonderful world of communication and transportation with new eyes. It is the breaking down of physical barriers to union. Political treaties and trade agreements go one step further. Not only are barriers removed, but a common life is established. The technological, political, sociological, and religious aspects of the world in which we live are like a vast mirror. They reflect what is going on within man, deep inside each one of us. The tendency toward union is being mirrored in the physical world about us, as man structures it into his daily life and dealings with his fellow man. It is a reflection on the surface of a far deeper miracle that is taking place within the depths of the human heart.

Man reaches out for his fellow man. He finds that as a person he can live only in the world of other persons. He finds that he must begin to tear down those obstacles that separate him from his neighbor. The first obvious barriers are those of distance.

As these dissolve, however, he suddenly becomes aware that there are far more subtle barriers that he carries about *within himself*. Obstacles to the personal union of one man with another reach deep into the heart of human nature. They are the heritage of Adam. He is still with us; we are all Adam. We feel humanity's weakness every time we encounter within ourselves those excessively defensive reactions and self-centered ways of thinking that prevent us from dealing with one another in the openness of the life of the Spirit. This happens even though we are physically close together. Is this not the experience of the lonely crowd? We have been gathered in our cities and pressed together with the stifling closeness of physical proximity; yet we are alone. We have surmounted the barriers of space only to find within ourselves further blocks to the union for which we pray.

It is this desire for deeper union that is at the heart of the birth of the Whole Christ. The reason why the cells, veins, and vital organs of the new creation are to be found in our personal dealings with one another is that this is the area of growth. Here the barriers to life are coming down—barriers to the new life, the common life, the life of the Spirit, the life of the Whole Christ in *agape*.

Each one of us, unique as we are, nonetheless shares in this growing awareness of the unity of the family of man. We are becoming one. We are being drawn ever closer together. Inevitably this causes pain in our psychic life. But the pain makes us aware of the deeper untapped sensitivities and potentialities for union that lie within us. If we are in pain, we are not completely oblivious to the sensitivity that is being hurt.

As these new realities gradually emerge into the common life of the family of man, we must adjust the external structure of society and education in order to foster and preserve them.

The task of today's Christians is to become aware of and proclaim the Good News that the technical growth of man's civilization, together with his marvelous ability instantly to communicate around the world, is an external manifestation of the building up of that Body referred to in the Pauline Epistles. But this is just the surface. What of the soul of this new creation? It is here that we find the central reality of the presence of Christ and His continuing incarnation in the human experience of twentieth-century man.

It is Christ who is behind the evolution of our common consciousness of the unity of our race. The growth of man's psychic life is the strongest witness to the presence of the Spirit whom Christ has sent to draw us all into union with Himself. "I pray . . .

that they all may be one just as you, Father, in me and I in you, that they also may be one in us. . . . I have even given them the glory that you have given me so that they may be one, just as we are one—I in them and you in me—so that they may be made perfectly one" (Jn. 17:20–23C). We must learn to plumb the depths of this experience. We must not pass it over. We must learn to "see," with spiritual vision through material eyes, what happens in each of our daily dealings with one another.

We must realize that the growth of consciousness in the human family is reflected in every one of us. The personal fulfillment that all seek will come only as we grow in awareness of the presence of Christ at the heart of our own experience and as we open ourselves in a personal response. Presence must lead to dialogue, and dialogue to the mutuality of a "We" encounter.

This is that sensitivity to Christ, to the Whole Christ, which is based upon an understanding of the implications of His Continuing Incarnation. It is the risen Christ as Head who is the source of new life in the Body, and yet it is the Diaphany of the Whole Christ, the birth of the Whole Christ that is occurring within the world of our experience. It is here that we must develop sensitivity. Our practical everyday spirituality must *realize* this great truth. "His gifts were that some should be apostles, some prophets, some evangelists, some pastors and teachers, for the equipment of the saints, for the work of ministry, for building up the body of Christ, until we all attain to the unity of the faith and of the knowledge of the Son of God, to mature manhood, to the measure of the stature of the fulness of Christ. . . . We are to grow up in every way into him who is the head, into Christ, from whom the whole body, joined and knit together by every joint with which it is supplied, when each part is working properly, makes bodily growth and upbuilds itself in love" (Eph. 4:10–16,RSV).

The effects of the Incarnation ripple outward through human history to touch every life and transform it. As the People of God, we are becoming ever more conscious of the fact that we are His Body. We are becoming ever more sensitive to the Christ who hovers just beneath the surface of our experience, breaking through at moments when we least expect it. We are suddenly realizing with St. Paul not only that "we are found in Him" but that He is a growing reality in us. "I do not mean that I have already achieved this or that I have already become perfect. But I am hastening on to try to grasp it, having been myself already grasped by Christ Jesus" (Phil. 3:12,C).

CHRISTIAN IDOLATRY

Whenever we face the mystery of Christ, we are presented with the practical problem of our own personal relationship to Him. The root of the mystery, in terms of our own experience, is twofold. As human body-persons we are limited by the experience of corporeity and "bodiness," while at the same time God, the transcendent one, is totally other. When trying to contact God, the mystery would be insoluble were it not for the person of the Whole Christ who bridges the gap.

Christ, however, is a mystery because He is at one and the same time both the transcendent risen Lord, Head of the Body, and the whole reality. He is the Head, but has a Body. We are the Body of Christ, and when we seek to establish a personal relation of communion with Him, we become confused in a twofold direction. We say: "Christ is the Head, I must relate to Him as risen, glorified Lord. But Christ is also the members and I have to relate to Him here. Yet there is only one person, Christ."

Ultimately, what frequently happens is that we split the two apart because of the difficulty of keeping both in balance. We establish a relation to the transcendent Head as well as a relation to the members, and soon we end in an ascetical dualism that places primary stress on the development of a relationship first with Christ as transcendent Lord and Head of the Body. Then, and only then, do we begin to consider going out to the Body to establish a relationship with the members of Christ. It seems that the language of the horizontal and vertical, or of the transcendent and immanent, existence of Christ unintentionally continues to propagate this split.

One of the reasons we continue to foster this dualism is that we really cannot take God at His Word become flesh. We are unable really to believe that the Totally Other, the invisible transcendent God, would become man. This mystery is so painful to live with and personally realize in our own lives that we tend to oversimplify matters.

If we analyze the Christological heresies of the early Church, we find that in most cases they were attempts to oversimplify the Hypostatic Union. Rather than live with the tension caused by trying to keep God and man together in a duality of nature but unity of person, the heretics stressed either the human or the divine to the exclusion of the other. They thus manifested their inability to live with the *mystery* of the union of the two within the person of Christ. But in each case, under the guidance of the Holy Spirit, the Church always made the precise theological distinctions that in the end preserved the true mystery of the Incarnate Word of God.

Today we may not be troubled with Christological heresies in large segments of the Church, but we still have the same basic human problems of trying to accept and live with the mystery of Christ in our own personal lives. We may believe, because what is taught is a dogma of the Church; but as far as making it personally real for ourselves, we are faced with many of the same problems that may have initiated some of the historical heresies.

What we sometimes tend to do in order to simplify the mystery of Christ as both transcendent and immanent is to choose one of these two qualities as the main core of our spiritual life. Then we work out our personal relationship either with a predominant stress on Christ as the transcendent, risen Lord, or else, if we should grow tired of prayer because it does not seem relevant to the things that occupy us in our daily life, then we may begin to fashion an ascetical life stressing the service of our neighbor. Without the balance of our understanding of Christ as risen Lord, this latter can soon descend to being mere altruism or humanitarian interest, a kind of philanthropy which is basically secular. It can become activity for activity's sake, what has classically been referred to as *"effusio ad exteriora."*

The living Christ is the risen Christ, whose visible Body is the

People of God. In the Church we have the tangible presence to us of the Body of Christ in its fullest expression.

The problem here is not in service to one's neighbor, but in the kind of *presence* that is involved in it. Mere presence is not Christian prayer-life. The whole reality of our "graced-life" in the Lord is in our free and conscious response to the "we" aspect, the interrelatedness that is the mutual encounter in selfless love between the divine self-gift in Christ and ourselves. Presence, therefore, involves a personal faith-response; and the more this response is a free, self-gift in love to a Divine Person, the more this interpersonal relationship becomes a religious sacrament.

It is important to note that this religious, sacramental presence is always selfless, and therefore it is a *sacrificial* presence to the other. It was Christ's ultimate sacrificial presence to mankind and to the Father that brought about our Redemption, and it is only through this same enduring presence that we in our selfless, sacramental presence to the Whole Christ in His members effect the continuing salvation of one another in His Body. A religious response in faith to the one, risen, and glorified Lord *as revealed* to me *in His incarnate members* is essential to a spirituality that is Christian. Just as the early Councils of Ephesus and Chalcedon articulated and preserved the richness of the Hypostatic Union, so too, the Second Vatican Council, taking up where they left off, extends this doctrine in an explicit manner to the union of Christ and His Church.

> Christ, the one Mediator, established and ceaselessly sustains here on earth His holy Church, the community of faith, hope, and charity, as a visible structure. Through her He communicates truth and grace to all. But the society furnished with hierarchical agencies and the Mystical Body of Christ are not to be considered as two realities, nor are the visible assembly and the spiritual community, nor the earthly Church and the Church enriched with heavenly things. Rather they form one interlocked reality which is comprised of a divine and a human element. For this reason, by an excellent analogy, this reality is compared to the mystery of the incarnate Word.

Just as the assumed nature inseparably united to the divine
Word serves Him as a living instrument of salvation, so, in a
similar way, does the communal structure of the Church serve
Christ's Spirit, who vivifies it by way of building up the body.
(Cf. Eph. 4:16.)[1]

However, when we seek to realize an "experienced" union with
the person of the transcendent, risen Lord, head of the Church,
we often neglect the development of a sensitivity to the only true
source of a personal meeting with Christ—namely, His Body,
the Church, the People of God. Historically this is the problem
men have always had in finding God. After the Ascension, if it
were not for Christ's identification of Himself with His members,
we could have no more visible, concrete personal experience of
God in our lives than man had before the Savior's coming. The
visible expression of the invisible God now is in the efficacious,
sacramental encounter of the Christian with the Body of Christ.
We have always understood this in the cultic sacramental expression of our Lord's Eucharistic Presence. But what we have perhaps neglected in our daily life is this same sacramental expression
in the struggle to create Christian community, which inevitably
involves man's growth toward the capacity for other-centered life
and interpersonal dialogue.

When Christians search for the person of Christ, they must
be able to find Him as a Body-Person. We instinctively recognize
that He is not someone whom we adore "out there" in the depths
of space, nor is He totally identified with the neighbor. Somehow
He is transcendent and yet manifests Himself to us in the body-
person of our fellow man. "Truly, I say to you, as you did it to
one of the least these my brethren, you did it to me" (Mt.
25:40,RSV). If we are to meet Him as a living person, both
elements of transcendence and immanence must be present.

When attempting to work out our spiritual life exclusively in
terms of a relationship with Christ as transcendent Head without
integrating His visible presence in the Body of the Church, the

---

[1] *The Documents of Vatican II,* p. 22.

People of God, we run the risk of a very subtle form of idolatry. Since man is by nature incarnate-spirit, he can personally meet spirit only *as incarnated*. This is his *natural* way of interpersonal life. In other words, as a body-person man cannot personally encounter pure spirit. (This does not deny the possibility that God could choose to communicate with individual men and women in some other manner. But if the Incarnation is any indication of the way in which God has elected to disclose Himself, it would seem that He has chosen to reveal Himself according to man's way of knowing.) "Since therefore the children share in flesh and blood, he himself likewise partook of the same nature" (Heb. 2:14,RSV).

If I should therefore seek to establish a personal relationship with Christ exclusively as the Transcendent One, apart from His visible presence to me in the People of God, then, since I am by nature a body-person, *I must construct His Body in order that I may meet Him.*

Since I can meet him only as a Body-Person, I determine the moments and the places and times when He will appear to me. I fashion His bodily presence to me according to my own standards. Whether this creation is largely a picture of the historical Jesus, tailored to my own needs (the perennial pitfall of apocryphal piety), or my own determination to find Him *exclusively* in the chapel, during Mass, or formal times of prayer, these become like so many oases spread through the dry desert of my day. They are wellsprings in the midst of the "non-Christ" hours that surround me. We do not mean to imply that Christ is not present during these times or in these places, but if He is exclusively present to me *only* during these 'holy moments' and not during others, then I have opened myself to a great deal of self-deception.

Most of us acknowledge intellectually that He is present throughout the day. But the real question is: Do I acknowledge it as a *whole body-person,* which means that I know and experience His presence in more than a conceptual way? Man as incarnate spirit is open to many levels of knowledge and experience, to many avenues of receiving God's self-communication and presence, and of growing in a "reflective-body-person-aware-ness" of this presence. The problem is that of giving a whole body-personal assent *to the Person* that is present to me through-out the day, *not merely to the truth that the Person is present.*

I need a great deal of honesty and self-awareness if I am not to fall into one of two oversimplifications of the mystery of Christ in my daily life. I can either limit my presence to Christ, whether personal or speculative, to the "holy moments of my day," or I can substitute intellectual assent to the "truth" of Christ's presence for the assent of my whole body-person. In either case I have determined when He will be a Person to me. I have limited His bodily manifestations, and by doing so have really fashioned His Body to my own demands. I have not done it in such a crude form as to make a golden calf, but I have made Him over as a Person into an image of my own liking. I like to be alone, so He is a God who is most intimate and meaningful to me in aloneness. I like to be calm and serene, so He is a God of serenity. During time of stress I call on Him to deliver me from stress and return me to calmness. I never think to look for Him within my experi-ence of the stress itself. He is always outside of it. He is a God whose Bodily manifestation is only one of serenity. When stress comes it is not a Bodily manifestation of God, it is an interruption in my communion with the god whom I have made and with whom I commune in peace and tranquility.

There is a point of human growth here that we have missed. Whenever we find areas of our life as body-persons in which we cannot find the personal presence of Christ, it is usually because we ourselves cannot be persons in these areas. When we cannot bring ourselves to situations, people, or circumstances as whole body-persons with that kind of "reflective-body-person-selfless-presence" that is necessary for a real encounter, then we will be unable to discover Christ, since the interpersonal relationship *is* our encounter with the Body of Christ.

But the encounter is frequently so threatening to me that I cannot really be truly present to it as a whole body-person. I have to protect and wall myself off with various defenses. If someone is so threatening, boring, or painful to me that I cannot attempt being present to that person as I truly am without acting it out, if I cannot have a kind of "reflective-body-person-selfless-presence" to the other precisely because that person is for me the sacramental "Thou" of my encounter with the Whole Christ, then I cannot truly be present to the Whole Christ in this moment of my life.

Usually those areas in which I cannot find the presence of Christ are the situations that threaten or cause me to close myself off in some way, so that I do not bring myself to the situation or person as a whole body-person. I am present to them only in a protected, intellectual, uninvolved way, behind my barriers, façades, and the various defenses that I use to shield myself in these situations. Consequently, I am not truly present to the Lord as He is present to me in this situation. I am not really with Him as I am, as a whole body-person. I am not present in faith trying to be open to Him. I am not selflessly present believing that He is there to be discovered, that at this moment I can enter into a genuine interpersonal, I-Thou encounter with the Whole Christ.

As we have seen before, I will discover Christ only when I can risk leaving myself open in the face of the threat and the forces that cause me to close in on myself. Only in such circumstances do I truly have to live as a man of faith, believing that I will discover the Person of Christ in this risk. However, such a faith-response, which involves my being truly authentic and present to Christ *as I am* and present to Him *as He is,* needs considerable elaboration.

WAYS OF RELATING THROUGH
VARIOUS LEVELS OF AWARENESS

At this point we should try to understand, at least in general, some of the ways we relate to people through our various levels of awareness.

We might first speak of the predominantly sensory awareness of a person as an object in contact with us through touch, sight, smell, sound, or through our feelings and emotions. We can perhaps experience this type of sense awareness most forcefully when we face a vicious, barking dog that will not let us through a gate. The dog is a threatening sense-object to us. We frequently view people in much the same way. We are so threatened by their actions or attitudes toward us that we really cannot consider them to be "persons-for-us." They are mere sensory objects.

Secondly, there is the predominantly intellectual consciousness of either an idea I may have of the person as object, or a truth to which I assent that this person is what he is. For example, I may have an idea of my superior as an efficient administrator. I build up an image of the man that, while it may have some foundation in reality, is more *my idea* of him than he really is in himself. I relate more to my image of what he is rather than to him. I project my image onto him and then relate to this concept, thus reducing him to the status of an object.

Thirdly, there is a predominantly imaginative awareness of the person as object through the phantasms I have in my imagination. For example, I may think this way about someone whom I have only met in passing or whom I have never met at all, but greatly admire. I take the information that is available to me and embellish it in a legendary fashion. I recreate the person, adding or subtracting qualities at will. The phantasms that many people have about movie stars are often created in this way.

We should note that in designating these "ways of relating," we are stressing only certain predominant ways of being aware of other people for the sake of clarifying a kind of pattern that our own unique makeup tends to lean toward. It is characterized by a more imaginative, intellectual, or sensory overemphasis in the interpersonal relationship at the expense of what we will now attempt to describe as the more humanly integral way.

This latter approach is what we have called "a reflective-body-person-awareness of myself as related to this person as subject." We use *reflective* here in order to preserve the true intellectual content of this awareness, or self-consciousness, rather than the word *conscious,* which might cause some to read a too strongly intellectualist emphasis into the phrase. With the term *body-person* we hope to preserve the unity of man as incarnate-spirit and at the same time include the rich gamut of his nonconceptual ways of knowing (emotional, sensory, etc.).

The complete phrase is then spoken of in terms of "myself." We are concerned with a type of reflective self-consciousness that is the essential part of man's capacity for interpersonal growth. It is only because he is capable of knowing that he is related, and at what level he is relating, that man has the ability to make the free choice to preserve this relatedness or to go even deeper into more profound levels of meeting. This is man's self-consciousness of his openness to all of reality and of his freedom to take on the task of sharing himself in relatedness to more and more of all that exists. This level of relationship involves the reflective, or knowing, whole body-person.

This does not mean, of course, that we cannot be conscious of our own way of meeting another person as, for example, primarily through the habit of attending more to the sound of his voice, or perhaps to the content of his speech, or the visual impact that he makes on us. This is not incompatible with a more integrative and comprehensive level of relatedness, but is simply an expression of my own unique style of meeting. At the same time, we must go one step further.

The deepest and most truly human way of relating is the specifically personal, which we will designate with the word *encounter* and which is spoken of as the "I-Thou" relationship. Here I do not merely meet an individual with an awareness of our relatedness as being predominantly intellectual, sensory, or imaginative. My presence to the other is the full "reflective-body-person-awareness" of myself not as related to an object "out there" but as encountering another self, as being open to and sharing myself with a "Thou." This is the level of potential love-relatedness and of human growth in becoming a person; that is, of becoming a human being capable of giving and sharing himself in "other-centeredness" and self-gift. This is a stage of relatedness in which man struggles to become more than he is alone, to go beyond his limitations and to discover his true self by transcending his isolation.

By his very nature as incarnate-spirit, man is more than the reality enclosed within the limitations of his physical body. His spirituality seeks to carry him beyond himself into a personal realization and fulfillment which he, as a single body-person, can never achieve alone. As long as man remains locked within the world of relating to others as objects, this essential need of his deepest being remains unfulfilled, and he is incomplete as a man. He cannot grow into becoming a person.

In order to avoid confusion and to dispel some of the naive thinking that tends to disillusion many concerning this I-Thou level of encounter, it should be clearly stated that many of the people we come in contact with may be incapable of or simply not choose to enter into such a relationship. In many instances they choose not to respond at such a level because of their social, cultural, or religious patterns of life, or simply because the casualness of the meeting does not provide them with an opportunity to dispel their initial inhibitions and fears. Such is the world of human relationships in which we all live, and we should not only be realistic about it but must also respect the freedom of others and not impose ourselves on them.

However, this does not mean that we should not struggle to be *available* and present to all men as a potential friend at the I-Thou level of encounter, even though to all appearances they do not or will not respond in like manner. The very witness of the religious life demands a level of availability to all men that is characterized by consciously attending to them as human beings, not as objects. The other may ignore me, even reject me with violence, but still I must struggle to be present and remain available to him at the I-Thou level of encounter. This is my invitation, although it may always remain one-sided, since I receive little or no human response from the other person.

However, if my I-Thou availability and presence to the other is reciprocated, then a whole new reality is born. What begins to happen is the creation of a "We." There is now an "interpersonal happening," a mutual sharing, a reciprocal give-and-take between two people as whole body-persons.

At this level of encounter, the self-consciousness that I had of myself in isolation is minimized, both because of the direct sharing of myself with another and because of the focus of my consciousness on the other. Yet there is now an even fuller "reflective-body-person-presence" to myself that may at first seem paradoxical but is not, because it is the very gift of selfhood; it is the consciousness of finding and possessing myself most fully, precisely in the act of giving myself away. I find myself richer and more fully a person in the response of the other to me and in our mutual exchange between each other. The growth process is a mutually creative "We" realization. This sort of relationship is characterized by what we choose to call in this book a "reflective-body-person-selfless-presence-to-the-other."

The I-Thou encounter between men is a stage of interpersonal growth that for us has been caught up in the self-gift of Christ to man. The I-Thou encounter of Christ's invitation to all of us has fused our becoming a person *as* our "becoming a person in the Whole Christ." The two are no longer separable, for without the gift of selfless love (*agape*), this deepest and most truly human way of interpersonal realization cannot be achieved among men. This is our visible expression both of unity with one another, as well as our I-Thou encounter with the Father in and through the Body of the Whole Christ.

Our task as Christians is to discover and constantly deepen the "we" level of relatedness to the Whole Christ. This is especially an imperative for religious, whose vows are really the public proclamation of their total self-gift to the Whole Christ. We religious must never, either through ignorance or by default, substitute any other level of meeting as our ordinary way of "growing in Christ." If we do, then the gnawing loneliness of personal emptiness, of stunted human growth, and constant anxiety will take their toll.

To recapitulate part of our exploration up to this point, we have said that our availability to all men must be one of potential friendship in an I-Thou relationship, even though this may never be returned. Yet when another person freely chooses to reciprocate in like manner, then the "We" relationship is created. We can never force other men to respond in the intimacy and selflessness of an I-Thou encounter. But when another person freely

responds to us, and some experience of this is absolutely necessary for balanced human growth, then we experience that we
become more a person, capable of greater intimacy and involvement, more capable of selflessly sharing our whole body-person
with others. When we are fortunate enough to have had a rich
background of I-Thou involvement, the direction of our "way of
relating" to people is predominantly one of personal encounter.

We have been called by Christ to respond to His I-Thou invitation to each of us with a reciprocal gift of our whole selves.
Christ has already initiated this call of friendship, but now the
choice of response lies with us. This is the moment when we are
faced with many of the deceptive choices that, as history amply
corroborates, have confused so many religious. We have already
briefly discussed a few of them.

The fundamental theological truth behind our response is that
in answering Christ's invitation to encounter Him in a "We"-
relationship, what we actually encounter in our "reflective-body-
person-selfless-presence-to-Christ" *is the neighbor*—all those
people in my life who are for me the People of God, the Body
of the Whole Christ.

But as I look at my own life and the lives of those around
me, I begin to realize that this relatedness speaks to me of
manifold levels of interpersonal relationship, from the grossest
forms of inhuman exploitation and impersonal rejection to the
ecstasies of intimate union in mutual selfless love. Within such a
vast array of conflicting personal responses to me as my experience of the visible Body of Christ, how am I to develop a stable,
constant "We" encounter with the risen and glorified Lord?

This answer is very complex in the existential order, and the
purpose of this book is to attempt some new directions toward
a possible solution. Theologically the answer can be summed up
as simply *the free gift of divine faith.* How God communicates
this gift to us, in what way we open to receive it, and in what
manner we struggle to live an authentic human life in faith,
giving witness to its vitality—all this is as complex as the mystery
of man himself.

It is the "We" encounter that calls us out of ourselves to

transcend our own egocentricity and the innate pull inward to isolation, our heritage from Adam; this is the level of true "faith-encounter," involving the whole body-person in a commitment to another. The other, lesser levels of relatedness are not capable of a true, human "faith-encounter" because they simply do not involve the whole man as he really is. They are only partial aspects or elements of an authentic encounter. Insofar as our response is guarded and limited, or securely held in check by our own defenses *alone,* it does not demand the risk of that act of faith on our part which is the necessary ingredient making possible our true meeting with the Whole Christ.

As I daily face those aspects of the Body of Christ that hurt me or threaten me, sometimes literally hurling me back into isolation, I am confronted with the call to authenticity. It is a call to be true to my deepest self and to transcend my own limits and weaknesses in the truest expression of personal love—an act of faith in another. It is this moment of existential choice, in which I am called upon to affirm my movement toward becoming a person in Christ, that demands that I cultivate and sustain what we have called a "reflective-body-person-selfless-presence-to-the-other."

When threat or pain confront me, I must consciously be so "close to myself" and, therefore, to my emotions, body, imagination, etc., that I can know myself as a "needer." This "closeness" tells me that I require a power greater than my own if I am to risk being authentically present *as I am* to the other person with my feelings of fear, anger, or frustration—feelings that I must neither act out to his detriment nor attempt to "will them away" on my own. I am perhaps first of all a "needer" just in order to be capable of accepting these negative feelings as my own, together with the consequent limitations and inadequacies that they impose upon me.

We have all experienced the dissatisfaction and varying degrees of frustration produced when our needs are not fulfilled. Our emotional life, generally speaking, is an outcome of the satisfaction or non-satisfaction of personally felt needs. As we grow older, we tend to interpret frustrations as expressions of our personal limitations. We see them as negative reflections upon our value and worth as human persons. It is only natural, therefore, that we begin to erect defense mechanisms to protect our self-concept. This is our unreflective way of trying to tell ourselves (and others) that we are really worth something. It is a natural (and usually necessary, but rather primitive) struggle to search out and express our uniqueness that so yearns for affirmation and confirmation throughout life.

The whole question of mental health, as well as the deeper theological implication for my developing relationship to the Whole Christ, is bound up with the use I make of such mechanisms. To what extent do I have recourse to them in order to flee from reality, thus avoiding the risk, pain, and necessary tension that are essential to an increased growth in freedom and responsible decision? Most important of all, how often do I use these mechanisms to evade a healthy existential dependence on God's personal self-communication to me as the ultimate solution to my deepest need for the peace and integration that human self-realization seeks to achieve? To what degree do I erect barriers in order to isolate myself from the consciousness of my own real limitations, and hence from those needs of other people that usually bring my inadequacies out into the light of day in the first place?

It should be obvious to the reader at this point that there are far-reaching implications in this one area of our psychic life for an incarnational spirituality that is grounded in an openness and conscious response to the "needs" of the Whole Christ.

It must be remembered that these needs are my own, as a member of the Body of Christ, as well as those of others. However, the effectiveness of my response to the needs of another will be proportioned to that faith-response on my part which is, in the existential order, my risking being a "needer"; that is, being selflessly present to the needs of the neighbor with that kind of freely chosen body-person presence that is authentic because in faith *I believe that I am not alone*. In fact, as time goes on, I will find that I can risk being "real" with others without my defenses and all the answers; at the same time, I will actually experience the "We-ness" of my intimate relationship to the Whole Christ as a body-person. I can face threat and live with greater amounts of frustration because of a living relatedness to the Whole Christ, whose presence more and more permeates my entire body-person with *His* Peace.

Consciousness of myself as a "needer" must always extend beyond myself to the other needs of the Whole Christ, who calls me to let them be the sacramental signs of His everlasting desire to give Himself to me. So it is that frustration, pain, threat, joy, anger—everything to which I can grow more and more sensitive in my body-person—become for me the invitations of the Incarnate Lord, calling me to accept, encounter, and become sensitive to Him within my own incarnational response to another. "Oh that *today* you would hearken to his voice! Harden not your hearts" (Ps. 95:7–8,RSV). The psalmist's urgent cry expresses so well the existential character of Israel's struggle for a realistic dialogue between Herself and God.

Today is always the time of encounter. God speaks to us through the veiled needs of the present moment. It is here that we must commence our dialogue, discerning His voice with open hearts and freely choosing to risk finding Him incarnated in the needing Body that yearns for our love.

To a greater or lesser degree, these existential moments of choice throughout my daily meetings with people confirm me in a personal tendency in one of two directions. Either I move toward increased "opening up" and availability as an authentic, whole body-person, which means I must of necessity live a deeper life of faith to sustain me in such selfless presence and vulnerability; or else I regress by shielding myself and gradually turning back within myself into isolation. When we make the latter choice, faith is meaningless and unnecessary. There is no need to believe when we have sidestepped the risks involved in personal growth. The anxiety, neurotic guilt, and self-disgust that so characterize modern man are the inevitable results of a choice against a human faith-encounter with the Whole Christ. And we must truthfully acknowledge that these tragic defects have not remained outside the rectory or the cloister walls.

In summary, let us state that it is at the level of the "We"-encounter that my life in the Whole Christ must be lived. It is here that I must be authentically present to the Whole Christ as He is truly present to me. The direction of my growth as a person in Christ (my so-called "spiritual life") must be toward the development of a capacity for "reflective-body-person-selfless-presence" to the Whole Christ.

This means that I freely and knowingly choose to make myself available as I really am as a whole body-person. I actually take myself into the presence of the other (or others) with a conscious awareness of my whole body-person. I truly put myself as I am at the disposal of others. I am vulnerable and open to the Body of the Whole Christ as He is actually present in my world. This presence is mediated through all those people whom I contact in the day-by-day existence that makes up my life chapter in Salvation History. I consciously choose to encounter the Body of Christ with a truthful and authentic gift of myself in and through a "selfless presence." I seek to live an openness to the needs of the Whole Christ, and I desire to give myself to those needs.

At this level of encounter there is an *effective* participation of my whole body-person in the very being of another. He is transformed, in a sense, and recreated by my relatedness, if he can be open to receive me. This efficacious self-gift in and through my whole body-person is the foundation of the sacramentality of our interpersonal relationships. To be humanly efficacious, our meetings must be "encounters"; that is, they must involve on each part a genuine "reflective-body-personal-selfless-presence-to-another." There is present here an interlocking exchange of actions that is mutually causal. Here we must stress the role of reflection in this whole growth process. It is necessary to grasp my experience intellectually so that I can continue to make those free choices to remain open and available as a potential I-Thou friend with all men. For example, after some personal meeting I can perceive through reflection that I was closed off, that I allowed my feelings of threat, pain, or desire to isolate me from the real "need" of the person. As a result, I related to him as an object, as a means to my own ends, or else I may have tried to reconstruct him to fit my needs of the moment.

The values preserved by the traditional, formal "spiritual exercises" with their stress on "recollection" assume even greater importance for the prayer that would result from this way of encounter with the Whole Christ. These moments of formal prayer or recollection are the time when I can pull my faculties together and in faith, under the Spirit, try to reflect lovingly upon my experience of the Whole Christ, discerning what has happened and is happening "between us." Those moments should help me to become more sensitive to what is needed if I am to move toward a life of greater involvement with the Whole Christ, sharing in the intimacy of a more total body-person union with Him.

As human beings, we are not just sensing or intellectualizing creatures. We are human persons whose various levels of awareness, those beautifully complex ways of knowing proper to an incarnate-spirit, are always open to be given or not given to another in a consciously free choice. We need to become more and more sensitive and open to the clues disclosed to us by our pre-reflective experiences. We must learn to let our bodies, our feelings, and our emotions speak to us about our capacity for selfless encounter. Once this heightened consciousness becomes a reality, however, the fact will always remain that we still must make the conscious free choice to bring or not bring our whole body-person into a "We" encounter with the Whole Christ. Knowledge alone is never a substitute for the free, personal response of faith and love.

5. Being Present to the Whole Christ

DEEPENING FAITH IN AN "AUTHENTIC" PRESENCE TO THE WHOLE CHRIST

AT THIS POINT the reader may be asking the following question: How can I be authentically present to another member of the Body of Christ when I am filled with feelings of anger or hostility, without either acting them out, creating defenses, or trying to repress them? We pointed out that no one can ever truly develop a relationship with the Whole Christ unless he can be consciously present with the very feelings and thoughts that are authentically his as he relates to the Body of the Whole Christ here and now. In order to do this, we must live such an existential presence to the Body of Christ, to the presence of the Whole Christ in *faith, that we can risk living with ourselves as we truly are.*

I must be so open to the needs of Christ's Body and to the power of selfless love, *agape,* which I experience in His Body and in myself, that these become the personal presence of Christ to me with such force, at the level of body-person reflective awareness, that they overcome my feelings of threat, anger, fear, and tendency to retreat into isolation. In other words, my faith becomes strong enough so that I can afford to be truly present as a body-person, with all my feelings of anger and hostility. Through the gift of faith I am enabled to see the other as the sacramental Thou of my encounter with Christ.

To the extent that I have my barriers up or repress these feelings from my consciousness, I am incapable of the openness and authenticity required for a personal encounter with the Whole Christ. I am not truly present to the other person, who for me is the Body of Christ. Nor am I present *in faith* to the real Christ, because there is no risk involved. I have my defenses up. *Psychologically* I am not existentially present to the other person because I have a mask on; and *theologically* the façade is the very defense that eliminates the necessity for a lived faith-presence. Without risk there is no faith.

It is the very struggle for personal integration brought about primarily in our dealings with others, where freedom is challenged and risk is demanded, that presents us with the marvelous opportunity of discovering Christ as the source of our human development. Every attempt to risk finding Him in what we fear most or where we least expect Him is a part of the way of faith mapped out for all Christians. Once we begin to realize the true meaning of "growth as a person," we awaken to new areas of possible encounter in our life where we will be called on to make acts of real faith.

The prophet Isaiah teaches us a magnificent lesson when he has God address Israel in the following manner:

"Fear not, for I have redeemed you;
 I have called you by name, you are
  mine.
When you pass through the waters I will
  be with you;
 and through the rivers, they shall not
  overwhelm you;
when you walk through fire you shall not
  be burned,
 and the flame shall not consume you.
For I am the Lord your God. . . .
Fear not, for I am with you." (Is. 43:1–5,RSV)

The Israelites were a primitive people still struggling with the violent forces of nature that refused to be tamed and that brought death and destruction in their wake. But now God commands

His people to find Him in the turbulence of the rushing waters, in the terrors of fire and lightning that burn and consume. In other words, God manifests Himself as Body-Person in the very forces of nature that the primitive mind saw as sources of death and destruction. God commanded His people to risk finding Him in the frightening power that they feared most. His only promise was "I am with you." Our security is always that He is Emmanuel God-with-us. Our risk is that we must meet Him as Body-Person in situations, people, and personal experiences that are not always to our liking and that sometimes are downright terrifying.

Isaiah shows us that God did not remove the element of risk from Israel's life as a people when He gave her a vocation. As a matter of fact, if we read the Bible with some attention, we see that from the very moment God called His people out of Egypt to offer sacrifice in the desert, this vocation was an invitation to risk and to hazard. Israel's real greatness, her fidelity to this vocation, was demonstrated neither by being sheltered and protected, nor by achieving security through a withdrawal from the difficulties and hazards of life. Rather, she manifested her fidelity to the Covenant by accepting risks with faith in the promise that God had extended to her: "I will be with you." From the first to the last, her God was Emmanuel. This is perhaps Israel's most characteristic conception of God—the One who remains faithfully with her in the midst of trial.

The parallel between the trials that Isaiah describes as presented to the Israelites and those that we face in our discovery of God-with-us in the threatening aspects of our interpersonal life within the Body of Christ are obvious. The more primitive Israelites were forced to find God in their struggle with the violence of nature. But man has since biblical times evolved politically, socially, and scientifically; Salvation History has taken *the* definitive step forward. However, we are still called to a life of faith and an even more profound belief in Emmanuel now that we live in the last days of the continuing Incarnation.

God is still the great risk in our life; He will never be discovered "with-us," at our present level of human evolution, until we are willing, in faith, to enter into the processes of human growth. These are now the waters through which modern man must pass. This is the flame wherein he must risk finding the living God.

SUFFERING, DEATH, AND RESURRECTION

"All this is that I may know Christ and the power flowing from His Resurrection; that I may know how to share in his sufferings by being formed into the pattern of his death, in the hope that thus I may also arrive at the resurrection from the dead" (Phil. 3:10–11,C).

As Christians of today struggle for personal maturity and self-identity, they must be helped to view this life experience as an integral part of Salvation History filled with the presence of the Spirit. Unless they perceive that the death of Adam together with their own self-centeredness is an indispensable prelude to a deeper, more mature life as a human person, and that this natural growth can only be accomplished in the Whole Christ, then they will never see any reason for embracing the threats of interpersonal encounter as the Salvific Cross which is our way of growth into union with God. St. John understood the dynamics behind this death-resurrection sequence and its connection with human growth when he wrote in his First Epistle that: "We have passed out of death into life *because* we have loved the brethren" (3:14, RSV). (Italics ours.)

Let us for a moment reflect on two types of daily death that we all experience. The first is a prelude to resurrection and new life, while the second reinforces us in the isolation that is our heritage from Adam. We can perhaps best distinguish these two types of death by first reflecting on the true meaning of the death which is at the heart of Christian mortification. A subsequent reflection on the miracle of "personal" resurrection will then draw both into focus.

REFLECTIONS ON MORTIFICATION

When treating of sensuality and the need for mortification, ascetical literature has frequently failed to distinguish between our sense *feelings*—both bodily and emotional—and their *self-centered use and expression.* The point we wish to make clear is that it is not the feelings themselves which are to be condemned, but rather the sinful, self-centered way in which they can be acted out.

We should carefully explore our feelings in an effort to come closer to the truth of what they can tell us about ourselves. First of all, our "raw" feelings, so to speak, express *both* the transcendentality as well as the self-centeredness of man and therefore cannot be sweepingly categorized as suspect, let alone totally self-centered. Secondly, when these feelings are integrated with our conscious awareness of them, they can tend to make us self-preoccupied. But these "known-feelings" may also be the principal motive behind a desire to thrust "outward" in search of higher personal fulfillment. Thirdly, if the feelings are allowed to remain in one's consciousness, there will be a tendency to act them out in a self-centered manner unless some measures are taken. This very crisis can, of itself, provide motivation for choosing either the dehumanizing possibility of suppression and defenses or the development of one's self-consciousness as a body-person *within* that which characterizes personal life, namely, an *interpersonal relatedness.*

For the Christian to consider man's bodily and emotional feelings as merely self-centered, and then to maintain that if they should remain in our consciousness they would inevitably be acted out in a self-centered manner, would be to consider man apart from Christ. This would be no more than a rather naive psychology founded upon purely secular reasoning. Such an attitude misses the significance of the Incarnation and the power that Christ has loosed within the family of man through the sending of His Spirit. It fails to realize that we now have a force *within,* allowing us to be authentic, to acknowledge consciously and accept our selfish feelings; and yet, rather than acting out their self-centered drive (which would be natural for man), we can live in faith with the power of Christ. We can be conscious of our selfish feelings and also conscious of a power within that enables us to act out the life of God, *agape,* and not the life of

Adam, self-gratification. It is perhaps a paradox, but we can become most conscious of this vital force of God *within our personal growth* when we experience it contrasted with that self-centeredness which, if allowed to be consciously present within us, we instinctively recognize we would, of ourselves, act out. When I can allow all my self-centered feelings to be consciously present, and then, aware of myself as I authentically am, take myself to the Whole Christ in faith and in this "faith-presence" to the Body of Christ discover a power that enables me to be conscious of my naturally selfish feelings *without acting them out*—but in fact enabling me to act out the exact opposite, selfless love—then I experience a power in me that is "Other" than myself.

When the Word became flesh, He took upon Himself all of the basically self-centered forces within man, and yet by living out His life in a completely other-centered manner, always obedient to the will of His heavenly Father, He bore witness to the power of God in His life that enabled Him to be a man (to feel all of our weaknesses) and yet to live with the life of God—to be, in fact, the God-man. "For we have not a high priest who is unable to sympathize with our weaknesses, but one who in every respect has been tempted as we are, yet without sinning" (Heb. 4:15, RSV).

Ascetical literature has frequently misunderstood the role of Christ in the integration of our vital feelings within a balanced and mature human personality. So often He has been called on to help us *not feel* the feelings that well up within our bodies. Christ has become a principle for repression of the feelings themselves rather than the *Living Presence enabling me to remain open to the selfish feelings*, while at the same time unselfishly acting out the love that is the power of God within me, *agape*.

In the one case a temptation, the desire to use the feeling in a self-centered manner, is identified with the feeling itself; and Christ is called upon to blot out the entire complex. In the second case, the feelings are recognized for what they are, something basically good that I *can* use either in a self-centered or other-centered manner. The role of Christ is not to remove, suppress, or repress these feelings, but to help me *consciously* live with them, while *at the same time* turning outward in a selfless expression of *His love within me.*

The death of which we speak as a principle of growth is not the death of the feeling, but *the death of the self-centered expression of the feeling.* The resurrection which follows this death is the elevation to a higher level of mature personal life wherein I can begin to incarnate more and more a selfless love, the love of Christ within my body-person sacramental expression to the world.

THE MIRACLE OF DAILY "PERSONAL" RESURRECTION

Paul stands in awe of the "power flowing from His resurrection." Although the ultimate manifestation of this power is in Christ's physical resurrection from the dead, we make a mistake if we restrict it to this alone. We must learn to become sensitive to the power of this resurrection at work during the course of our own daily life.

Our Lord left us an experiential legacy of personal resurrection and new life summed up by two statements as the substance of the Continuing Incarnation. "I came that they may have life and have it abundantly" (Jn. 10:10,RSV), and "Love one another as I have loved you" (Jn. 15:12,RSV). This new life and love is the life we have in Christ's spirit.

In the seventh chapter of his Epistle to the Romans, St. Paul describes the state of man facing the problem of human maturity without Christ. The law of God, an external force, constantly reminds him that the way of self-fulfillment is through other-centered activity; while the law within him, the law of his members, clamors for fulfillment in terms of self-gratification. This tension in the flesh cannot be resolved by man alone. It draws from Paul the agonizing cry, "Wretched man that I am! Who will deliver me from this body of death?" (Rom. 7:24,RSV). He acknowledges the hopelessness of his situation and the need for a Redeemer, someone from outside who will enter into his struggle between the law and himself. It is with great joy that he can conclude his lament with the relieved cry: "Thanks be to God, through Jesus Christ Our Lord" (Rom. 7:25,RSV).

By becoming man, Christ took upon Himself the tension that we all feel. But in living out a life of obedience to the will of His heavenly Father, He never consciously ratified self-centeredness as a way of personal fulfillment. He lived a fully human life in which all of His vital forces as a man were centered on God the Father and lived out even to death in a selfless manner. The Resurrection was not only a sign of God's acceptance of this pleasing sacrifice, but also signified that a force had been irrevocably loosed in human history whereby man could now begin to live an other-centered life, not merely because of the coercive power of an external law, but because of a new law in his members enabling him to live for others *as a man.* He could now begin to break out of the heritage of personal isolation bequeathed to him by Adam. This new gift within him made the possibility of Resurrection a reality.

It was because Christ possessed the Spirit in union with the Father during His life on earth that He could always consciously turn His human capacity for love outward rather than inward. He was able to transcend the isolation and self-centeredness of Adam through the dynamism of the Spirit's presence at the heart of His human love-life. The Resurrection was the sign that Christ had definitively conquered the death of isolation. By rising from the dead, Christ in His humanity forever broke through the wall of self-centeredness separating man from God.

Then in His glorious ascent in power, together with the Father He sent the same Spirit into His Body to continue the resolution of the state of division which had already been healed within the humanity of the Head. It is the Spirit at work in the hearts of the faithful who now enables them to turn outward toward one another.

Psychologists and theologians are in agreement that human maturity is found in the growing capacity of man to transcend personal isolation. But this is an activity accomplished in the Spirit. Thus any kind of lasting human maturity is irrevocably linked with the gift Whom Christ and His Father have sent us. It is the Holy Spirit who is at the center of our human development as persons, because it is only in and through the Spirit that we can transcend the tendency we all have to seek fulfillment in isolation.

What is an experience of daily resurrection in concrete terms? How do we develop sensitivity to this language of resurrection, this voice of the Spirit who has come to bring us to life in greater abundance?

Perhaps a few examples will help to clarify this matter. Frequently there occur moments in our life when we desperately want to be ourselves, to express how we really feel, but we cannot because we are confused or afraid. Or there may be times when an objective situation demands that we prudently but courageously speak out in defense of someone, even at some cost to ourselves, yet we do not. All the while we feel the struggle that reverberates throughout our affective and intellectual make-up. We acknowledge at this moment that we are in a state of division. We are also aware, in remaining silent either by reason of conscious choice or sheer weakness, that we have missed an opportunity to grow as a human person. By holding back within ourselves, we remain in a kind of isolation and state of death.

It is at this precise point of experienced tension that Christ calls us to life and to a life of more abundance. The sacrifice to which He calls us is *death to that part of ourselves that wants to close back in isolation.* Our acceptance of this call to sacrifice brings a resurrection to a new life of greater personal openness, awareness, and other-centeredness. It is the "more abundant life" of the person who can really be himself as other-centered. It is the fullness of cooperation with the Spirit in our response to the Whole Christ that enables us to "become a person" through the growing ability to transcend isolation as a way of self-fulfillment.

Here we see the two deaths of which we spoke earlier. They are in direct confrontation with each other. Resurrection depends upon the flooding of Adam's isolation with the light of the Spirit. It is a death to and liberation from self-imposed darkness and loneliness.

Paul prays: "... that I may know how to share in His sufferings by being formed into the pattern of His death, in the hope that thus I may also arrive at the Resurrection from the dead" (Phil. 3:10–11,C). His prayer is that he may pass through the death that leads to resurrection rather than remaining in the definitive death of isolation. The pattern of Christ's death, a dying to our desire for isolation as a way of personal fulfillment, is always before Paul.

As Christ became a life-giving Spirit only after the Resurrection, so too we can give love only in proportion to the death and resurrection that we have undergone in our growth toward becoming a person in the Whole Christ. "It is expedient that I go to the Father, for if I do not go away the Counsellor will not come to you; but if I go I will send him to you" (Jn. 16:7,RSV). Death was the condition of His Resurrection to that new life wherein He could give the Spirit to us. This pattern of death and resurrection in us leads to maturity in personal life. The daily death and resurrection involved in the dynamics of our human growth as persons within the Body of Christ follow the same path as the Head. The gradual Christification of Adam, the evolution of the Whole Christ, and the suffusing of the members with the dynamic life of the risen Lord take place only through death. To the extent that the individual members begin to live with the life of the Head, they too become life-giving Spirits. They can extend this *gift* to others. "Love one another *as I have loved you*" (Jn. 15:12,RSV). (Italics ours.) The point is that He loved us with a selfless love. Only Christian *agape* can enable the family of man to transcend the isolation of Adam.

In this brief discussion of death and resurrection, we have tried to indicate man's incarnational experience of the power flowing from the Resurrection by showing the way that he must "... share in Christ's sufferings and be formed into the pattern of his death" (Phil. 3:10,C). This is not realized by the suffocation of our spontaneous desire for life, but only by a death to their self-centered demands. The experience of resurrection is found in the growing ability consciously to live with myself as I authentically am, acknowledging my selfish feelings and emotions, yet at the same time remaining open in my personal union with the Body-Person of the Whole Christ in order to receive and live with that power of God's life which enables me to transcend my own selfishness and death-filled isolation.

To do this is to experience in our human growth the first dim intimations of that life of glory which is gradually catching us all up into the life of God. To open ourselves to the force of Christ at the heart of our personal development is our way of joining with St. Paul in ". . . hastening on to grasp the perfection of the resurrected life" (Phil. 3:12,C). But we can do this only because we ourselves ". . . have already been grasped by Christ Jesus" (Phil. 3:12,C).

We hope these pages have shown that the Christian values traditionally recognized in "abnegation" and "mortification" are as true today as they ever were. However, religious have often failed to show the relevance of these values to modern man, both in the way they present them as well as the manner in which they live them.

The cross of Christ cannot be imposed on man from the outside under the guise of penitential practices adopted from another century or culture. Neither can it be found through imitation of the external penances of some holy individual, which may stand as a sign of his unique and saintly integration of the mystery of suffering into his life. The Cross must be found *within* each person's own life experience; and for modern man it must be found within his experience of himself as struggling toward self-fulfillment as a person in the Whole Christ.

Man has always had difficulty locating the true source of evil that is at the heart of the mystery of suffering and the Cross. Paul speaks of the "secret power of wickedness" at work within the world which "the Lord Jesus will annihilate by the radiance of his coming" (2 Thes. 2:8*). Our Lord testified to the divisive force of evil somehow present in the very core of human existence when confiding to His disciples that "[The World] hates me because I testify of it that its works are evil" (Jn. 7:7,RSV).

* NEB: From *The New English Bible, New Testament.* Copyright The Delegates of the Oxford University Press and Syndics of the Cambridge University, 1961. Reprinted by permission.

We ourselves experience the effects of this wound when feeling the disorder between ourselves and others, and among men of different races, nations, and colors. In a word, man and the whole of his universe suffer from a deep disunity and confusion in their relationships.

Perhaps a more primitive people tended to place the source of evil outside of man, in the physical forces of nature or a social structure that oppressed them. The Jews awaited a Messiah-King who would liberate them from Roman dominance. Even after His Resurrection, the disciples still naively asked Christ: "Lord, is this the time when you are to establish once again the sovereignty of Israel?" (Acts 1:6,NEB). They had not yet come to realize, as Paul would a short time later, that Christ had come to liberate them from evil within themselves, from sin and death. He had come to establish a new kingdom within men. But the disciples' concept of evil was so primitive that they did not realize that Christ's Incarnation and sacramental revelation of the Father, expressed through His interpersonal relationship with them, was the power that was capable of definitively ending the reign of evil in the heart of man. "The Lord Jesus will annihilate [sin] by the radiance of his coming."

Our Lord's response to the disciples when they questioned Him about the restoration of Israel was simply to tell them: "It is not for you to know about dates or times, which the Father has set within his own control. But you will receive power when the Holy Spirit comes upon you; and you will bear witness for me in Jerusalem, and all over Judaea and Samaria, and away to the ends of the earth" (Acts 1:7–8,NEB).

In the power of His Spirit, they would witness in a far more profound manner to the "restoration" of Israel. With the coming of the Spirit, the New Jerusalem had begun; the Kingdom of God was firmly rooted in the hearts of men. But the Cross would always remain as the way to restoration and the path to resurrection. "If anyone wishes to be a follower of mine, he must leave self behind; he must take up his cross and come with me" (Mt. 16:24,NEB).

Perhaps today we are at the point where our gradual growth as persons in the Body of Christ has made it possible for us to

understand that in order for every crevice of the human personality to be implanted with the dynamism of His selfless love,
Christ's redemptive power of *agape* had to penetrate just as
deeply into the heart of human personal existence as had the
selfishness of Adam. This *agape* is the life of God, but what we
have difficulty accepting, *as* did the Apostles, is that this divine
life is, above all else, *personal*. Its communication, therefore, will
be within man's *interpersonal* life. For the first disciples this
interpersonal life was their relationship to Jesus of Nazareth, but
for us today this continuing interpersonal life is with the Whole
Christ.

The mystery of the Whole Christ is the unifying power that
brings wholeness into our lives and into the world. This mystery
continues as God re-establishes the unity of all things by reconcil-
ing them to Himself in Christ. Only by existentially deepening our
union with the Whole Christ do we today become one with the
Father, capable of revealing the mystery of Christ crucified and
risen. Only by becoming *ourselves* the mystery of death and resurrection do we "preach the hidden secrets of God" in an
effective, sacramental witness.

Modern man will not even pause to consider the "foolishness of
the Cross" unless we approach him where he deeply feels the need
for unity, integration, and wholeness in his personal life. The
mystery of Christ crucified, which is a sign of contradiction because He is the perfect embodiment of Divine Wisdom (1 Cor.
1:17–2:16), confuses modern man. But today, more than ever
before, this confusion is open to our witness because many men
deeply feel the need for unity, even though they sometimes look
upon the necessary means as dehumanizing and beneath human
dignity.

There will always be those for whom the "foolishness of the
Cross" is a contradiction, simply because it involves pain, selfless
love, and a radical dependence upon God. But these are not the
men of whom we speak. There is a great surge within mankind,
especially among the young, toward an appreciation of the human values present in sacrifice, dedication, and self-gift to some
cause or ideal of human betterment. Tragically, however, it is

this same group that often views our Christian witness of Christ crucified as a barrier to the achievement of their human values and social goals.

The "hidden secrets" of God's self-gift to men through the mystery of the crucified Christ can be effectively revealed to these searching people only when we, as body-persons in the Whole Christ, meet their deepest personal needs through our healing, sacramental, resurrected presence—a presence that, although a seeming sign of contradiction, meets their deadening "pull-to-isolation" and replaces it with the power of Christ's selfless love.

It does little good merely to talk or preach about penance today. But the very body-person wholeness of a Christian apostle becomes the most effective sign of the mystery of the crucified and resurrected Lord. When men are confronted with a person whose life reflects a death to self-centeredness and resurrection to a fuller capacity for mature human love, they are drawn by the power of the new life in him. This is the way that we must *live* Christ, and so "Put on the Lord Jesus" (Rom. 13:14,RSV).

We must preach Christ crucified and resurrected with the sacramentality of our lives, because the very meaning of sacramental encounter is—a meeting that touches the whole man. To be effective sacraments, we must have unified the spiritual and the material, the death and resurrection, into the oneness of our own body-person.

Too often we have lost sight of the fact that the Cross is meaningless without the Resurrection. To consider it in isolation from the new life that follows is basically un-Christian. But we have also sometimes forgotten that the Resurrection can only be effectively preached by a *resurrected person*. The Christian must effectively sign, in his sacramental presence to the world, the presence of Christ crucified and risen. His body-person must sacramentally witness to the death that has led to new life and to the faith that enabled him to risk "being conformed to his death in order to finally arrive at the resurrection from the dead" (Phil. 3:10–11,C).

Sacraments are meant to express our whole body-person experience of faith and to signify and engage a response from others in the same way. Sacraments are bodily expressions of the reality that we believe and live; as such, they signify an affective, imaginative, as well as an intellectual experience of faith. Hopefully, if our interpersonal communication is sacramental, it will engage the same human qualities in another person's response. Fortunately, effective human communication is not limited to an exchange of concepts. The unity of man's psycho-physical system, in the interdependent and inter-related activity which is human life, can be meaningfully grasped only by sacramental communication. Anything less will leave his imagination, his feelings, his affectivity (and, paradoxically, much of his most creative intellectual capacity) untouched.

As the extension of the mystery of Christ's death and resurrection, Christians can lay hold of the hearts of contemporary men only when their human wholeness speaks with compelling force to all that makes another individual human. We must speak especially to each man's interior struggle between selfish isolation and "other-centeredness" as he cries out to "become a person in the Whole Christ."

Only a Christian energized with the divine *agape* of Christ can live out the daily death that such sacramental communication demands of us. This is the real Christian penance of the whole body-person (*metanoia*—the whole-man's turning to God), a penance with the necessary interior disposition and necessary penitential acts turned toward God in and through the Whole Christ.

MAN'S CALL TO SHARE IN
TRINITARIAN LIFE

The fact that God communicates Himself to us through our interpersonal life is something that does not dawn on many Christians. The truth that human growth has now been caught up into the economy of God's self-communication to man in and through Christ has not been clearly stated. But it has always been an integral part of Salvation History as God gives Himself to man in Jesus Christ. Our problem today is the same as it has always been. We still cannot fully appreciate the significance of the Incarnation and the Hypostatic Union.

God gives Himself to us in this interpersonal growth in order that we may ultimately participate in the interpersonal love of God, the Trinitarian life. We are called into this life, this community of Persons, this perfect sharing of ourselves which is our unity, through God's free invitation. When Genesis speaks of our creation in the image and likeness of God, we must understand that we have been created like Him not just in our being and existence, but also in our doing and acting, in our free choices. It is especially within this particular aspect of our "likeness to God" that we are called upon to grow. We have been given the gift of a free will and an intellect, which makes personal growth in freedom possible through the personal gift of self, as in the life of the Trinity. This is why some theologians hold that we cannot really say of a person that he is *imaging* God and living out his human vocation, or that he has responded to God's call to him in creation to "be" in His image, until he has committed himself to another person as a "vocation to be lived out." It is in this manner that marriage through its sacramental nature completes man. It is the same with the life of the religious vows and a total commitment to the Whole Christ. Both vocations presuppose this public gift of self to another, together with the historical living out of this value, which then effects within the persons that "image and likeness" to the Community of Persons that is the Triune God.

Trinitarian life, God's life of love, is the communication of Person to Person, the gift of self in its perfection to the Other. It is into this life that we are invited by the Father in Christ through His Spirit. The real living out of this life of love in the present era of God's relationship with man, this "fullness of time," is now within the Body of the Whole Christ. It is lived between all men who have been joined to and caught up in Christ.

When we reflect on what happens to people as they fall in love, we realize that there is a real union that takes place within them and that grows as love grows. At the same time, we experience an increase in personal freedom, in self-identity, in self-realization, in a kind of independence within the dependency of inter-relatedness and union.

Our capacity for this phenomenon stems from our creation in the image and likeness of God's Trinitarian life. God has structured into us this innate ability to grow in union with our fellow men when He created us as incarnate spirits, capable of developing in human love and freedom with one another. But He also "waits on our response" to His gift of Himself to us through the Whole Christ in order to perfect this capacity.

The point we want to stress is that God has given us a human foundation for our participation in His life and has structured it into the very process of our human love. When we live our experience of interpersonal communion, in faith, as involved in the life of the Whole Christ, we become a true Incarnation of Trinitarian love-life and, as such, are intimately caught up within the life of God. Within the Trinity, the gift of Self to the other Persons *is* their union, whereas in man it is the love-relationship between human beings, acted out selflessly in faith within the Whole Christ through the Spirit, that effects the union both between the persons themselves and between the persons and God. We can never consider a union of persons "in Christ" as a relationship somehow or other apart from God. If two people are united in Christ, their personal union *is* their union with God. "I pray . . . that they all may be one just as you, Father, in me and I in you, that they also may be one in us, that the world may believe that you sent me. I have even given them the glory that you have given me so that they may be one, just as we are one—I in them and you in me—so that they may be made perfectly one" (Jn. 17:20–23,C).

God communicates Himself to me now within the Whole Christ, in and through my human growth as a person as I try to become mature enough to be capable of receiving and in turn giving selfless love. This very facility is in itself the gift of God's own life, something which I do not deserve. But it is communicated to me in the very process of sacramental interpersonal encounter. This begins in the very early stages of life when a child first receives care and selfless love and is accepted and valued as a person, even though he is self-centered. This kind of selfless love, given in the face of the child's own egotism, sustains him and ultimately enables the child gradually to identify with that selfless love that is present to him in the Whole Christ through those people who love him.

THE TRINITY, THE HYPOSTATIC
UNION, AND THE WHOLE CHRIST

Our relation with the Triune God must be both articulated and lived in such a way that we in some way witness to the Hypostatic Union existing within the Whole Christ. The crucial problem we face in developing a spirituality that is theologically accurate and at the same time according to God's plan of self-communication to man, is in maintaining within this spirituality of the Whole Christ that unity which is more than a mere extrinsic imitation of the Hypostatic Union. This is a delicate theological point, and the Fathers of the Second Vatican Council show great tact and prudence when they discuss it.

> For this reason, *by an excellent analogy,* this reality (the Church) *is compared* to the mystery of the incarnate Word. *Just as* the assumed nature inseparably united to the divine Word serves Him as a living instrument of salvation, *so, in a similar way,* does the communal structure of the Church serve Christ's Spirit, who vivifies it by way of building up the body (cf. Eph. 4:16).[1] [Italics ours.]

The union of the divine and human within the person of Jesus of Nazareth is *compared, by an excellent analogy, in a similar way* to the unity of Christ's Spirit with the Church. Just as the former is no extrinsic union, neither is the latter. But just as the Fathers of the early Church concerned themselves with the relationship between the human and divine natures in Christ, so it will remain for the theologians of a "new Chalcedon" to spell out in greater detail the quality of the relationship existing between the person of Christ and His Body the Church.

For our present purpose, let us say only that we are attempting to formulate a statement which *reflects in some analagous way* the mystery of the Hypostatic Union within the Whole Christ.

---

[1] *The Documents of Vatican II,* p. 22.

As members of the divine incarnated Person and identified with the Body of Christ, the Church, we must now articulate concretely by our lives, as effective material signs of His presence, the mystery of the union of Christ and His Church. Our spirituality must be based on the reality of the Incarnation and the "Continuing Incarnation" of the Whole Christ within the family of man. We must preserve the mystery of transcendence and immanence without overemphasizing one to the detriment of the other. In discussing the union of the risen Lord with His Church in this book, if we spoke of the "transcendent Christ" and the "immanent Christ," we would leave ourselves open to the possibilities of fostering that dualism which contributes to the spiritual excesses of modern-day idolatry. Possibly the following statement might better maintain the unity of the human and the divine within the Whole Christ while at the same time preserving the absolute transcendence of the glorious risen Lord: *Human beings cannot meet the person of Christ, the transcendent risen, Lord, apart from the Body in which He is present to them.* Articulating the truth in this way, we are attempting to include in our statement about man's discovery of the person of the transcendent Lord the very body-personal experience within which we find Him in our human development.

The Christian will hopefully be less likely to separate the two if he tries to realize that his body-personal experience of the Whole Christ *is* his interpersonal life in faith with the People of God. Just as Christ is the sacrament of our encounter with the Father, so mankind is the sacrament of our encounter with the Whole Christ.

A PEDAGOGICAL ILLUSTRATION
USING A GESTALT

Through the Incarnation, Christ has become so intimately involved in our personal growth that to become a person and to grow in Christ have really become two aspects of the same reality. In the existential order they are inseparable.

A Gestalt image, with its fluctuating change of "figure" and "ground" can be used to illustrate *pedagogically* the Christian's realistic experience of the Whole Christ. One must, however, seek to verify this simple visual experience on the level of interpersonal life. The only purpose of the image is to give some idea of the integrated and organic character of our faith-experience of Christ within the flesh-and-blood realities of our daily life.

"Figure" and "ground" mutually support each other. I either see a white goblet on a black background, or else I perceive two black faces staring at each other across a white background. The figure of the goblet demands the ground of the black faces if it is to be seen, and conversely the opposed black faces as figure depend on the ground of the white goblet. In other words, we cannot visually see one element without the other.

If I did not know that the picture was a Gestalt, I might tend to rest content with the first figure that I saw and make no additional effort to discover the other dimension. I would remain satisfied with the one isolated figure and not plumb the further depths that change it into the ground of the second figure.

It must also be noted that I need not go outside of the picture to find the two images. All of the ingredients for discovery are present within the Gestalt itself. The only external aid necessary is for someone to reveal to me that this is a Gestalt, and that I must make the added effort to go beyond my first primitive and isolated experience of the one figure. At the same time, I cannot divorce myself from the first image, because it serves as the ground for the second.

We frequently have difficulty realistically experiencing the presence of Christ and our incorporation into the Whole Christ, because we live our daily moments of joy and suffering in isolation from Him. We do not find a person *within* our experience. We rest content with the figure of our isolated daily life without ever being any more than *intellectually* aware that there is another dimension to it. We never know, with the totality of a "body-person-reflective-awareness," that our human experience *is* the ground for our discovery of the personal presence of Christ-for-us.

Whether we choose to be conscious of it or not, Christ has caught up and incorporated all of mankind into His Body. What we must now struggle to develop is the existential experience, an "in-faith-reflective-body-person-selfless-presence" to the reality of the Thou of Christ present in my relationship with another person. The thou whom we meet in our neighbor is not apart from the Thou of the Person of the Whole Christ. We cannot divorce our experience of the Divine Person from His members who are, for us, the incarnated sign of His presence, His Body filled with love and needs. This is the Whole Christ of our human experience. The long, difficult struggle in faith, to which every Christian is called, is growth in the development of a capacity to pierce the surface of his everyday life in order to see it as the ground where he meets the Person of Christ. Ultimately this capacity is a pure gift. But the ground for our life of glory, which is actually beginning now through the Continuing Incarnation and the divine Diaphany, is the life we live with one another in the Body of Christ Jesus.

"For this reason I bow my knees before the Father, from whom every family in heaven and on earth is named, that according to the riches of his glory he may grant you to be strengthened with might through his Spirit in the inner man, and that Christ may dwell in your hearts through faith; that you, being rooted and grounded in love, may have power to comprehend with all the saints what is the breadth and length and height and depth, and to know the love of Christ which surpasses knowledge, that you may be filled with all the fulness of God" (Eph. 3:14–19, RSV).

6. Man-Made Composure versus the Peace of Christ

PURITY OF INTENTION— A SINCERE BUT LIMITED RESPONSE

IN ORDER to describe the discovery of the "Thou" of Christ, one must carefully make certain distinctions regarding what has traditionally been referred to as "purity of intention." The interpersonal dynamism, or interaction, of which we speak in this book is a "reflective-body-person-selfless-presence-to-the-other," rather than a physical action that is "baptized," so to speak, beforehand with purity of intention. Too often this latter is merely a mental act. Intellectually we say to ourselves: "I want to perform this action with and for Christ." The difficulty is that frequently this purely rational awareness does not overflow into our affectivity. It is true that a human response to Christ is grounded in our understanding and free choice to give our whole selves to Him. The intellectual and volitional faculties of man must always be preserved and developed, but they are not the totality of man.

It is unnecessary to stress the fact that philosophically and theologically we acknowledge the *truth* of the wholeness of man and the unity of his body-person response both to his fellow man and to God. Scriptural studies are continually uncovering the richness of this truth as they plumb the depths of the Hebrew people's understanding of their relationship with Yahweh. Knowledge and love were never abstract qualities for the Semite. Man knew and loved God not as an intellect and a will but as a dy-

namic union of body and spirit. St. Thomas himself never lost
sight of the unity of man in the midst of his detailed analysis of
human intellectual and volitional life. The orthodox teaching of
the Church has always preserved this unity in man's being and
way of knowing as incarnate-spirit. Her pastoral, liturgical, and
sacramental life, stressing symbolic gestures, color, sound, light,
and scent, has always witnessed to a profound awareness of
man's integrity.

It is sometimes useful to discuss man's component parts so as
better to understand him in his relationship to the world and God
as an incarnate-spirit. In the existential order, however, man
does not exist in little pieces, each operating somewhat inde-
pendently from the other. Those who speak of the "war" between
matter and spirit within man frequently make it sound as though
man were really identified with his spiritual part, making war on
the body as "other than himself." It is almost as though man
has to subdue the body as a foreign agent, as though the body
were outside of what he really is.

Perhaps we have misunderstood the doctrine of the immortality
of the soul. Since the soul is immortal, we tend to identify man
with it, forgetting that even the separated soul is still oriented
toward matter in order to express itself. Man is created *incarnate-*
spirit. As a person, he is made to live in the world of other persons. For him to be person is to be interpersonal. To be an
"incarnate-spirit-person" is to be "interpersonal through matter."
This is the natural way of interpersonal life for man. God may
suspend these laws in the case of the separated soul, but we must
never build our philosophy of man upon this somewhat unnatural
state of being. To do so would imply that man's personal life is
really quite independent of his body. This would deny the entire
sacramental way of life in the Church and the efficacy of Christ's
redeeming action upon the Cross. The bruised body of our Savior,
together with its transformation in the glory of the Resurrection,
is the efficacious sign of the Father's love for man and our incorporation into Trinitarian life. We are caught up into the interpersonal life of the Trinity through the Body of Christ, and our
own body is no peripheral accessory to this union with God.

Unfortunately, we have inherited a subtle attitude that affects our whole stand toward reality and interpersonal life. It is an implicit dualism, including a tinge of Manichaeanism, that is handed on in a kind of nonverbal, pre-reflective way. It is never found in the official, orthodox teaching of the Church, but sometimes subtly pervades the writings of many ascetical authors, who are frequently responsible for the "attitudes" of popular piety.

There are usually far more warnings against the excesses of the body than against those of the spirit. At the affective level, we tremble at the possibility of falling into sins of the flesh far more than we fear excesses in the opposite direction. Few of us lose much sleep over the possibility of being swept away by spiritual pride, but we do live with the constant threat of being pulled down into matter, of becoming gross and carnal, of trading our spiritual birthright for a pot of pleasure. If there must be excesses, most of us would rather have them in the realm of spirit. Perhaps we unconsciously feel that here, at least, the battle is more interior, less open to the critical eye of our peers and superiors, and certainly less likely to involve us in scandal.

The struggle may be less visible, at least to the uncritical eye, but we pay the same high price in lack of maturity, lack of integration, and lack of sound apostolic effectiveness. We may not be giving scandal in the usual sense of this word, but our very inability effectively to communicate Christ is a far greater scandal. It witnesses to the sad fact that He is not the principle of our integration, and that our life, for all of its vaunted sacrifices, is really quite empty.

Perhaps we have used purity of intention to take up the slack in our want of wholeness and personal integration by cultivating a kind of growth in conscious "intellectual wholeness" as our asceticism. Could it be that we have somewhat unconsciously inherited this undercurrent of Manichaean dualism and not realized that, without critical evaluation, purity of intention can easily cloak and foster it?

When our thought patterns are tinged with this uncritically accepted dualism, and we are thrust into tension by the ever-present task of attempting to integrate our incarnate-spirit into a dynamic unity, then the anxiety this produces seeks a resolution. This is especially true if we should experience a strong tendency to identify our "real self" exclusively with the "spirit," lest we open ourselves to the possibility of literally "falling into the body" and becoming able to find our real identity *only* there.

Perhaps in the past we have attempted to reconcile this necessary tension in growth, this "body-personally-felt-need-for-wholeness" with the oversimplified and fragmented approach of the excessively rationalistic person. We simply *will* to be whole; or, in other words, we *make* ourselves whole by having the intention of being whole. This effort can be quite sincere, and usually is. Yet it is, at best, a rather primitive attempt to respond as a sacramentally efficacious sign of the presence of Christ. The intention is good, but intentions do not make sacramentally effective signs in the existential order, unless they overflow into an entire body-person response to other men.

Since the material element in man has frequently been looked upon as "second class," we have often attempted to find our integration more in terms of a predominantly intellectual effort, which we sometimes feel is the "purer" element. We have sought integration more through a rational intention of being whole rather than through a lived wholeness involving our complete body-person.

We may have tried to achieve wholeness with purity of intention. We "baptized" our action with the *concept* or idea of being a body-person involved "in Christ." But the truth is that all too often we unconsciously used this as an easy way to escape from the painful task of daily struggling to become a genuine body-person present to the Whole Christ. This latter involves growth toward a truthful "being with" myself and others. Day by day I must work at responding with authenticity in my presence to the Whole Christ. This means that I must consciously *include* my body, its affectivity and wide spectrum of feelings, sensitivities, and needs *within* the more "intellectual" and "volitional" presence to others that possibly may have characterized my "learned way of encounter" in the past. Purity of intention has too often provided us with a safe and convenient means of affectively leaving the body "out there," while at the same time intellectually uniting it through intention to our apostolic involvement with others.

Should this be done in the name of a very acceptable ascetical principle, while beneath the surface it is largely motivated by an unconscious desire to avoid the risk of living with my body, then personal integration and growth in the Spirit through authentic presence to the Whole Christ has been bypassed. And yet this growth and integration are the very "stuff" of any genuine prayer-life. When we have cut ourselves off from effective growth at the body-person level of our relationship to the Whole Christ, prayer often becomes merely an empty exercise; in some cases, it is a kind of compulsive ritual to alleviate neurotic guilt feelings. The kind of neurotic anxiety that seeks "to get such and such a number of prayers said each day" is a pathetic caricature of the teaching of Our Lord to "pray always."

Unfortunately, the common interpretation of purity of intention does not foster a growing body-person awareness of the presence of God, and does not lead to a clearer awakening of the sense of God in every man's own body-personal relatedness to all of reality. The "way of prayer" of which Christ speaks in "praying always" is an invitation freely to participate in the gradual Diaphany under the Spirit of the *musterion* of the Whole Christ. It is a call to *live with* God-Incarnate. But it can in no way be a life *apart* from my body or the materiality of inter-body relatedness.

Purity of intention is a hazardous means, at best, of reaching maturity in Christ, because it too easily falls prey, as we have said, to a naive resolution of the necessary tension involved in growth itself. My body, with its many avenues of knowledge and its ability to contribute sensitivity to subtle levels of non-verbal communication, is the primary source of my contact with reality; consequently, it is the incarnate expression of my presence to reality.

This "body-presence" is the sacramental presence of my whole body-person. It becomes for other men either an *effective* or *ineffective* experience and contact with the sacramental presence of the Whole Christ in their lives. If I am unable to bring an integral body-sensitivity, united with my intellectual and volitional awareness, into a dynamic oneness of presence to others, then my "intention" of total self-gift is but an illusion. I must commit myself to Christ as He is actually present to me in those around me, the Christ of my experience. What I give must be the *totality* of myself to the *Whole* Christ.

Authentic body-person presence to Him is the efficacious sign of my intention to be truly sacramentally involved with His continuing, saving, Incarnation. An integral body-person presence to the Whole Christ is essential to any sincere expression of self-gift toward the Whole Christ.

The original idea behind the use of purity of intention was certainly to foster greater personal involvement with Christ. Because, however, this particular ascetical principle is very susceptible to an over-intellectualist interpretation, it has frequently been terribly misunderstood and tragically misused. Even when the proper distinctions have been made, they have rarely been comprehended in such a manner as to offset the possibility of the one-sided emphasis that seems to be an inherent weakness of this principle.

Ultimately, of course, it is the Triune God who makes up for my deficiencies. He is the One who takes up the slack in the insufficiency of my fully integrated body-person wholeness. But the Divine Persons do not take up this slack by stepping outside of our created human nature and its intrinsic laws of development. The psycho-physical systems in man have an interdependency and interlocking dynamism in their organization that underlies the unity of our body-spirit indivisibility and integrity. The Divine Persons do not come to dwell in the depths of man to effect growth in "graced wholeness" only within the realm of the non-material, let alone the intellectual and volitional.

The doctrine of purity of intention has often led us to approach the question of personally integrated growth in Christ in a manner which is both psychologically as well as theologically unsound. To attempt an asceticism in which I go as far as I can on my own toward "getting my feelings in order" so as to be an effective sacramental sign to another, while at the same time calling on Christ to fill the gap in what is still needed, borders perilously close to semi-Pelagianism. Few of us can afford not to reflect seriously and meditate upon this tendency.

We do not work at becoming an effective, sacramental sign by acting as if we develop the capacity for interpersonal life on our own, and then call on Christ because we have not had time to complete the integration ourselves. As this book has repeatedly tried to point out, my very growth as a person is always a gift to me—a gift of selfless love from another, and ultimately The Other. I cannot will to become a person. I can only humbly, gratefully, and lovingly accept the gift as I receive it through my lifelong contact with those who for me are the Body of the Whole Christ. Consequently, Christ is involved from the very beginning in my growth as a person and my growth in the capacity to be a sacramentally efficacious sign of His presence.

Man's very being is a becoming, and mature integration is not instantly accomplished. Instead, the growth of my personality is a task, and there will always be deficiencies, gaps, and areas of non-integration where I have not fully received, or been able to receive, the selfless gift that makes me a whole person.

The question, then, is: How does Christ fill up my lack of integration, especially in those areas where my own mature wholeness is incomplete, in order that I may effectively manifest His presence? Is it sufficient to baptize my lack of integration with purity of intention? Can I make up for the feelings of anger, fear, boredom, and excessively strong attraction with the "pure intention" of communicating Christ? Does the addition of this intention to my feelings make me an effective, sacramental sign as a whole body-person?

In most instances, we must frankly admit that we make the intention of performing an action for Christ but must then still struggle with our strong feelings. Purity of intention does very little to heal our disorderly emotions. Consciousness of the abstract truth that Christ fills up my deficiencies is not enough to deal with a sudden surge of anger or fear that sweeps over me as I confront a threatening person. My intention may be to communicate Christ, but my whole affective body-reaction is totally against it. How can I witness to Christ when I am this way?

Most of the time in my dealings with others, when I find it difficult to be truly "present" to them, I am conscious of a pull into isolation or of strong feelings in the opposite direction from what my purity of intention or genuine attitude wants to be. How can I risk being truly sacramentally present as whole body-person to another when I have the vivid consciousness of my affectivity going in the opposite direction from what I want to do by intention? If I am authentic and do not either repress or in some way put down the feelings that well up within me, I am faced with the difficult task of attempting to live with them. How can I be authentic when I am really hostile, threatened, or bored without either acting out these feelings or retreating behind defense mechanisms that effectively conceal my real feelings from all but the practiced eye?

The answer to this question demands a somewhat careful analysis of the way in which we are sacramental signs of the presence of Christ, precisely *as weak* and filled with personal deficiencies. We obviously cannot do this by merely 'baptizing' our adverse feelings with the intention of communicating Christ. Moreover, since we all recognize that we cannot act out our feelings of anger or fear and still effectively communicate Christ, we try the next best thing. We consciously attempt to suppress the feelings. (We are not referring here to the psychological mechanism of repression.) We try to "get hold of ourselves" so that, for example, a meeting with another will not be a total catastrophe. We even pray that Christ will "take away the hostile feelings" so that we can confront the other person in a state of calm, and thus, as we think, effectively communicate Christ-likeness.

Neither pure intention nor suppression of feelings, however, enable us to be effective signs of the Lord's presence. In the one instance, the feelings get in the way; and in the other, there is no visible sign of the presence of the power of Christ in us. We have suppressed the very feelings that, if felt and lived in a reflective-body-person-"We"-presence to the Whole Christ, could have manifested within us the presence of the power of the Lord.

God communicates Himself to men through the sacrament of the whole man, through the visible, material sign of man's total body-person presence to all of reality as his response to the mystery of God's self-gift. If I am so threatened or affectively disoriented that my defenses are up, I cannot witness to the power of God's love that sustains me in my threatened state.

By suppressing the strongly adverse feelings of fear, hostility, or boredom through the use of consciously developed defense mechanisms, I witness to the fact that, like most other men, I have compensated for my weaknesses. Over the years I have developed certain ways of protecting myself when threatened. But this says nothing about the power of Christ at work in me. It merely says that I am a man, and that I behave like most men when threatened. (We are not speaking here of unconscious defense mechanisms, for they usually call for professional psychotherapeutic care.)

The very tension created in trying to live a conscious, authentic type of existence is an effective witness to the presence of the power of Christ in my life; I risk being myself with Him and at the same time am involved in my work with others as "We"-related.

This ability to be consciously aware of my own unsuppressed needs and feelings, and yet at the same time show by my actions a genuine concern for the needs of others, witnesses to the efficaciousness of God's relationship to me when I authentically respond to Him as a "needer," that is, as one incomplete and not fully integrated. My feelings show that I am a needer and weak, yet my actions are not those of a weak person. It is thus that I witness to the power of Christ within me. I witness as one who needs to be resurrected, as one who is willing to risk in faith living in openness with myself as a "needer"; the "real me" is threatened and strongly feels dislike or hostility, but nonetheless I risk being present this way to the Whole Christ.

This is the point at which we can truly say with St. Paul, "It is no longer I who live, but Christ who lives in me" (Gal. 2:20, RSV). "I live now," I am really alive to myself, not walling off unacceptable areas of my life, but consciously taking myself as I am in weakness into a faith-encounter with the Whole Christ. Then a transformation takes place: "It is no longer I who live, but Christ who lives in me; and the life I now live in the flesh I live by faith in the Son of God." His life becomes manifest in me, His power surges through me. I am consciously filled with my weaknesses, yet I *live* with *His life.* I am weak and strong at one and the same time. This is an extremely powerful witness.

People instinctively recognize when we are weak. We sometimes pride ourselves on how clever we are at masking our true feelings, but sensitive people see them in us. Man of course communicates in non-verbal ways. His every movement or non-movement reveals something about the state of his inner being. Yet when I can acknowledge and be aware of my weaknesses and still be an effective, healing, sacramental presence of Christ's *agape,* then the only possible source of this power must be my union with Christ Himself.

This "being-with" the Whole Christ is the oneness of a simultaneous presence to myself, my neighbor, and to the Transcendent Lord in the Triune God, whose expression to me is so clearly and humanly manifested through the needs of His Body. I can then beg Christ, with a kind of authentic presence, for a sharing in His *agape*-life, so that I will not act out my feelings in a self-centered way but may remain open to the needs of His Body with a selfless presence.

In the last section of this book, we will discuss further the implications of this "awareness of myself as a needer" for a sound Incarnational spirituality. Suffice to state here that in any encounter with my neighbor I must be present as a body-person. However, in an encounter that involves my feelings and emotions, I must be even more consciously present as a body-person in a selfless way. I must be aware of my body-person as "in-faith We-related," as "We-present" during my awareness of certain strong feelings, such as, for example, fear or possessiveness. At the same time, I must also be reflectively aware of my body-person desire to be selflessly present to the person before me, to be present as gift and not to hurt, to heal in spite of my opposite feelings. It is in these circumstances that the Divine Person of this "We" relationship will effect in me the body-person sacramental sign of our friendship.

I must, however, truly be present *as I am,* living in the midst of the tension aroused by consciously allowing my feelings to be alive in me and yet at the same time being present in faith to this experience, believing that I will meet the person of Christ within the very forces that threaten me. Both of these realizations, the awareness of threat and the desire to discover and communicate Christ, must be consciously present in me so that I may, in faith, be a sacramentally efficacious sign of the presence of Emmanuel (God-with-us). I must take myself to others and be present to them in a way that gives witness to the reality of divine life in me. I must witness to a power at work in my body-person that enables me to transcend my own strongly felt needs, not by defense mechanisms of my own making, but through my efficacious integral involvement with the Whole Christ.

When my weaknesses shine through and are visible, when I am authentically present as one who himself needs to be healed and yet at the same time as someone who effectively heals another, then this is a way that Christ's love can truly be seen in me according to what I truthfully am.

When another person can perceive my weaknesses, my self-centeredness, my insecurity, my hostility, my boredom—and yet at the same time really experience me listening to and healing his needs at the body-person level of human communication and existence, then I am a living witness to a power at work within me that could not possibly stem from myself alone. Of myself, in isolation, all that I could do would be to react to the demands of my own feelings toward the person or situation.

If I choose effectively to suppress my feelings, then the person with whom I am in contact is not led to ask any questions about that power that he did not experience within me. It does not take the power of Christ to manipulate feelings. It *does* take the power of Christ consciously to live with certain strong feelings in such a way that I not only do not act them out but I can even transcend them, and so efficaciously listen to the needs of another that I heal him.

This "agape-action" is not just a purity of intention on my part (in an intellectual sense), but is the expression of faith in a lived out "reflective-body-person-selfless-presence-to-the other."

The paradox of this sacramental way of prayerful encounter with the Whole Christ is that I am a sign of God's presence *precisely because of my weakness.*

This is what St. Paul means when he speaks of a glorying in his weaknesses. The Apostle was very sensitive to those moments when his consciousness of the presence of Christ was heightened. Like anyone, he realized that moments of "contrast" were perhaps the most effective times when one could develop sensitivity to the presence of God. Paul did not glory in his being a Hebrew or a Son of Abraham as much as he gloried in weaknesses: "If I must boast, I will boast of the things that show my weaknesses. . . . I will all the more gladly boast of my weaknesses, that the power of Christ may rest upon me. For the sake of Christ, then, I am content with weaknesses, insults, hardships, persecutions, and calamities; for when I am weak, then I am strong" (2 Cor. 11:30, 12:9–10,RSV).

In weakness he discovered the strength of the Lord within himself. It was especially at these moments that he could say: "It is no longer I who live, but Christ who lives in me" (Gal. 2:20,RSV). This was the time when he could contrast the power of God effecting some good with his own weakness that, of itself, was enough to hinder the good. By not hiding behind a defense mechanism, he risked allowing the power of God to become consciously felt in his life. When we are perceived as being "body-person weak" but nonetheless are found capable of communicating the strength of Christ, then we are effective, salvific, sacramental signs of a power greater than ourselves.

Perhaps this is why Christ chose the "poor" of this world to be the effective salvific signs of His presence on earth. We do not have to be towers of personal integration in order to mediate the love of Christ effectively. But in our weakness we must be able to risk in faith an authentic encounter with the *Whole Christ*. We must risk being *needers* and at the same time risk opening ourselves to the needs of others, both to heal them and to be healed ourselves, precisely *because* our *mutual needs* are seen in faith as those of the Whole Christ. This faith-encounter is what enables us to live consciously aware of our feelings without acting them out in a way that would be harmful either to ourselves or our neighbor.

If we are able to perceive only our experiences in isolation from the Whole Christ, then we can never really discover Him in our human moments of falling in love, being afraid, or strongly desiring to use another person for selfish needs. Just as the prophet Isaiah tried to express his vision by using the imagery of a language familiar to a primitive people, so in his Epistles did St. Paul when he boasted of the weaknesses in which he discovered the power of Christ. Scripture reveals to us that it is principally through the risk of opening ourselves in faith in the midst of threat and human inadequacy that Christ will reveal Himself as being truly present. To the nonspiritual eye there would seem to be nothing present except an isolated human reality. It would not be the ground and sign of something deeper.

St. John invariably speaks of the necessity to act out our intentions. When living the Christian life of *agape,* we must actually *become* what we intend. "If anyone says, 'I love God,' and hates his brother, he is a liar" (I Jn. 4:20,RSV). We must so incarnate our intentions that they overflow into our entire body-person response. Perhaps this is why we instinctively recognize that there is more to charity than the intellectually pure intention of being charitable. The Church's stress on faith *and* good works, or the emphasis of some spiritual writers and saints, like Ignatius of Loyola, on the value of body-posture in prayer, shows the importance of an incarnational response.

The purity of intention that is often little more than an intellectual "baptism" of my action, leaves me as an ineffectual, fragmented sign. My interpersonal actions are sacramentally effective signs of the power of God only when they involve the totality of my personal presence, that is, a "reflective-body-person-selfless-presence-to-the-other." I cannot be a sacramentally effective sign of Christ's presence when I am only half there.

The effort to develop a "reflective-body-person-selfless-presence," which is a real prayer of faith in the Whole Christ, at once brings me into the world of my lived-out experience. This can involve me in an intensely exciting discovery. The growing awareness of my ability to be so "close to myself" that I can consciously recognize my instinctive reactions to others, as well as become aware of the gift of a growing capacity, within my whole body-person and within those I love, to heal with Christ's love and live with His life, is a thrilling experience. I can consciously and prayerfully observe the intimate Personal presence of God ripening within my life.

As a religious, the entire purpose of my life is to become close to this process of growth in union, and to commit myself to it more and more as the source of my self-identity, so that those with whom I come into contact may find this same meaningful, deep identity within their own lives. Our Lord said: "I came that they may have life and have it abundantly" (Jn. 10:10,RSV). The abundance here is precisely this total body-person involvement in the *agape*-life of the Whole Christ, which the Christian and especially the religious seek to live at its deepest level. It is fundamentally an interpersonal life with a self-identity deeply rooted in the reality of Emmanuel.

MAN-MADE COMPOSURE VERSUS THE PEACE OF CHRIST

We are not attempting to describe an asceticism that escapes pain or sacrifice. On the contrary, it is only by being authentically open, sensitive to, and in faith accepting the very existential situation that threatens us, as being the "ground" of our experience of the Whole Christ, that we will be able to relate in an I-Thou way to the person of Christ as He is now truly present to us in His Body.

Whether we like it or not, each of us, according to his temperament and life-situation, will experience attraction, fear, repulsion, etc., in our daily encounters with others. It does no good to use the defense mechanism of an assent to the *truth* of Christ's presence in place of a full commitment of ourselves as body-person, with very real feelings and emotions, to the Whole Christ as He presents Himself to us through the obscure signs of His Body.

Defense mechanisms can be a substitute for real faith when they are consciously fostered in order to avoid the risks of mature growth toward finding Christ in what threatens us. We might paraphrase St. Paul and say that "if justification were through consciously fostered defense mechanisms, then Christ died to no avail."

There is a kind of situation where, when I feel myself becoming threatened, I can "will" my own peace. I can so structure the interpersonal meeting that it is non-threatening to me, and then a kind of peaceful calm will come on the surface. This does not, however, witness to the presence and power of God's love in me. I detour out of the area of the body-person threat and bring my own peace to the menaced affectivity. This failure to live with a threat and to remain open in spite of it does not, however, witness to the fact that it is the power of Christ that heals. Our Lord says: "Peace I leave with you, *my peace* I give to you" (Jn. 14:27, RSV). The peace that the Lord gives is not the peace of the world. The peace that the world gives is the peace that *we make* by getting out of the body-person threat through our own efforts. The peace that the Lord gives is the peace which enables me to live with threat and still be authentic as threatened, because I have found Him in this experience and can communicate His love in and through the faith-witness of my "reflective-body-person-selfless-presence-to-the-other."

What our Lord wishes to tell us about His peace is that: "I give you the gift of my peace. This is my abiding farewell to you, my peace, my own life, my selfless love, my *agape;* such as the world cannot give, so that you will not have to live in anxiety and fear." As Christians, our peace must not be the peace that the world gives, but rather that peace which comes from finding our self-identity in the capacity to live with risk and threat *because* of our relationship with the Whole Christ. We do not live with the insecurity of having constantly to manipulate reality by setting up false values and our own defenses in order to create a kind of artificial peace.

THE WHOLE CHRIST—NEEDING
AND LOVING

To say that "we act," Christ and I, is not some speculative ideal of Christian perfection which can become a realized part of our lives once we intellectually acknowledge it. Unless we begin to grow in our awareness of "His felt-presence" in all that we do, unless we gradually realize that our every action, sin excepted, is an integral part of the building of His Body, then we have scarcely begun to live the Christian life. As Christians we are called to the realization that we are no longer alone.

When the agonizing cry, "My God, My God, why have you forsaken me?" (Mt. 27:46,C), was wrung from Christ on the Cross, it was the cry of a Divine Person who in His humanity had allowed Himself to experience the full effects of man's sin, without Himself having sinned. He let Himself feel the utter loneliness of man, locked in the isolation that is part of our heritage from Adam. Once man is encapsulated within a life of self-centeredness, his experience of every action rings with the hollowness of personal loneliness. But in His Resurrection, Christ forever broke through the barrier separating man from God. We now live in Him, but we must still grow in our awareness of this fact. This is the Christian life, a growth in consciousness of how we have ". . . already been grasped by Christ Jesus" (Phil. 3:12,C).

If we are to risk the kind of open body-person presence in pain, threat, suffering, and objective evil in which the gift of faith is deepened and we discover Christ as a "Thou-for-us," then we must recognize that our ability to find Christ Incarnate in the threatening circumstances of life is built upon our previous faith-experience of Christ in and through the selfless love that has been extended to us through His Body. Experiences like these resurrect and build up our whole body-person capacity in such a way that

we can desire the gift of a deeper faith to search for Christ and
want to find Him in the threatening reality that confronts us.

This is a kind of "growth-in-love-process," a faith-in-love response to the Body of the Whole Christ. It needs to be prepared
for by having experienced the gift of *agape* (selfless love) in the
Body of Christ during our early life. As human beings, we grow
through others. This growth is so "*agape*-conditioned," because of
our need for the experience of selfless love from another human
being, that even biological and physiological maturation and the
very learning process itself has been shown to be retarded in
children deprived of this experience. This growing capacity for
faith and love comes to us in the whole developmental growth
process—as a baby, child, adolescent, and young adult—of our
interpersonal relatedness to other persons. Our growth in faith
should, in a sense, chronologically mature with and complement
our entire human growth in both its physical and interpersonal
development. No one would expect a baby of three weeks to with-
stand the threat of physical pain, interpersonal hatred, or evil of
any kind. We would, however, hope that a grown man could bear
a certain amount of physical suffering and would have matured
sufficiently in his self-identity and psychic strength to be capable
of living with some rejection and evil in his daily interpersonal
contacts.

When I meet people, my felt-experience may be one of exces-
sive attraction, pain, threat, fear, or sadness. More often than
not, this is anything but what I would consider to be the consoling
presence of the Lord to me. In the hospital I am conscious of
suffering and being hurt. I am frequently aware of enduring some
injustice or of being annoyed by someone's personality that clashes
with mine. My body-person sensible contact with the signs around
me often interprets them as conveying rejection and hate. There is
a deeper existential presence beyond this surface experience. It is
perceived only through the gift of faith as we risk searching for,
pleading for, asking for a more profound level of I-Thou encounter
with Christ in our very openness and listening to this particular
experience, which is the "ground" that manifests His presence. This

might be called a kind of phenomenological-existential asceticism of the Cross.

To reject the evil of self-centered activity in another while at the same time staying open to the somewhat threatening needs of this selfishly acting person, because such needs are seen in faith as those of the Body of Christ, involves a tremendous risk. Our faith that we will discover the person of Christ manifesting Himself in our threatening brother involves us in a real martyrdom when we live it out. We must risk discovering the God of love in the Body which has not yet been so perfectly transformed that it loves with the love of God.

Experience of the Body of Christ, for most of us, is not of course restricted exclusively to its threatening aspects. We do experience *agape*. However, when I am confronted by the selfless love of another, I am at the same time present to one whom I know is not the radical source of this love. I know that he shares the same human weaknesses as I and the same strong pull inward to selfishness. I am not present to the fullness of unselfish love when I receive *agape* from another. Instead I am aware of a twofold reality which is there—the free gift that is being extended to me, but also some aspects of the person that are quite the opposite. This darker truth is as much a part of my real knowledge of another as is my joyful reception of his selfless gift. In other words, I am not present to the purity of selfless love which is the perfection of what I experience.

Just as I must bring faith to my experience of threat, so I must approach the experience of unconditional acceptance and selfless love from another in faith. I require faith in the first instance to believe that I can find Christ present in the threatening person or situation. I need faith in the second instance in order to believe that it is Christ who is present as the *agape* source of the selfless love that I experience from another. In the second case I experience the presence of Christ because I know that the person who extends this selfless love of *agape* to me is just as incapable of giving the gift as I am. That deeper dimension, the Gestalt of this incarnated love in my neighbor, is the person of the Whole Christ.

Christ is the reality of my neighbor's gift to me. His self-communication, to which my neighbor has freely opened himself, is now being freely communicated to me. My neighbor is deeply involved and is not merely a passive instrument in this building of the Body of the Whole Christ. Nonetheless, what is received and communicated is not identical with this human person.

Man's self-experience includes an apprehension of his capacity to transcend himself and unselfishly love another, together with a parallel tendency to be self-centered by pulling into isolation and refusing co-existence.

Our experience of the Body of Christ is also a kind of twofold experience. We experience the gift of unselfish love as well as the self-centeredness and objectively evil actions of others. The Christian must develop a sensitivity to the presence of Christ in both of these experiences. He must discover that God can communicate Himself through the needs and lack of perfection of the Body just as much as He can in the clear manifestations of selfless love. Obviously, God is never identified with the evil or imperfection, but the human experience of these realities is potentially a faith-encounter with God.

PART III

PART III

7. Personalism and the Search for Christ

UP TO THIS POINT in our discussion we have been concerned with developing an understanding of the Whole Christ from a psychological and theological point of view. We must now begin to consider the authenticity of our own response to God through an interpersonal relationship with the Whole Christ. The following portion of the book will be devoted to discussing the extension and mediation of the life of *agape* to the Body by a person who is trying to live with an ever-deepening awareness of the mystery of the Whole Christ. We will continue to discuss God's ongoing self-communication to man in and through the Body of the Whole Christ, but now the emphasis will be more upon our capacity to participate in this divine communication to other men. It is here that the *sacramental* nature of our interpersonal life with one another as well as our entire life of prayer must be discussed, since it is in this dimension and sphere we become contemplatives in interpersonal living.

BIBLICAL PERSONALISM, LAW, AND THE SEARCH FOR CHRIST

In the first sections of this book we have simply taken for granted the increased evidence from modern psychology that personal development can be attained only through interpersonal relationships, and most fully through I-Thou communication, which hopefully is experienced as a "We" dialogue with certain crucial persons during the lifetime of each man or woman. This psychological growth does not simply parallel our growth in Christ, but rather *is* the human expression of our experience of growth in the Whole Christ. To be truly receptive to others and genuinely selfless in the gift of oneself, a man must surrender his life to find it, must surrender the "I" to the "Thou" in order to attain the "We." "Whoever seeks to gain his life will lose it, but whoever loses his life will preserve it" (Lk. 17:33,RSV). It is this law of human, personal growth, which involves risk, trust, and a commitment in faith to the "other," that our Lord enunciates as the way toward an interpersonal relationship with Himself.

"Whoever cares for his own safety is lost; but if a man will let himself be lost for my sake, he will find his true self" (Mt. 16:25, NEB). "What will a man gain by winning the whole world, at the cost of his true self?" (Lk. 9:25,NEB). In these texts St. Luke clearly takes account of the necessity for that absolutely essential psychological foundation upon which a realistic self-concept rests. It is given to us by those who have truly loved us selflessly and have therefore bestowed upon us the capacity for an other-centered love, one that is directed outward in the gift of my full body-person as loveable. St. Luke tells me, as I read his Gospel, that I will not lose my deepest self or forfeit my personal identity by seeming to lose it in the sacrifice of self-gift to the person of the Whole Christ. Instead, I will find my most profound identity not in a kind of external possession and acquisition of material things but in the gift of my "I" to the "Thou" of Christ. My human capacity for self-gift, for selfless love, and for an other-centered existence (what we might call the "personal center," using Paul Tillich's term) can rule my whole body-person, because it is united with the personal center of the divine person, Christ.

A kind of biblical personalism is evident throughout both the Old and the New Testaments because, as we have said, God chooses to give Himself to us on *our* terms, according to *our* way of communicating, which is objective as well as personal. Once the personal communication of God had been received into the society of man, it became embodied in the laws, rituals, codes of moral conduct, customs, and traditions within the Judaeo-Christian heritage. These are some of the necessary objectifications of God's presence that human society requires as a kind of constant reminder to *live* personally with His presence and His life. External codes and traditional structures have an important educative value and also serve as norms and external sanctions for those who wander from the right paths.

But man sometimes has a tendency to look on the law and its external observance as an end in itself. This is especially true if he has not matured sufficiently in his personal life to be able to relate to God in the manner that St. Luke described in the above-quoted passages. Because of a lack of experience in interpersonal living, we frequently find it difficult to discover the "personal" content of the law, and therefore we concentrate more on the rubrics of external observance rather than on union with the person of the lawgiver. St. Paul mentions this tendency throughout his letters, while at the same time stressing the true source of all justification: "For his sake I underwent total loss of all things and I value them as mere dung so that Christ alone may be my wealth and I may be found in him, possessing not my own justice based on observance of the Law, but that justice which comes through faith in Christ, the justice which comes from God and is based on faith" (Phil. 3:8–9,C).

To the extent that law is an external, coercive force, it is incapable of justifying man. Paul again puts it well in his letter to the Galatians when he says: "If justification were through the law, then Christ died to no purpose" (Gal. 2:21,RSV). It is only when man lives with the inner life of the Spirit and accepts the death-resurrection sequence in his own history, as God's life floods through his body-person, that he can really begin to believe in the risen Lord who is present to him in the Body of the Whole Christ. This faith is the source of all true justification.

Our attitude toward the law, however, frequently presents a problem to our growth in human maturity as well as to our increase in sensitivity to the person of Christ. The gift of the Spirit is the only true inner cause of justification, rather than any external observance of a law that coerces man from outside.

We must live the life of incarnation, death, and resurrection from within. We are not coerced into it from without.

Even though Christ has given the Spirit as an interior source of justification, there still remains an element of law in the Christian dispensation. The morality of the New Testament does not lack obligation or sanction. The teachings of the New Law can also be written down and codified. To the extent that this is done, the New Law can justify no more than the Old Law. As an *external* force, the commandments of Jesus are little more than a norm of conduct. They are not a principle of activity. We might there-fore, ask: Why does the Christian religion require a code of laws? Why maintain alongside the unwritten Spirit who justifies another written element that can never justify? St. Paul answers that: "The law is not laid down for the just but for the lawless" (I Tim. 1:9,RSV).

The law is always a pedagogue for those who have slipped, helping man to recognize that he is a sinner by making him more conscious of the tension between the law of self-centeredness within him and the law of God saying that he is made for other-centered interpersonal life. Since we are all "of Adam," of the Total Adam, we all need the law. But insofar as we are "of Christ," of the Whole Christ, Paul can say to us that: " . . . you have died to the law through the body of Christ, so that you may belong to another, to him who has been raised from the dead in order that we may bear fruit for God. While we were living in the flesh, our sinful passions, aroused by the law, were at work in our members to bear fruit for death. But now we are discharged from the law, dead to that which held us captive, so that we serve not under the old written code but in the new life of the Spirit" (Rom. 7:4–6,RSV).

Individual Christians who commit themselves to a life of the vows embrace what has classically been termed "the way of perfection." Obviously this perfection of life is in no way different from that to which all Christians are called. The mode of life is dictated by the three vows, although it is ultimately the union with God incarnated in the life of charity which is the perfection that is sought. With certain conditions present, the vows should allow men and women religious to witness in a striking manner to the personalizing force of Trinitarian love that is now operative within their lives. To the precise extent that they become rich, warm, vibrant human beings, while at the same time foregoing what most people consider to be the most personalizing of forces in human life—for example, a spouse and their own children— to that extent they can directly witness to the personalizing force of the One with whom they live, the Whole Christ. How can these men and women be so human without the needs of their own family to call forth their capacity for love and affection?

This is perhaps one of the most striking elements in the witness of the religious life. We can become deeply human and remain open only by living intimately with God, and this because the God with whom we live is not far away. He is neither an abstraction nor someone whom we meet for the first time only at death. Instead, He is discovered as a flesh-and-blood, vibrant part of our daily life. Without in any way destroying God's transcendence, the Incarnation has forever made our God, a *God-with-us*. The *eschaton* to which we witness is not just *something in the future*. It is the Kingdom of God here present as the grain of mustard seed. It is a witness to the Christ-life that has already begun to grasp mankind through the Continuing Incarnation of the Whole Christ. If anything, it is by becoming as completely human as possible that religious bear witness to the presence of Christ at the heart of their own human growth. Their perfection as religious *is* their perfection as human beings when it is accomplished through a lived faith-encounter with the Whole Christ.

Many people are genuinely perplexed by the Gospel command to "be perfect as your heavenly Father is perfect" (Mt. 5:48, RSV). This applies especially in their attitude toward the law. We need a certain amount of mature growth in freedom and interpersonal life before we are able to realize that justification does not come through observance of the law alone. Spiritual directors must constantly ascertain the degree of human maturity and freedom with which an individual Christian approaches his encounter with the law as an external codification of Christian life. This will usually be a good index of how they relate observance of the law to the command to be perfect.

If the level of their interpersonal life is mature, they will have no problem in seeing that their Christian perfection lies in the presence of the Christ-life within them, and that their experiential grasp of this presence is mediated through the death and resurrection at the heart of their growth in union with the Whole Christ. They will place their security in the person of Christ and their experience of His love and needs mediated to them through His Body. Their observance of the law will be an overflow of this love into their daily action.

The command to be perfect is really an invitation to growth in our interpersonal union with God. But the immature individual who hears this command can become confused if he is not sure of what human growth entails. It is all too easy for him to substitute the category of a *quantitative observance of the law* for the difficult process of human growth in the Whole Christ. The more immature the person, the more primitive will be his category of growth. One who begins to know how to love, realizes that growth involves the gradual ability to transcend isolation and live with the love of Christ in an other-centered manner. He places his security in the presence of the Spirit and his daily interpersonal life with the Whole Christ.

To the immature, who are more self-centered, the law poses a threat to their way of selfish fulfillment. Without guidance, they tend to place their security not in the person of Christ *but in their own exact observance of the law*. Insofar as they fulfill the precepts of the law they feel secure. The external code ceases to be a threat to them. They are assured of its fulfillment if they can reduce the precepts to quantities that can be measured. Morality becomes more and more legalistic and even ritualistic. Gradually security returns—a security based on the minute fulfillment of every precept contained in the law. They then go one step further to interpret growth in perfection as a measurable increase in their obedience to the rule. Ultimately, in some extreme cases, the impersonal category of quantitative fulfillment of the law even begins to replace the personal response of charity.

Not only have these individuals unconsciously worked out a system whereby they "possess their own justice based on observance of the law" (Phil. 3:8–9,C), but this very attitude tends to harden them in a kind of self-centered moral life. They have placed their security not in the person of Christ but in the *measurable* fulfillment of the law, in the quantities that can be seen and calculated.

This is one of the reasons why we are sometimes faced with religious who, while they have lived a life of *perfect observance,* nonetheless acknowledge quite candidly that they are empty inside. No one has ever shown them how to grow as persons and how Christ is to be found at the very heart of this human development. As a result they have been forced to fall back on their own primitive solution to the problem, at times with disastrous results, to say nothing of endless years of loneliness, debilitating frustration, and needless emptiness.

The quantitative approach to spiritual growth is basically a very primitive attempt to solve a human problem. It fails because it can never help the person to transcend his own isolation. Such people never have to risk committing themselves to another person's freedom. They have never grown enough in love to be able to risk placing their security in someone who loves them, because the other is free and *could* reject them. This can be the source of great insecurity. The person who has allowed himself to be loved and to love, however, knows (with that experiential "knowledge" of St. Paul) *that the very nature of the true lover is not to reject the beloved.* Once this experience is a firm part of our make-up, we can then risk placing our security in the free gift of love mediated to us in the Body of the Whole Christ. This means allowing ourselves to be drawn out of our isolation. Of itself, the law cannot do this, and this is its basic weakness. Those who place their security in an external observance of the law alone ultimately end by reinforcing themselves in their own isolation. Observance of the law must be the *result* of an overflow of true love if it is to be a justifying action. Only then is it an effect of the life of the Spirit.

The law cannot justify because it does not require us to make an act of faith in itself. Faith is an *interpersonal* reality. I believe in another *person,* and only because of this in the truths that he reveals. Thus freedom is an integral part of faith.

The justice that comes through Christ is the new life which courses through us by reason of His presence in our personal life. It is this presence that enables us to risk the same death which He underwent for us, so that in Him we too might slowly begin our resurrection to a new life in the Spirit of love that opens us to others. In this act we become life-giving-incarnate-spirits and thus actively participate in the growth of the Whole Christ. The direction of our perfection is toward a totally personal, other-centered life, which cannot in any way be reduced to quantitative analysis and measurements.

It is a relationship to the Person who embodies the law, and whose will is contained within the law, that frees man for a truly personal response to law itself and to the living out of his social relatedness in conformity to that law. Moreover, if it is to be truly effective, this personal relationship to the lawgiver must be the interpersonal I-Thou communication that fully develops man's nature as created in openness to receive God in and through all of reality. Its effectiveness depends upon a conscious relatedness to God in the very dynamism of divine self-gift. If God is to be encountered as a person and not an abstract law, He must be discovered in each man's experience of the persons within his own unique history. Since this is man's only knowledge of the personal as an incarnate-spirit, it is not surprising that the God who is so fully a Person communicates Himself to man principally in and through the interpersonal relationships of his life, in and through the Whole Christ.

Those critical persons in my life who have truly loved me have also transformed and given personal meaning to all the social laws that govern our relatedness. A self-sacrificing person brings life to the law for me and communicates the law to me as something not apart from the vitalizing personal power of love, which must be, to the degree that it is selfless, a participation in Christ's *agape*.

In God's self-communication, the Word Incarnate is expressed to us as a Person and only secondarily in the words of a person. This simply means that God is so Personal that we can see what He is only in a personal life. God can Incarnate Himself as man because man is person and because God is Personal. In Christ, the human, personal manifestation of the Divine Persons reveals to us what it means for man "to become a person" and to "become a person in the Whole Christ."

SPIRITUAL EXPRESSION THROUGH MATTER

We have seen in previous chapters how God communicates Himself to man in and through the Whole Christ, and that this self-communication is primarily within man's human growth as a person. We must now begin to explore man's nature as created in openness to receive God in all of reality, together with his capacity to become conscious of this self-communication. A clear understanding of these two qualities of man's wholeness as a body-person is essential in order to grasp the theme of this book and to facilitate each reader's own personal free choice to take on the task of becoming a fuller person in the Whole Christ.

This somewhat philosophical subject has been treated in depth by many competent authors, and we do not intend to review their works here. Our plan is to highlight only those insights that we feel are important for an understanding of interpersonal related-ness to the Whole Christ.

The two above-mentioned values must be understood more as *possibilities* that are *to be realized* in man's existence rather than as fully achieved realities. As incarnate-spirit, man must grow into these God-given potentialities. He must "become a person" by surpassing and transcending his numerical aloneness through the selfless gift of himself to others, and thus "become a community." His individuality must strike root in others through self-gift, until his own personal identity is realized through relatedness to them.

We are not born with a full-flowered capacity for self-gift nor with anything but a primitive consciousness of our potential. Human growth includes our expanding self-consciousness as we evolve through personal interaction with the created world around us. We are dependent upon matter for both the content and the manifestation of our self-consciousness. To express ourselves, we must take up the material world around us so as to communicate our interiority and spirituality. Man therefore makes use of what we have come to know as the *symbolic,* or sign, actions of human communication.

The material world into which my spirit is incarnated through my body provides me with the concrete possibility for "spiritual expression through matter." This is the great dignity and special calling with which man, above all other creatures, has been gifted. He is ordained in his inmost self to "act matter" and to express his being, as imaged in the likeness of the Triune God, by accepting and living out his role as a "man-sort-of-spirit." The freedom that he seeks in self-expression is therefore a freedom of the spirit, not *from* matter but a freedom *for* matter. It is a freedom for incarnation. Man finds himself only when he incarnates; paradoxically, man *liberates himself* when he can incarnate. So many err when they mistakenly believe that the human spirit finds freedom through separation from matter. They miss the delight of the human spirit when it incarnates itself. A man feels joy that rushes through his entire body-person when he finally masters a difficult stroke in tennis. The ballerina or the pianist, the linguist, the poet, or the singer are most free in their art when they have mastered their subject matter, when they can incarnate the vision of their spirit with ease and joy. This is the freedom of incarnate-spirit—a freedom for matter. Our technological, medical, and social advances are but a further manifestation of this necessity and delight with incarnation. All men are called to ever-increasing expression as incarnating-spirits. This is the way we are created to image God. This is the *life* of man, the incarnate greatness to which he is called—and it is *in* this activity, not apart from it, that he finds His God, Emmanuel. The so-called "limitations of matter" are for each of us, as incarnate-spirit, the very possibility of "our-kind-of-spirit-expression." Matter-spirit expression is at once the condition and the possibility of our self-development, of our answer to the question: What am I to become?

Personal encounter for man must therefore take place in the

way that is natural to him, that is, through his body. We enter into our personal encounter with other men through physical realities perceptible to human senses. Just as man must find external freedom by mastering his environment through technology and science, so too must he achieve freedom within himself in order that his interpersonal actions will also be the free expression of incarnating-spirit.

However, this kind of "inner freedom for interpersonal incarnation" is not something that he accomplishes by himself. It is always a gift from another. He must *be freed* for interpersonal life and the kind of incarnate self-expression that is the heart and soul of this communication. Ultimately, the task of all religious education is so to free man that as *incarnate*-spirit he may discover God-with-him. The Christian life is built upon our corporate growth in this kind of capacity for free, incarnating, body-person response to the Whole Christ.

As religious, our growth in the Whole Christ is not taken out of the human existential world of relatedness nor out of the stream of dynamic orientation toward human self-fulfillment. Instead, it is accomplished in this milieu and must then be expressed and symbolized within this context. In other words, we must become sensitive to the presence of God within our human world of meaning by giving it human expression and letting the Word become Flesh in our daily lives.

The essential foundation of our ability to become a person lies in our ability to transcend isolation and to share ourselves as free gift with another. This capacity for openness to all of reality, the hallmark of every spiritual being, is the essence of man as person, providing him with potentialities for human growth that are unlimited. It is also the "ground" of our capacity for religious experience, making it possible for God to give Himself to us through a sharing in His divine life, and ultimately in the fullness of open friendship with Him.

Other created realities on the face of the earth are totally confined by their materiality to a particular sphere of space and time. In this lack of openness to *all* of reality, and an inability to be conscious of this openness and relatedness, lies the essential distinction between man and the other creatures of the earth. Man's human nature might be called an unqualified interpersonal availability to God. By reason of his spiritual endowment, he is created with an openness to be the recipient of God's own free self-communication, and in turn, to share himself with God. But it is always a sharing through man's spiritual way of being—incarnated, fleshed, visible, tangible spiritual expression in matter.

THE PERSONAL GROWTH OF AN INCARNATE-SPIRIT IN HISTORY

If human nature were essentially bad and corrupt, as some have held, then a strong system of tight interpersonal control would be absolutely necessary. This would then largely determine our social morality and the tone of our interpersonal relationships. In a nature from which only evil could proceed we would conclude that there should be as little spontaneous, free expression as possible.

Another school of thought has looked upon our human nature as, at root, both good and bad. The goal of social relatedness is an eventual victory of the good, with the means to this end being the supernatural aids together with a strenuous development of the powers of will and intellect.

There is, however, a third view which asserts that man, by his very nature, strives for self-realization. This does not mean that he lives a good life without expressing any selfishness, but rather that there are constructive forces within man urging him to realize his given potentialities. The goal of his morality, and therefore of his interpersonal relatedness, will be to *outgrow* the destructive forces in himself by opening out to the "others," to the source of his salvation and self-realization. As we have so often pointed out, we cannot consider the "others" in our life apart from the Whole Christ and God's continuous self-communication to us.

This latter view of human nature takes a fresh approach to the problems of man's "becoming a person" and is filled with insight for the Christian who seeks to "become a person in the Whole Christ." It aims at releasing our *natural* desire to know and give ourselves to another, to proceed more from privilege than from obligation, more from inner responsibility than legal restraint, more from a spirit of love than the pangs of fear. This is a view of man which believes that he seeks for his true good, and from this belief there springs a basic desire to be able to trust in human nature.

What we are saying is that man, by nature, is dynamically oriented toward self-realization, and that a man must truly understand his condition of existence and act upon this understanding if he is to attain his fulfillment. Such a view of man is fully compatible with our Christian heritage. It takes into account the powerful force that pulls us into isolation, "the law within our members"; at the same time, it recognizes that there are other forces in us that tend toward fulfillment through union. Nor is this a Pelagian view of man, a view that man can pull himself up to God by his own bootstraps. Man *absolutely* depends upon the *free* gift of self from another for his radical development as a human person.

We might say that an individual human being must be called into personal existence by someone who, in a sense, *transcends* him, who is outside of him. We cannot reach self-fulfillment in isolation. Just as an individual human being is called to personal life only by one who transcends him, so too, the family of man as a whole is called to personal life by the free gift of love from One who totally transcends it. In fact, the very capacity of individual men and women to be selfless with one another is due to that first act of selfless love of a transcendent God for His people. We can never really love until we know that we are lovable. The faithfulness of Yahweh in the face of Israel's infidelity, the figure of Christ teaching men to "love one another as I have loved you" (Jn. 15:12,RSV), and the bleeding Savior on the Cross murmuring: "Father, forgive them; for they know not what they do" (Lk. 23:34,RSV)—all this gradually began to make an impression on large segments of the family of man. We are the beloved of God; we are His people. Our capacity for human love absolutely depends upon this first act of divine love. Only in virtue of this love can we too begin risking the kind of life that Our Lord led, a life of self-sacrificing love in which, paradoxically, we find both ourselves and our God.

Man's personal self-expression in matter must be done in a manner that is natural to him, and the connecting link between his "spirit-matter-condition-of-being" and his interpersonal relatedness is what we have referred to as "authenticity." Another way of expressing this is "the real me," or "the authentic I," or "the real self," as opposed to the idealized or neurotic self.

The word *authenticity* is filled with an atmosphere of a certain self-knowledge, an attentive listening to *all* the forces at work within myself and a kind of openness to listen to myself honestly as an incarnate-spirit. I do not choose to close off other people or areas within myself that I find too threatening to live with. It is only when I can confidently rest in the genuine, personally experienced love of another that I can really risk being authentic. Until I know that I am lovable, I cannot chance listening to those aspects of myself that I instinctively recognize are unlovable.

Once I am able to be my authentic self, then I can avoid the pitfalls of the neurotic self, the self which I construct in isolation by carefully carving and shaping it so that areas of threat and pain will be excluded. Whenever man attempts to fit the self into this kind of a straitjacket, the deformed wreck that results is a clear sign to all the world that he is truly a "self-made man."

The reason that authenticity is the true expression of my incarnate-spirit is that it is the only true manifestation of those two human values which make me most a man, namely, my openness to all of reality and my capacity to be conscious of this transcendentality. Only when I am authentic can I really be open to all of reality and in this very act become aware of my capacity to transcend myself as well as the limitations of space and time. The true expression of my "real self" is, therefore, the expression of a spiritual being incarnated in matter.

I am truly *self*-conscious in the way that is proper to an incarnate-spirit. My consciousness penetrates and includes my body, my affectivity, my feelings and emotions. I am conscious with my whole self, not with my intellect alone. Life is more than logic. Hence our consciousness of life must be more than logical. How do you *feel* about yourself or another person? is an extremely important question. It does not imply mere sense knowledge alone. Instead, it is our stumbling way of attempting to recognize that there is another dimension to knowledge that must be included within the realm of consciousness if we are to be truly authentic and knowing in the manner proper to incarnate-spirits.

We have perhaps been a bit naive in our interpretation of the dictum of St. Thomas that "Nothing is in the intellect which was not first present within the senses."[1] We have acknowledged the dependence of intellectual activity upon sensation, but then we tended to leave sensation by the wayside—as though it had finished its task and the intellect took up the higher work of spiritual activity. We have even acknowledged that this spiritual activity of the intellect completely depended upon a constant contact with the life of sensation. But this contact was rather like the relation between the sea and a merchant ship. If you take the vessel out of the water, it will not operate; when you leave it in the water, it goes by itself.

We have recognized the priority of sensation and have acknowledged the need for contact with sensible reality while the intellect operates, but we have perhaps not sufficiently explored the fact that one of the tasks of the intellect is to *penetrate sensation with intellectual consciousness*. We know as a whole body-person, not just as an intellect and not merely as a sensing body. Intellectual activity is not wrapped up within itself as the vessel in the sea. It must reach out to matter, to the body, and penetrate it with self-consciousness. We have lived with so much of our sensation without reflecting upon it! We are not truly conscious as body-persons. So when we ask: How do you feel about someone or something? it is an extremely important question. It is an attempt

---

[1] St. Thomas, *Summa Theologica*, I, 84, 3.

to bring a certain wholeness and authenticity to our knowledge of reality. It is an attempt to help us become "close to ourselves" as an expression of incarnate-spirit.

This expression is most fully realized in the "We" communication of an I-Thou relationship, characterized by mutuality, directness, trusting openness, and presence. It is only in this relationship that a human being comes into the fullness of his personhood and can begin to realize his potential self. To the extent that a man is closed in on himself and isolated from other people—and, therefore not psychologically present to the Persons of the Triune God—he cannot find his real self as "community." We discover ourselves only insofar as we find ourselves related to another. Any effort to develop the self within and by the sole power of the self fails, because it does not make that vital *selfless* thrust out into the world of the *concrete other*.

The "I-it" relationship will not draw out from a man, as incarnate-spirit, the deep human response of which he is capable. We respond to a call according to its value, and when we are confronted with a spiritual being, the only response worthy of that person is a total gift of my whole body-person as incarnate-spirit. The "I-it" relation, in Buber's terminology, is one of "monologue." Only the I-Thou is a relation of "dialogue." Only the communication of the "We" is that mutual achievement of unity, a reciprocal "bringing-to-be" of a living, personal relationship involving the *authentic* presence of both persons to each other in a free, responsible, grateful, gift-giving-mutual-openness. Such interpersonal communication develops the deepest level of our incarnated-spiritual-nature and opens us in our totality to be transformed and become the "community" that is our most profound yearning.

To be a man, then, is to be a body-person having a history, a history that is not just one static moment in time but an ongoing history in the making. From an initial myopic self-centeredness as a baby, and concern with the preservation of physical self-identity as my total conscious world of meaning, I can grow to an ever-greater awareness of my human self-realization as a "We." Only in terms of the "others" in my on-going history, and in terms of my increasing capacity to take my psychological stand as fundamentally "other-centered," will I become a person. Human existence is a process of becoming other-centered and of gradually resolving the tension of that pull into isolation and self-centeredness through the "We" involvement of my total body-person with the Whole Christ. The task of human existence is to respond with an open listening to the constantly changing pattern of call and response in the creative act of God's love, and to the continuing creative gift of Himself to me.

Man exists, then, with all the manifold relationships and links that comprise his world of meaning. To speak of my human existence is to say that I am not encapsulated and enclosed within myself, but rather that I stand out and am beyond myself. I am a reality *in the world,* and *through my body* I am present to and expressing myself in this world. I am also conscious of this presence and of my relationship to this world of meaning. My human way of knowing and receiving is through my body-person contacts in this world of relatedness, and my self-identity and self-concept come to me through this same relatedness. My human nature is such, therefore, that I can receive a spiritual gift, a spiritual life, a spiritual person, and share that life in and through the concrete material realities that come into contact with me as I live in space and time.

The glory of being human is that I am open to the nonmaterial through the material. The material can therefore serve as sign to me of the hidden reality that is signified. We are not limited to matter, although we need the material in our ordinary way of knowing. This ordinary way of knowing according to our nature is what we call "sacramental." That is, we are open to knowing the material sign as well as the spiritual reality expressed through it, and of being conscious of our knowledge of both. Thus, we are capable of receiving God's communication of Himself, if God so chooses, in and through the created realities of our earthly existence.

Of profound importance to us as religious is our natural openness to all of reality, both the spiritual and the material. For this is the foundation of our incarnational prayer-life and our human encounter through a faith-response to God's gift of Himself to us as human. We will develop these ideas in relation to prayer toward the end of this book.

MAN AS NATURALLY SOCIAL IN
THE WHOLE CHRIST

With this brief but more philosophical exploration into our human nature completed, let us now begin to reconstruct the important elements of our growing synthesis as we have seen them up to this point.

Just as an interpersonal response was necessary with the historical Jesus in His concrete, visible, human nature if His contemporaries were to relate to Him in love, faith, and mutual friendship, so this is still true for us now in our relationship with the Whole Christ. We must continue personally to meet Christ, but Christ as He is now, the Whole Christ.

If we are to respond to the self-communication of God through union with the Whole Christ, we must first be able authentically to share ourselves with Him as He is today. When attempting to do this, we immediately find that this kind of dialogue involves our entire personal history. As unique individuals we find ourselves situated within concrete time and space relationships having many limitations. Each of us was born during a certain historical period and has lived with various people and events that shaped and formed us.

I find that I am dependent on other men for my capacity to respond to God's gift of Himself to me through Christ. Why is this? Simply because God has freely chosen to communicate Himself to me in terms of the very nature and way He has created me. He does not usually reveal Himself to me outside my created nature, which is social. Salvation is social because man is social. Man can be a man only by being related, and therefore to be saved is to be saved in relationship. God does not choose to redeem man apart from the reality that he is, a being who *is* in "becoming," and who, at the deepest point of his religious aspirations, is social in Christ. This is the vocation that he is created to live out. The profound corollary that each of us must personally reflect on throughout our lives as the cornerstone, so to speak, of our growth in the Spirit, is that God communicates His salvation to us both in our "relatedness" and in our "becoming" as human persons. Our salvation is corporate because man is corporate—and corporate in Christ. Man can exist as human only by, in, and through his relatedness to other men, which now, in God's economy, *is* his relatedness to the Whole Christ. But it is a relatedness based upon the gift of self, and of personal life, which is *agape*. This is the Christ-life in the corporate family of man. Our "becoming a person" is through another's selfless gift to us and through our own gift of self to others.

God comes to man on man's own terms in order to complete and integrate his created nature. Thus God communicates Himself to me in and through other men in the Body of the family of man. Opening to God and receiving God therefore means opening myself to man and receiving man. Receiving and giving is another way of saying being related as a human being. Becoming a man and becoming holy means entering into relationship and mutual self-gift. This cannot be achieved apart from God's self-communication in and through the Whole Christ.

Growth in the Spirit is intimately bound up with growth in the Body of the Whole Christ. This latter is equally dependent upon our human body-person growth, which in its turn can develop only in contact with created reality. The whole cosmic evolution of man must never be profaned by fragmenting it into isolated segments, as if Head and members were only haphazardly joined, as if "all things were [*not*] created through him and for him," as if "in him all things [*did not*] hold together," or as if it were *not true* that "in him all the fulness of God was pleased to dwell, and through him to reconcile to himself all things" (Col. 1:16–20, RSV).

We have long recognized that "individual differences" are key values to be developed if one desires to effectively unlock any child's unique potentialities for learning and human growth. Perhaps what we have not seen with equal clarity is the relationship between this principle and the unlocking of every man's own unique approach to God.

Moreover, we have not made the study of this relationship a

value in our ascetical training so that our very interpersonal lives and their levels of communication become growth-producing encounters. In other words, we have been slow to develop a spirituality that values and cultivates every Christian's unique body-person presence to another as the sacramental sign that, if responded to in faith, is capable of stimulating and motivating the other person to seek out further his own unique relationship to the Divine Persons within his concrete life-experience.

Theologically, we have known that a man's ultimate value is given to him by reason of his absolutely singular created relationship to the Divine Persons. Throughout his life he is continually being created and loved in a way that is uniquely and personally unlike that of any other human being. But somehow the human experience that should be at the core of our Christian prayer-life, enabling the above-mentioned theological truths to become fleshed in our lives within the practical order of human inter-relatedness, has been badly neglected. We might make use of the generic phrase "the experience of acceptance," which, although it admittedly encompasses many levels of meaning, can nonetheless describe the concrete experience in our encounter with another that brings the conceptual word of theological truth into the flesh of human experience.

The reason an experience of acceptance at any level is so important is that this human, experienced sign, which unlocks our God-given human potentialities for self-realization, is at one and the same time the effective, sacramental way of realizing the theological truth of God's presence within our development as human persons. Moreover, because it is sacramental (an *effective, incarnated, personal presence in matter*), the invitation to learning is directed toward the whole body-person of man as incarnate-spirit.

The experience of acceptance, whether at the profound level of actually healing, which is discovered to some extent in any genuine experience of selfless love, or at one of the many stages of "unlocking" the latent growth capacity of a talent, is always an affirmation of man's own uniqueness. It exposes something more of the real self that actually comes into being in the relationship. The experience of acceptance at even such levels as the encouragement of individual creative expression in the arts, athletics, or any similar human body-person form of communication opens each of us to more of our real self, and to the possibility of exploring new avenues in deepening this discovery.

The experience of acceptance, then, at any one of its myriad levels of communication, is to some degree an expression of selfless love and respect for the uniqueness of the individual, which is so in tune with God's own unique creative relationship to this person that it is truly a religious experience for him. It is in harmony with the most profound theological meaning of the Incarnation. It is indeed unfortunate that so many Christians are conditioned not to recognize the living God within these small, but sometimes almost ecstatic, moments of self-affirmation by another.

There is a reciprocity of growth in the Whole Christ, whether I am either receiver or giver of selfless love. In either role, if I am unable, in faith, to see human want as a real need of the Body of Christ, demanding a self-sacrificing kind of love in response (which alone I am incapable of giving), then I have, in fact, closed myself off from God's self-communication to me through these very needs of His Body.

The gift of *agape* that I, as self-centered, so desperately need throughout my life if I am ever to be able to transcend my pull inward is given to me in human inter-relationships, but only to the extent that those who influence me are alive in Christ, living with His own *agape*-life and responding in faith and love to the needs of the Whole Christ. If they are closed off to me, I will not have received the sacramentally effective power of God's love that enables me to risk being authentic and accept myself as I am. If I am not yet sure of who I am, I may at best have only a very negative self-image to fall back on.

Moreover, I will not be able to accept myself in the necessary tension between self-centeredness and other-centeredness, which is the healthy existential challenge to further growth, and the opportunity for developing responsibility and exercising greater personal freedom. If I do not have the experience of acceptance, I will find it difficult to identify with my self-centeredness as well as with my capacity for transcendence, which together give me a truthful self-concept.

The task of becoming more a man, which is the vocation of every human being, involves me in the tension of gradual transformation. I am always both "of Adam" and "of Christ." My chapter of Salvation History will be the living out of this tension in such a way that Adam is transformed into Christ as selfishness yields to an other-centered way of life. I must open, in faith, to the life of the Spirit in order that my capacity for transcendence (my spiritual nature) may be *consciously* integrated into my life as a Christian.

Without the gift of selfless love from another, involving their capacity to transcend themselves and to listen to me, I will never be able to risk discovering the same capacity for transcendence within myself. I will continue to seek personal fulfillment almost exclusively in terms of self-gratification. If no one has ever provided me with the experience of acceptance *just as I am,* involving both my self-centeredness as well as my drive to self-realization (which must not be confused with *selfish*-realization), then I can never respond selflessly to the needs of another and allow my potential for other-centeredness in Christ to be realized. I can only identify myself almost exclusively in terms of my self-centeredness, and obviously who wants to make a gift of selfishness to another? In order to affirm me and give me my self-identity, someone has to love me *as self-centered,* realizing that this is not the entire reality of my "becoming-person." When I experience others loving me in this way, then I can begin to do the same. This experience of acceptance transforms me, so that I can risk living with the tensions of growth, open to them and seeking resolution in a personal integration through acts of entering into a "reflective-body-person-selfless-presence-to-the-others" in the Whole Christ.

One of the most difficult truths to be grasped, and even more to be lived out in an incarnational spirituality, is the fact that in order to be open to God's self-communication, I must enter into an interpersonal relationship with the Whole Christ *as I am.* This may sound banal, but in reality such an open, truthful encounter is a lifetime task, involving many complexities both in my conscious and in my unconscious ways of relating.

At present, we must let it suffice simply to point out the connection between this fundamental principle and what we have just discussed. Each of us will find it difficult to enter into an authentic relationship with the Whole Christ, in our human world of personal relationships, to the extent that we cannot accept ourselves as we truthfully are.

As a consequence of this lack of self-acceptance, I am not open to reflect upon the tension between self-centeredness and other-centeredness, which will hopefully grow toward a resolution in the Whole Christ. The paradox is that the only way I can ever come to accept myself as I am, is if I can risk opening up to the healing love of the Whole Christ who, in and through the accepting love of other persons, accepts me as I truly am. This *is my experience* of the love of the Whole Christ, the *agape* that the transcendent Lord expresses to me in a member of His Body.

Not only do we ourselves grow this way, but the truth of this significant plan of God's self-communication must also sufficiently impress itself upon us so that we can responsibly assume, in faith, the lifelong task of sacramentally communicating this divine life to others. My personal experience of the Whole Christ, as well as the experience of other men, is truly most meaningful in terms of the sacramentality of another's selfless love.

This is the significance of Christian community. It is an invitation to the life of *koinonia* with Jesus Christ. "It is God himself who called you to share in the life of his Son Jesus Christ Our Lord; and God keeps faith" (1 Cor. 1:9,NEB). This common life is meant to be the conscious experience of a life of *agape* in interpersonal living, whose source is daily commemorated and effected in the Eucharistic Celebration. The life of love of the Christian community finds its most radical cultic expression in that liturgical action wherein the members of the community gather to celebrate their growing experience of a daily *life* together in the Whole Christ.

The religious communities within the family of the People of

God are intended to be powerful sources of this effective sacramental transmission of the life of *agape* within the Body of the Whole Christ. The witness that we give to one another is not just a sign that a God far away loves us. Instead, in faith, we become for one another the effective, visible sign of the presence of the loving God.

SUMMARY

We have said that we must share ourselves and enter our interpersonal relationship with the Whole Christ as we are, i.e., as authentic. We must be able to share our "real self" with the Whole Christ, as opposed to the neurotic expression of what has been called the "idealized self" or the "unreal self." Only the "real me," as I am, can have a genuine relationship with another person. I cannot relate with only a part of myself or with a façade. The two persons relating must be authentic.

Therefore, my entire personal human history and what this brings to my capacity for interpersonal relationships must not be neglected in my growth in the Whole Christ. As we have said, salvation is social, and we are dependent on other men if we are to respond to the call of salvation. Man can be a man only in relationship and in becoming. Because man is social by nature, he can find fulfillment only in and through relatedness to others, and God communicates Himself to man within man's nature, not outside of it. He comes to our human nature, and therefore to our growth process, in order to help us fulfill our vocation to become a person with the capacity for self-gift. God communicates Himself to us in order that we may come to maturity and to that degree of personal integration which brings our human nature into a sharing relationship with others.

This sharing relationship with other men, which is characterized by selfless love, is possible only when we are participating in God's own divine life and in the gift of *agape* communicated to us through the Whole Christ in the Spirit. This takes place principally within the entire growth-process of man's self-realization. Therefore, God communicates Himself to man in and through other men within the human, interpersonal life of the Whole Christ. This mode of communication is what we have called "sacramental" because it is according to man's body-person way of interpersonal communication. It is in terms of revelatory sign-actions that we efficaciously achieve personal communion with one another. Since God seeks a mutual, intensely personal communion with each of us, His plan of self-communication utilizes the whole process of human interpersonal growth, so that our development into "becoming a person" is one with "becoming a person in the Whole Christ."

Two results flow from this growth-process, if it is experienced in our own lives as the sacramental presence of Christ mediated to us in and through others.

First, a growing self-identity in the Whole Christ, grounded in the personal experience of myself as loved, and as therefore lovable by the person of Christ in His Body. That is, I am loved by the important people in my life, giving me an identity and providing me with a growing self-concept that I can accept because I am not threatened by its withdrawal. This is my human experiential foundation for what Revelation can tell me of the reality of Christ in my own personal life, if the Word of God is preached to me.

When I say "I," I do not say it as one who has no experience of the concrete presence of the Body of Christ. I may have little theological understanding of this, but I have had the human experience. When Revelation tells me more about my human experience, and I can respond to the Word of God in faith, then I have the human foundation for identifying with the Whole Christ through the total gift of myself in response to the gift of Himself to me in and through His Body. Thus I have the foundation upon which my prayer-life as a Christian and my commitment to Christ in the religious life is grounded. The religious life must, then, become the public expression of my body-person desire to deepen this self-identity with the Whole Christ.

The second aspect that should result from the growth process, if experienced as a sacramental presence of Christ mediated to me in and through others, would be a growing capacity for entering into deeper levels of interpersonal life. My self-identity, as rooted in the experience of being loved and therefore lovable, allows me to share myself with others. The deeper my identity as lovable, the more I can afford to risk making my "sharing" a truly authentic one. This involves both the good and the bad in me, that is, myself as I authentically am. I come to realize and to accept that I am more than my own selfishness, that the real "I," which involves both good and bad, has been loved and accepted. Therefore, this same "I" can enter into interpersonal life, and I can share myself as I am with others, even though they may at times reject or threaten me in my attempt to be available to them in an authentic way.

Living this "way of openness" in authenticity and faith can bring about the gradual integration and healing of those self-centered and selfish expressions of my affectivity and feelings. This very integration, so that I can risk loving selflessly and authentically without fear, is a part of my growth in Christ. Growth in the Whole Christ touches me at the very center of my struggle for personal integration. Ultimately, therefore, the One who integrates me is God. This is our reconciliation to the Father through "becoming a Person in the Whole Christ."

That reconciliation is not something which stands outside my human growth toward becoming a person. My union with the Father is effected in and through reconciliation with my fellow men, who are the Body of Christ for me. This is the way of God's self-communication, the gift of Himself to me mediated through the sacrament of interpersonal encounter. Having received the gift of agape and having responded, I now become capable of mediating this same divine gift to others.

Membership in the religious life, therefore, by reason of its very function and witness among the People of God, requires the ability to relate to the Whole Christ; it also involves taking on the risk of developing this relationship in greater breadth and depth with the totality of one's developing person.

8. The Meaning of Agape

WE HAVE already stated that man is open to the nonmaterial through the material, and that matter can therefore serve as a sign to us of the hidden reality that is signified. We are not limited to the material, but we need matter for self-revelation and interpersonal dialogue. This way of communicating, according to our nature, is what we called "sacramental." That is, we are open to knowing both the material sign as well as the spiritual reality behind it, and of being conscious of our knowledge of both. Thus we are capable of receiving God's communication of Himself, if He so chooses, in and through the created realities of our earthly existence.

This brings us to the formulation of several essential reflections on what we might call our thumbnail sketch of a philosophy of interpersonal communication. Let us trace just an outline of these thoughts step by step.

Men communicate in order that they may share something with one another, and in sharing create a bond of union, so that their need for each other may be satisfied. We seek to be fulfilled in our social nature by finding self-realization and redemption through one another. Man attempts to become community, that is, to discover himself, by becoming one with an effective, realized bond of union between himself and others.

We are speaking here of "community" in the sense of human beings joined together with an effective, realized bond of union

149

that is possible only when these persons are living a sacramental life. Our concern, then, is with community as a source of personal growth, and we would describe *person* as someone who has the capacity to lead a basically other-centered life with some constancy. A *person* is able to listen and respond selflessly to the real needs of others.

By *sacramental* we mean an intentionally truthful and genuine interpersonal communication, made possible through authentic material signs and symbols that not only signify a communion but also create union.

The communication we are reflecting upon is of a special kind. It is the shared gift of self with another and the constant attempt at a mutual exchange of selflessness and other-centeredness as a way of life.

This specifically human communication, however, is effected (made possible) only through the *authentic* signs of interpersonal relationships. These are the symbols that must not only signify the reality of other-centeredness and the attitude of selflessness behind them, but must also be capable of revealing this as the authentic disposition of the persons involved.

Moreover, for authentic signs to promote and foster interpersonal communication leading to real communion between persons, there must be the opportunity and willingness for the sharing of real human experiences. By this we have in mind persons present to one another and sharing themselves with one another as they really are. They are present to each other in such a way that they are open to and able to accept the other as they truly are right at the moment of their encounter. However, the artificial nature of many social gatherings frequently prevents the emergence of such authentic presence.

For example, most social functions today have as their objective almost any conceivable goal from the relief of boredom or the achievement of social status to political persuasion and mate-hunting; they do not provide the occasion for an authentic sharing among people. Frequently the atmosphere in which I must socialize has certain rather strongly felt, rigidly pre-conditioned "right ways" of speaking, feeling about things, expressing oneself on issues, or "maintaining the approved image or party line" through subtle (or sometimes not so subtle) means to insure conformity. In such instances, there is not much tangible evidence given on the part of those who determine such conditions, and even less on the part of those who conform, that the "programmed" occasion will afford them the opportunity to meet and share themselves with one another as they really are. The tragedy is that many of us are never permitted by our environment to grow into mature persons through an authentic presence to one another in such a way that we can learn to be open, to listen, and to accept each other's God-given individuality and unique response to life. The poverty of personal growth and richness that results in restricted circumstances such as these has found its expression in popular parlance through derisive slang to describe such unfortunate human beings.

The kind of realistic human experience about which we are speaking also means allowing ourselves to be both present to the situation or experience as it really is and accepting it as such. Moreover, this includes a kind of listening to and accepting each person's particular mode of feeling, a reacting to or understanding the same shared relationship or situation. In other words, there must be a willingness to search for and listen to a *unity* deeper than the diversity of "individual differences" brought to each shared experience.

We are all unique in our reactions to people and events, and we each incarnate the mystery that is ourselves in a slightly different way. But we find our radical unity in the capacity to accept and share in one another's uniqueness by actually helping to create it. This is how the walls of individual isolation are broken down. By helping one another to be authentic through the experience of acceptance, we bring it about that the signs of human communication effectively unite rather than further divide us. Without authentic signs, men are isolated and unfulfilled. But when these signs are authentic, they reveal the unique persons communicating with one another, and "community happens." Martin Buber put it well: "Community is where community happens."

However, granting the opportunity and the willingness to share genuine human experiences, this is possible only through effective material signs; or, in other words, a sacramental mode of communication and interpersonal exchange. All human communication is sacramental in this sense.

Relating this sketch to what we have already discussed earlier in the book, we might conclude that in man's struggle to be authentic, he must listen to and accept himself as he really is; he must give himself as he truthfully is to the needs of others; he must create the environment for real human experiences; and he must share this struggle with other men so that a community may grow.

GOD'S CREATION—A TRUE SACRAMENT

In their pastoral Constitution on *The Church in the Modern World,* the Fathers of the Second Vatican Council clearly indicated that the entire economy of salvation is the sacramentally efficacious sign of the presence of the Lord.

> The people of God believes that it is led by the Spirit of the Lord who fills the earth. *Motivated by this faith, it labors to decipher authentic signs of God's presence and purpose in the happenings, needs and desires in which this People has a part along with other men of our age.* For faith throws a new light on everything, manifests God's design for man's total vocation, and thus directs the mind to solutions which are fully human.[1] [Italics ours]

No element of creation, sin alone excepted, escapes this sacramentality. We can choose to view certain elements of creation as isolated from the Continuing Incarnation. We can look on them as being profane in the sense that they are outside the sphere of sacramentality and do not possess the capacity to be efficacious signs of the presence of the living God. But then we have failed

---

[1] *The Documents of Vatican II,* p. 209.

to appreciate the significance of St. John's insistence that "*all things* were made through Him, and without Him was not anything made that was made" (1:3,RSV). In like manner, St. Paul asserts that: "In him everything in heaven and on earth was created, not only things visible but also the invisible.... And he exists before everything, and all things are held together in him.... For in him the complete being of God, by God's own choice, came to dwell. Through him God chose to reconcile the whole universe to himself ... to reconcile all things, whether on earth or in heaven, through him alone" (Col. 1:16–20,RSV).

Father Schillebeeckx expresses it in much the same way:

> The whole created world becomes, through Christ's incarnation and the God-man relationship which is consequent upon it, an outward grace, an offer of grace in sacramental form. As a result of Christ's visible manifestation of Himself in the world—a manifestation which embraces the whole world—the preaching and the sacraments of the Church can be regarded simply as the burning focal points within the entire concentration of this visible presence of grace which is the Church.[2]

Because of the totality of creation in Christ, we must honestly acknowledge that if we personally are unable to approach certain threatening aspects of this same creation in a spirit of faith, believing that they are not isolated from the ambit of God's sacramental expression of Himself to man, then *we* are the ones who have made them exist in profane isolation. We are the ones who have deprived them of their sacramental efficacy for us. We are the ones who have failed to recognize that they can serve as the "ground" for our discovery of the "figure" of Christ. We have arbitrarily determined that particular material signs signify the presence of Christ. But by closing off certain portions of creation to the sacramentality of His efficacious presence, we have once again slipped into the sin of idolatry. By determining where the

2 Schillebeeckx, *op. cit.*, p. 268.

Word will become Flesh-for-us in His Continuing Incarnation, we
have sought to mould an image of His Body that is more pleasing
to our particular tastes.

At times we fail to understand the true significance of "efficacious signs." We have been taught that certain cultic actions manifest the presence of God and are efficacious *ex opere operato,* by
reason of the dynamism of the divine presence and the will of
Christ. We see cultic sacramental signs as efficacious because
Christ has willed them to be so within the sphere of worship and
official ecclesial activity.

We frequently fail to recognize, however, that the cultic sacramental actions are not separated from life, and that their efficacy,
as being the true manifestation of the presence of Emmanuel, is
based upon the far more profound truth that all of creation is a
sacramentally efficacious sign of the presence of God. Because of
the Incarnation, the entire created universe has, in the words of
Father Gerard Manley Hopkins, been "charged with the grandeur
of God" that "will flame out like shining from shook foil," if
only the truth is preached to us, and we, in turn, can humbly beg
for and grow in the capacity to have eyes to see and ears to hear.
The world is an efficacious sign of the divine presence even though
man has been slow to grasp this deeper dimension of material
creation.

THE CHURCH—SACRAMENT OF
THE WHOLE CHRIST

One of the more significant theological developments we can
observe in the Old Testament is a growing appreciation of the
meaning of the principle of *interiority*. This principle is the soul
of any kind of authentic personal presence. The ever-present vice
that prophet after prophet vehemently condemned throughout
Israel's turbulent history was the lack of authenticity in her worship of Yahweh. Unless the motives of the heart were in accord
with the significance of the external action, the worship was vain
and empty. The authenticity of the sign was an integral part of
its efficacious character.

Even in the sacrificial worship of the Israelites there could never be the perfection of interiority, because the priest and victim were separate beings. Priest and people transferred their intentions to the victim, which was then offered to God as a pleasing holocaust, a cultic representation of the attitude of worship and humble supplication in the hearts of the People of God. The sacrificial action was an efficacious sign of the union of Yahweh and His people, simply because God had said that this was so. There was nothing intrinsic to the blood of goats and bullocks that could unite man with his Creator.

With the coming of the Messiah, the perfection of interiority, heralded in Malachy's prophecy about a pure offering in the Messianic era, became a reality. In Jesus Christ, Priest and Victim become one. Christ offered Himself. As Son of the Father, the Word of God become man had the ontological capacity to be mediator. Yahweh Himself had laid the sins of the people upon Him, and Jesus' intention was to perform the will of His Father. His action was efficacious because He ". . . did not exalt himself to be made a high priest, *but was appointed* by him who said to him, 'Thou are my Son, today I have begotten thee' " (Heb. 5:5–6, RSV). (Italics ours.) Christ is presented as both Priest and Victim. His own humanity is the place of expiation and reconciliation of the People with God. The veil that covered the place of the presence of God, and which was sprinkled with blood by the high priest on the Day of Atonement to effect a reconciliation of the People with God, is, in Christ, His own humanity. "But now Christ has come, high priest of good things already in being. The tent of his priesthood is a greater and more perfect one, not made by men's hands, that is, not belonging to this created world; the blood of his sacrifice is his own blood, not the blood of goats and calves; and thus he has entered the sanctuary once and for all and secured an eternal deliverance. For if the blood of goats and bulls and the sprinkled ashes of a heifer have power to hallow those who have been defiled and restore their external purity, how much greater is the power of the blood of Christ; he offered himself without blemish to God, a spiritual and eternal sacrifice; and his blood will cleanse our conscience from the deadness of our former ways and fit us for the service of the living God" (Heb. 9:11–14,NEB).

The Epistle to the Hebrews notes that both the intention and action of Jesus as Priest and Victim are authentic: "In the days of his earthly life he offered up prayers and petitions, with loud cries and tears, to God who was able to deliver him from the grave. Because of his humble submission his prayer was heard: son though he was, he learned obedience in the school of suffering, and, once perfected, became the source of eternal salvation for all who obey him, named by God high priest in the succession of Melchizedek" (Heb. 5:7–10,NEB). His human cries and tears were the visible, efficacious, authentic expression of His desire to undergo suffering and death in order to unite all things through His life of obedience to the heavenly Father. All things were created in Christ, but now, through the human nature of Jesus, creation was brought to a higher level of supernatural life by being given the capacity to share in the interpersonal life of God through the Son's relationship with the Father. "It was clearly fitting that God for whom and through whom all things exist should, in bringing many sons to glory, make the leader who delivers them perfect through sufferings. For a consecrating priest and those whom he consecrates are all of one stock. . . . The children of a family share the same flesh and blood; and so he too shared ours, so that through death he might break the power of him who had death at his command . . . and might liberate those who, through fear of death, had all their lifetime been in servitude" (Heb. 2:10–15,NEB).

Thus there are four qualities with which we can describe Jesus as the leader who delivers us:

1. He is an *authentic* sign in whom the human manifestation of the obedience of the Son of God rings true.

2. He is an *efficacious* sign, for the Father Himself has made Him perfect as Priest and source of our eternal salvation.

3. He is the perfection of the *principle of interiority,* summing up in His own person the perfection of the New Law as superceding the Old.

4. He is the *Sacrament* of encounter with God, the visible

Incarnation and expression in the language of man of the Father's love.

Together with the Father in glory He then sends the Spirit of Love into the hearts of mankind, now adopted sons in Christ, so that they too may now begin to live out the same life of obedience to the Father and death to self-centeredness that was the vocation of the Leader who delivered us.

These same four qualities that we apply to Jesus during His earthly life are now used to describe the risen Lord as He exists together with His Body the Church, the Whole Christ.

As adopted sons of God, living with the newness of a Spirit-quickened life, men gradually discover the gift *within* of a capacity for obedience and love manifested through *agape*. Through faith and the experience of acceptance, they find themselves in touch with an inner source of strength that enables them to begin the life-long task of transcending their ever-present pull toward self-centered autonomy. As they grow in their openness to this new life, they are more and more capable of becoming authentic, efficacious signs—the sacrament of an encounter with the *agape* of the Whole Christ.

The Church, the People of God, as the Body of the risen Lord, caught up in the life of the Whole Christ, is the most perfect expression of an effective, sacramental sign of God's presence in the world. The *Constitution on the Sacred Liturgy* echoes this thought when noting that: ". . . it was from the side of Christ as He slept the sleep of death upon the cross that there came forth the wondrous sacrament which is the whole Church."[3]

Father Schillebeeckx has attempted to describe the intimate relation between the cultic sacraments and the over-all sacramental life of the Church as follows:

There are only seven official sacraments, but there are numerous forms of sacramental expression within the life of the Church. It would be wrong to identify the life of the Church with that life which is confined within the bounds of

[3] *The Documents of Vatican II*, p. 140.

the priesthood and the official sacraments. It is not exclusively from the sacraments that we derive grace—it also comes, for example, from fraternal contact between Christians and their treatment of each other and their fellow men. . . . The seven sacraments are there precisely so that the sacramentalism of the Church, in its more extended sense, can be fully realized in everyday life. The truly Christian life in the midst of this world is—for other Christians—an external and meaningful supply of grace, dogma, and preaching. Similarly, when non-Christians come into contact with those whose life is truly Christian, they are in fact coming up against the Church, as the visible and effective presence of grace in the world.[4]

Father Schillebeeckx then goes on to stress the essential polarity existing between *official* sacramental actions and the over-all sacramentalism of the presence of Christ in the life of the Church. Without cultic worship in our community life, we inevitably lose our sensitivity to the innate sacramentalism of Christian existence.

No man can stay open for very long to the effective signs of God's presence in the world by himself. Since the presence of God is always a Personal presence, man needs an *interpersonal* reminder that *effectively* enables him to remain sensitive to authentic signs of God's presence in the Whole Christ.

This is why the liturgical and official sacramental life of the Church is always a *community* celebration. We must never, even for purposes of abstract analysis, consider the sacramental actions of the Church in any way apart from the believing community that performs them. The People of God are essential to the action, even though the efficacy of the action is by virtue of the power of Christ. But the cultic sacrament, performed in its official, liturgical, interpersonal context, keeps us alive to the meaning of personal presence and, when we are open to the sacramental experience in faith as whole body-persons, actually effects in us the kind of sensitivity required for a true contemplation of God in the innate sacramentalism of Christian existence.

[4] Schillebeeckx, *op. cit.,* pp. 261–262

The indispensable role of the cultic sacrament in the life of the church is perhaps best seen in terms of the *anamnesis* which is at the heart of all sacramental and liturgical action. Father Rahner has provided a theological definition of this term and then briefly described it in the following manner:

> Anamnesis may be theologically defined as the ceremonial re-presentation of a salutary event of the past, in order that the event may lay hold of the situation of the celebrant. Unlike many liturgical acts in other religions, Judaeo-Christian anamnesis presupposes that although the event has and retains its historical uniqueness, it is at the same time present, that is, remains in force as an accomplished fact. . . . The presence of the Lord's death must not be reduced to the merely moral and juridical presence of an event in the past; to do so would exclude the real anamnesis which the Scripture declares to be necessary.[5]

It is through the official action of the Church, with her power to re-present the historical saving events of salvation in the seven cultic sacraments and Eucharistic Celebration, that enables us to maintain our sensitivity to the sacramentalism of Christian life and further plumb its depths, in order to experience and better articulate the presence of God at the heart of our interpersonal life.

TOWARD A THEOLOGY OF
INTERPERSONAL COMMUNICATION—
THE MEANING OF *AGAPE*

We discussed man's social nature before going on to develop our thumbnail sketch of a philosophy of his interpersonal communication, as well as our reflections on the sacramental character of creation and Christian life. It remains for us to deepen our discovery of what it means to become a person in the Whole

[5] Karl Rahner and Herbert Vorgrimler, *Theological Dictionary,* New York, Herder and Herder, 1965, pp. 19–20.

Christ by further exploring the theological dimensions of the sacramentality of human interpersonal communication.

The indelible *character* of the sacraments of Baptism, Confirmation, and Holy Orders tells us something about the deeper "life dimension" that is included within their cultic manifestation.

Through baptism I am caught up in the life of the Whole Christ. "For Christ is like a single body with its many limbs and organs, which, many as they are, together make up one body. For indeed we were all brought into one body by baptism, in the one Spirit, whether we are Jews or Greeks, whether slaves or free men, and that one Holy Spirit was poured out for all of us to drink" (1 Cor. 12:13,NEB).

The Christian community acknowledges that the child or convert is signed with the seal of Christ and given the vocation as an adopted son to imitate the leader of his salvation and live out a life of other-centeredness in faith. Baptism is not merely a historical fact in the life of the Christian. It is a vocation to be lived out in his personal history. This is the true meaning of the *character* of Baptism. It gives man an inner direction toward life in the Body of Christ as a value that is to be continually realized at ever-deeper levels of personal life.

The cultic ceremony of Confirmation, witnessed to in faith by the believing community, is an efficacious sign that the young adult has been further incorporated into his responsibilities in the Whole Christ by being given the power and mandate to mediate the Holy Spirit to the members of the Body through *agape*. Confirmation is an effective sign that one now has the ontological and, one would hope, psychological capacity to live that kind of other-centered existence that is a sign of the presence and effective communication of the Spirit. On the psychological level, as we have already seen, this capacity develops in man as he himself grows in personal maturity and the capability of self-sacrificing love.

The sacrament of Holy Orders initiates a man into the vocation of a specifically cultic service to the Body of the Whole Christ. The officially ordained minister fosters the Christ-life that is gradually laying hold of the family of man. In their daily lives, the People of God imitate the obedience and other-centeredness of

Jesus by continually responding to their call to be adopted sons and daughters. They follow in the steps of Christ who lived out His vocation of Sonship with a constant eye to the will of His Father. But as a Christian community they must always realize that this life activity, their growth as human persons, is never separate from the salvific action of Jesus and the presence of the Spirit whom He has sent.

The official, sacramental and liturgical acts of the Church, performed by the duly authorized minister, are at the service of this life-activity of the Christian community. The *anamnesis* that vitalizes all sacramental worship has a twofold function. It reminds the pilgrimaging People of God that the saving event of the Lord's life, death, and resurrection is at the heart of their human growth as persons as well as actually effecting their personal union with one another in the ever-present mystery of His Continuing Incarnation. The personal presence of one to another in the Christian community, as they break bread together in faith and charity and hope for the fullness of the Coming of the Lord, is a sign that the liturgical celebration not only represents but also effects their union. We go to communion "together." We must not approach the table of the Lord in psychological isolation from those who receive His Sacred Body with us. "When we break the bread, is it not a means of sharing in the body of Christ? Because there is one loaf, we, many as we are, are one body; for it is one loaf of which we all partake" (1 Cor. 10:17,NEB).

The efficacious sign of the presence of the Lord at the Eucharistic Banquet is not restricted to the Host. It *includes* the community and their life of faith, hope, and love with one another. As we mentioned before, the sign is not efficacious unless it is authentically incarnated in the whole human response. Just as we cannot divide man and hope for him to be an efficacious sign of the presence of God with only a part of himself, neither can we divide the cultic celebration and restrict the efficacious presence of the Lord to one part of it. The physical presence of Christ in the Eucharist is caused by the power of Christ and not by the isolated response of the believing community. But if this presence is truly to transform the interpersonal life of those who are present, then they must be open to the efficacy of the total sign that *includes* the people with whom they worship. They, together with the risen Lord, are the Whole Christ. The *personal* experience of this reality means actually being open to *this* man and *this* woman standing next to me *as the efficacious sign,* together with myself, of the worshiping Christian community. When approaching the altar, we must always be alive to the fact that we go to communion *together.*

Scripture is constantly speaking to us of those "breakthrough points" in our daily experience where the "grandeur of God" suddenly flames "out like shining from shook foil." Perhaps, most significantly, it is within the area of our interpersonal life that the writers of the New Testament seem to find the clearest manifestation of man's experience of "God-with-us," Emmanuel. It is only fitting that a God, whose existence is to be "Personal-within-Himself," should become manifest in that area of man's life where the latter is most capable of imitating divine life. The "between" of interpersonal life, where man meets his fellow man and discovers himself, is also the very "ground" of his meeting with God.

It is the experience of *agape,* together with the needs which evoke it, that most vividly thrusts us into the presence of Emmanuel. The cultic life of the Christian community celebrates, fosters, and is directed toward effecting this deeper union in *agape.* We come together in the liturgical assembly to celebrate the growth of Christ's *agape* among us; and in the very celebration, if we are open to the full efficacy of the total sign of the worshiping Christian community, this life is effected in us and we are transformed.

As a result of Jesus' presence among men and the sending of the Spirit at Pentecost, the Christian community began to become aware of an entirely new human experience that was happening among them. It was so different from anything they had previously known that there was really no word with which to describe it. It was a kind of love, but none of the Greek words in use at the time could adequately capture its total meaning. *Eros, Storge,* and *Philia* had overtones of sexual love, familial affection, or a kind of affectionate regard, all of which failed to convey the meaning of this new experience within the Christian community. Finally the inspired writers of the early Church seized on the word *agape,* rarely used at that time, as being best able to express in human language the richness of this gift of God that was being discovered in their new life together. They had all experienced the power of this love in the Christian community and hence could bring their experience to the new word.

A pagan, on the other hand, would have been quite mystified by the use to which this word was being put within the Christian community, since he would most likely not have experienced the effects of this new love. As he read the texts of the New Testament dealing with *agape,* he would probably have found them as puzzling as we find the writings of the great mystics. When St. Ignatius of Loyola attempted to describe the vision of the Trinity that he experienced on the banks of the River Cardonner, he fell back on the inadequate description of three notes played on the organ at the same time. For one who has not experienced the vision of Ignatius, the language is poetically beautiful but hopelessly inadequate to describe the contents of his mystical experience.

It is perhaps unfortunate that the Greek word *agape* is translated into English as "love" or even "charity," since both of these words carry the burden of so many connotations from our own culture. We can sometimes avoid the burden of having constantly to demythologize the meanings added by our own culture if we read the texts of the inspired authors but leave their own word in the original Greek. For example, if we slowly go through the following text from the First Epistle of St. John, substituting the word *agape* for the word *love,* we might be able to concentrate a little more on the attempt of the writer to communicate this radically new experience of the Christian community. In a way, the text may sound very much like the mystical writings of one of the Saints. But by remaining with St. John's own word, we may find it easier to stay open to the subtle distinctions which both he and other authors of the New Testament are attempting to include in their use of *agape.* It is good to meditate on this text, going through it slowly and attempting to reach through the words to the experience of the writer. We must begin by remembering that *agape* is a unique and new experience in the early Christian community.

> "Beloved, let us have *agape* for one another;
>   For *agape* is of God, and he who has *agape*
> Is born of God and knows God. He who does
>   Not have *agape* does not know God;
> For God is *Agape*.
>   In this the *agape* of God was made manifest among us,
> That God sent His only Son into the world,
>   So that we might live through Him.
> In this is *agape,* not that we
>   had *agape* for God but that He had *agape* for us
> And sent His Son to be the expiation for our sins.
>   Beloved, if God so had *agape* for us,
> We also ought to have *agape* for one another.
>   No man has ever seen God;
> If we have *agape* for one another,
>   God abides in us and His *agape* is perfected in us"
> (1 Jn. 4:7–12,RSV).

It is interesting to go back over the text and reflect on some of the qualifications that John introduces into his use of *agape*. The distinctions he makes tell us something about the experience of the primitive Christian community. He first identifies *agape* with knowledge of God, stating that he who experiences *agape* is born as a new creation and is caught up into a higher life. If we do not experience *agape,* we cannot experience our incorporation into this radically new life.

St. John then goes on to make the stunning remark that God is *Agape*. God had *agape* for us and sent His Son, *Agape*-Incarnate, to be the expiation for our sins. The long-awaited Emmanuel, God-Incarnate, now continues to be incarnated in our daily experience of the Whole Christ. My human interpersonal experience of Emmanuel as *agape* is centered in those people in my life who seek to live a life of selfless, authentic openness in faith to the needs of the Body of Christ. This is my daily sacramental experience of *agape*. God-with-me, the Incarnate Word made Flesh, the Whole Christ of the Continuing Incarnation, is discovered, experienced, found in the "between," the uniquely selfless love life of the Christian community as it seeks, in faith, to answer the needs of the Body of Christ. This psychological experience of *agape,* together with a corresponding faith-sensitivity to genuine human needs, as being the needs of the Whole Christ, is my experience of God-with-me.

John goes on to show that *agape,* although experienced in an incarnational human setting, is nonetheless not an experience originating from man as its radical and ultimate source. "In this is *agape,* not that we had *agape* for God, but that He had *agape* for us." *Agape* is always a gift of God. So to experience *agape* is to experience God and not some man-made reality. *Agape* is also discovered only in interpersonal life. John admonishes us to have *agape* for one another, because, as he has said earlier in the same epistle: "We know that we have passed out of death into life, because we have *agape* for the brethren. He who does not have *agape* remains in death" (1 Jn. 3:14, RSV).

Father Ceslaus Spicq, O.P., has pointed out that St. Paul frequently uses "in Christ" and "in *agape*" as synonymous expressions.

> The believer must live in love just as he must be and live in Christ. It is correct to say that the believer exists in charity (Eph. 1:4) and that he exists in Christ (1 Cor. 1:30). He lives and grows in and through love (Eph. 4:15–16) as he lives and grows in Christ. We are rooted and grounded in charity (Eph. 3:17) as we are grounded in Christ (1 Cor. 3:10–12). We are instructed by love (Col. 2:2) and by Christ (Eph. 4:21). We think and love in charity as Christ thinks and loves (Phil. 2:1–5). All our actions arise simultaneously from *agape* and from the Lord. . . . In most texts where St. Paul describes the Christian charity, the word "Christ" can

be substituted for the word "Charity" and an exact portrait of the Lord be created.[6]

Thus the human, interpersonal, sacramental experience of *agape,* nurtured by the cultic life of sacramental worship within the believing community, provides us with our most profound body-person realization of life in the Whole Christ.

Father Schillebeeckx further describes the Christian's growing experience of God's presence in the following manner:

> The man whose life is based on sacramental grace begins to realize how grace surrounds him and guides all his actions, and to see his most deeply personal spiritual intentions appear before him in an entirely new and surprising light—*as something that he can no longer understand simply on the basis of his own personality or explain in terms of human psychology. He gradually learns to realize that there is someone else at work within him*—"So is everyone that is born of the spirit" (Jn. 3:5–8) and, in the words of St. Paul, "And I live, now not I; but Christ liveth in me" (Gal. 2:20).[7] [Italics ours.]

As we have already seen, St. Paul has his own unique way of describing the experience of Christ's presence in his life. His Second Letter to the Corinthians (12:10) is eloquent personal testimony to the accuracy of Father Schillebeeckx's above-quoted statement. It was in moments of weakness and contrast that Paul discovered the strength of Christ. This was when he began to recognize that "there was someone else at work within him." Paul has perhaps shown best of all that the experience of *agape* is discovered most clearly in the moment of tension and sharp contrast when we know that the good which we achieve (or that is achieved in us) is beyond the human capacity of the giver.

If I am humanly weak and find myself acting in a strong man-

---

[6] Ceslaus Spicq, O.P., *Agape in the New Testament* (Vol. II), St. Louis, B. Herder Book Co., 1965, pp. 316–317.

[7] Schillebeeckx, *op. cit.,* 274–275.

ner, the appearance of this strength brings me up with a jolt. There may be certain people or situations that naturally threaten me. In many instances I am acutely aware of my weaknesses; nonetheless, I am actually able to listen to another's needs more than my own fear or self-preoccupation, and I am frequently able to heal the other person. At one and the same time I am aware of both strength and weakness within myself.

Perhaps I have also experienced other people acting in this same manner toward me. At times when I know they are exhausted or preoccupied, and their own needs have been clamoring for attention, they have, despite these compelling influences in the other direction, been able to listen to my needs more than their own. There have also been times when they could not. They have been too turned in and preoccupied to listen to me.

A force is at work in the first instance that I recognize as incompatible with the human weaknesses I know to be present in the other. This, again, is what Father Schillebeeckx is getting at when he says that a man "gradually learns to realize that there is someone else at work within him."

However, it is important to note that for Paul, it is only by being authentic, by remaining open to his own weaknesses and not seeking to bolster them with man-made defense mechanisms that he, or anyone else for that matter, is able to discover the power of Christ. Once we have erected impregnable barriers of protection, we will never be able to discern whether strength comes from our own makeshift defenses or from the presence of Emmanuel. The artificial barriers destroy that essential tension and contrast which is so necessary if we are to discover Christ. When we are weak, then we are strong. It is during these precious moments that the efficacious sacramental sign of God's presence shines through for us with particular brilliance.

Paul spent himself tirelessly in his struggle against people who wished to justify themselves by their observance of the law. He was always concerned for those who "wished to have a righteousness of their own," the ones who tended to find their identity before God in terms of their accomplishments.

In many ways they are like the individual who does not yet

have an inner sense of who he is. Consequently, he tends to find his identity too exclusively in terms of what he has—wealth, bodily health or beauty, talents, job, opinions or ideas, or even the perfect observance of the law, the rules of a religious community, or a school of philosophical or theological speculation. Such an individual tends to identify himself with externals. Recognizing his own weaknesses, he compensates by finding his self-identity in terms of some possession or capacity which he developed in order to achieve this personal identity. The surge toward discovery of the "real self" has been diverted into identifying more with what is possessed than by the discovery of "who I am." Such a person grasps for an identity by building it himself, rather than by risking opening to it as a gift given to him by another. In biblical language, this man is attempting to justify himself; he is attempting to become a person in isolation.

Whatever it is in life that we make into the principle of our salvation as a human person, to such an extent that our personal identity intensely depends upon it, *that is our god.* If our radical identity depends upon the gift of selfless-love from another, upon what we have called *agape,* then we are saved as a person. We have found God-with-us. But if our personal identity depends upon status, a "religious" image, our teaching talent, authority, observance of the rule, or any other external reality, then we have worshiped an idol. We have not found God but made one.

Idolatry has been the plague of man in his relationship with God since the beginning of time. The conversion from the idol to the true God, Paul's "losing all things for His sake" (Phil. 3:8, C), is an agonizing process. It is the *Via Crucis* which every man must tread as he renounces the absolute egotism that is his heritage from Adam.

Man truly finds himself when he is able to risk letting the gift of his self-identity be given to him through the selfless love of another. This is the way in which we begin to discover our radical identity in the Whole Christ.

PART IV

PART II.

9. *Becoming Contemplatives in the Whole Christ*

IN PRECEDING CHAPTERS we discussed the question of finding the "real God" in our life, rather than a god of our own finite conceptions or one whom we create and fashion to satisfy unfulfilled natural human needs. We also spoke of the Whole Christ as the "ground" of our critical search for a personal relationship with the Trinitarian Community who is God. In each succeeding section, we have tried to strengthen the reader's realization that the dynamics of human growth in the Whole Christ, personally realized in faith and responded to at ever-deeper levels of man's entire body-person, must be the movement of any Christian life worthy of the Incarnate Lord.

To break down the long-standing barriers of a nominalistic or over-intellectualized approach to a personal relationship with the Triune God—which, as adults, we have all absorbed to some degree from our environment—admits of no instant or easy about-face. Patterns of behavior and deeply ingrained "ways of relating" have an interlocking complexity within our whole personality makeup which defies quick change, even though the latter may be intellectually acknowledged as desirable. We can never again return to the wonder and openness of early childhood. Regardless of age, we can always work toward a more profound awakening of the sense of God within our own particular stage of human development.

Unfortunately, many adults tend to associate growth with either physical maturation, which they have for the most part completed, or with "spiritual growth," which can be rather nebulously thought of as "out there." However, we cannot remind ourselves too often that as human beings we are either in a state of "becoming" or we have atrophied. Our physical and formal intellectual development may be aspects of life that we consider to be largely completed. But these elements of human growth must never be confused with the ever-present task of "becoming more a person," which will remain as long as life itself.

We are beings in whom the process of birth never ceases. We pass through a lifetime of birth and rebirth. But when we finally reach the period of life that society regards as "mature," we must not be deceived into believing that we have reached the climax of our growth. Instead, as someone has said, we have reached only the "full grown way of growing."

To begin this deepening process we need go no further than that which is most intimate to each one of us, our own body-person. Even a brief reflection, focused upon the immediate awareness of myself as "becoming" and growing as a person because my "becoming" is one of relatedness, can help me to extend the consciousness of my related-body-person.

With this as background, we must now explore our understanding of the Whole Christ as He is revealed to us, so that we can develop a spirituality and a prayer-life of encounter with Him (and eventually with all Three Divine Persons) that is truly grounded in our existential experience. It is for this reason that we have stressed the theological importance of authentic "signs."

These signs must become, for us, the principal experiential avenues of our contact with the Whole Christ, and thus with the Spirit of His love and with the Father. The earthly life of Jesus was a continual incarnation of the presence of the Father's love. Jesus, the Father's Word become Flesh, was the authentic interpersonal sign of divine communication with mankind in these last days. "When in former times God spoke to our forefathers, he spoke in fragmentary and varied fashion through the prophets. But *in this final age he has spoken to us in the Son . . . who is the* effulgence of God's splendour and the stamp of God's very being" (Heb. 1:1–3,NEB). (Italics ours.)

Our Lord constantly stressed the sacramental aspect of His own presence as a sign that the Father was with men: "He who has seen me, has seen the Father" (Jn. 14:9). "Believe me that I am in the Father and the Father in me, or else believe me for the sake of the works themselves" (Jn. 14:11,RSV).

He then continued to teach them that they too, joined to Him in faith and love as members of His Body, would be present to men as a sign of the Father's powerful love. "Truly, truly I say to you, he who believes in me will also do the works that I do" (Jn. 14:12,RSV).

And these works will principally be the signs of *agape.* "If you have *agape* for me, you will keep my commandments" (Jn. 14:15, RSV); "This is my commandment, that you have *agape* for one another as I have had *agape* for you" (Jn. 15:12,RSV). Because, "He who has *agape* for me will be given *agape* by my Father, and I will have *agape* for him and *manifest* myself to him" (Jn. 14:21, RSV).

Here Christ described the further signs whereby the Christian would be able to experience and discover the interpersonal presence of the risen Lord in his life.

Sensitivity to these material, sacramental "signs," which are our tangible experiences of relatedness to the Divine Persons in our lives, must be cultivated as a "way of the Spirit," as an approach to a personal and living relationship with each of the Divine Persons. They are a way that is one with the rhythm of our personal growth as human beings.

What could be more in keeping with the beneficence of a personal, loving God than that our human climb toward self-realization should be "graced" by the self-communication of the Creator Himself? What could be more in accord with the creative love of God for us, than that the impelling thrust of human nature toward self-actualization should be open to man as his own unique way of encounter with God?

Few of us have developed a spirituality around the profound significance of this truth. The mystery of Christ, as well as the economy of salvation and redemption, is nowhere more beautifully revealed than within the evolution of man. It is not hard to imagine that if St. Paul were alive in our century, he would have been thrilled by the mystery of the growing Body of the Whole Christ revealed in the child developmental studies of a Piaget, a Montessori, or a Gesell. He might perhaps have even enriched his preaching and writing with the sensitive and articulate expression of "*agape*-action" in the growing personal life of the Body of His Lord, if he could have had at his disposal the description of "healing encounters" by such men as Carl Rogers.

Paul would have been so awed at the mystery of the Continuing Incarnation shining through the laws of human growth, which are gradually being unfolded by contemporary explorations into the psychology of man's "becoming," that he might have personally realized a new glimpse into the way in which men are: ". . . to come to the full wealth of conviction which understanding brings, and grasp God's secret. That secret is Christ himself; in him lie hidden all God's treasures of wisdom and knowledge" (Col. 2:2–3,NEB).

Christian prayer must not be something parallel to, or apart from, the growing sensitivity of the family of man to what it means to be human, to what it means to become a person in that evolution in which: ". . . the whole created universe groans in all its parts as if in the pangs of childbirth" (Rom. 8:22,NEB).

Paul goes on to add that not only creation ". . . but even we, to whom the Spirit is given as firstfruits of the harvest to come, are groaning inwardly while we wait for God to make us his sons and *set our whole body free*" (Rom. 8:23–24,NEB). (Italics ours.)

Note that Paul does not say "set us free from our body." He speaks of the redemption of the body, which for him, with his Semitic anthropology, *is* the whole body-person. We come to full self-realization as incarnate-spirit only through the gift of total adoption into Trinitarian life. The seeds have been planted, the firstfruits are budding forth, and the Christian community waits with eager longing and a growing sensitivity to the true significance of its ancient Eucharistic prayer: "*Marana tha,* Come Lord Jesus" (1 Cor. 16:22,NEB); (Apoc. 22:20,NEB).

Our consciousness of Emmanuel must not be exclusively a biblical image, nor a historical phantasm that comes to the imagination from seeing illustrated books or religious works of art. Rather it should be the reflective, experiential knowledge in faith of "God-with-me," discovered through my increasing sensitivity to the presence of the Divine Persons revealed in and through their *active participation in my life.*

The primary source of my discovery of the signs of God's creative, living activity in my life is by becoming open to, and aware of, the vast richness of body-person experiences that lie untapped within my daily contacts with reality. I am plunged into the material world of my body-relatedness from the very first moments of life, and as I grow in my ability to "read" the world of material signs in my new adventure into the world of person, there should be a gradual awakening to these same signs as the loving Father's own incarnated speech to me. My child's sense of wonder and awe was naturally open and ready to listen to the word of God in creation. But too often it was driven out of earshot by the noise of adult demands, adult concepts, and meaningless abstractions about God.

However, the consoling fact that each of us comes to appreciate more, as the years go by, is that in creating us human, God has gifted us with a life that is always a "becoming." It is never too late to unearth new dimensions of infinite richness in the divine self-communication by discovering the signs of God in *my life.* But to do this, I must begin with my own experiences, here and now, of myself as a human being.

What we are suggesting is not a kind of introspection or belabored analysis of motives and actions—that fatiguing "picking away at myself" that is so often associated with an examination of conscience. Instead, we are concerned with an actualization of each person's human potential for spirituality. By opening myself up more and more to such experiential phenomena as freedom, creativity, spontaneity, and wonder within my entire body-person relatedness to the people and things I contact each day, vast new worlds of meaning and richness can be personalized.

The realization of man's spirituality is not restricted to the traditional "church milieu." God's self-communication is not exclusively determined by these more traditional forms of religious encounter, most of which are man-made and have been constructed to meet the religious needs of a certain time within specific cultural settings. Historically, we know that the Church herself has made many changes in the outward expression of the cultic sacraments, and even in the Sacrifice of the Mass, in order more effectively to impress men with the theological truths that must always be re-incarnated in the continually evolving language of life.

In our Western culture, and particularly within the more pragmatic American version, the hurdles over which a growing child must leap in his race toward maturity are often the very barriers that gradually destroy or dull his innate sense of wonder, until its very existence is no longer a part of his conscious experience.

If we have lost this priceless ingredient for true wholeness as an incarnate-spirit during the course of our growth toward maturity, may we not legitimately raise the question that possibly our developing "holiness" might also be somewhat impaired?

How much of this background did we bring to the religious life, and was any effort made to reinstate the God-given "way of the human spirit" as our most normal approach to the Father's gift of Himself to us? And today, as products of their environment, what is the direction of spiritual growth that candidates for the religious life bring with them to the novitiate or seminary? How are they helped to develop an incarnational spirituality as they enter a life of dedication that demands both a profound sense of the presence of God in a world of conflicting values and social upheavals, and a deeply rooted capacity to encounter Him within the realities of their life-experience as it really is? How, moreover, do they not only encounter Him but also find Him so relevant to their own daily life-experience that they are caught up and set afire with this message?

We must honestly ask ourselves how much the "spiritual direction" that at present is given in our centers of religious formation attempts to cope with this problem, or in fact even recognizes it as a problem?

We believe that the answer to this latter question will only gradually be resolved as the present generation of older religious, both those responsible for the formation of novices and those whose influence extends throughout the apostolate, take upon themselves the gradual reassessment of their own prayer-life and struggle to find God in their lives in a way that is truly relevant to them personally. This must be done under the guidance of the Spirit with a kind of heroic availability, in faith, to the needs of Christ's Body—manifested in the people within "my area of life and work." Involvement with these people must first be characterized by an attitude of openness—to listen to them and to struggle with them for some direction, if not for an answer. But I must do this always mindful that I myself am a "needer" with, in fact, very few or none of the answers to *this* person's needs.

We religious today are, in truth, more the "needers" perhaps than anyone else, because we claim to know and love Christ. We claim to live in intimate friendship with Him, and yet how seldom we are able effectively to communicate this to anyone! How many of us are really helping another person or persons to grow closer to Christ by sharing with them not advice but the spiritual direction of a sacramentally effective body-person relationship? This sort of "spiritual direction" is full proof of the presence of God, because it is a "signed" effect of the incarnated Spirit within us. It does not depend on our theological or ascetical book wisdom, because it is the Wisdom of the Spirit. This kind of "spiritual direction" involves a willingness to *grow with* another, to accompany that person in his struggle for self-realization as a human being, and to be keenly aware that *both* of us *are growing*. In a word, this is a willingness to *give myself as body-person* to another. It is a sharing dictated *not on my terms* but by the other's *real needs* for growth. This demands a sharing of myself for which there is no substitute in word or action, although both of the latter may be included in the effective sign of this deeper reality.

Each of us must be so deeply involved with the needs of Christ's Body that we are actually pained, confused, and agonized over our inability meaningfully to communicate Christ to others, especially the young. Our inability really to "get through" to those whom we know deep down thirst to find Him, but cannot accept Him in the "image of their fathers," should be a source of genuine sadness to us.

How many adult Christians are there, even among the "professional religious," who are afraid to admit (especially to themselves because the truth is so threatening) how actually abstract and unreal God is to them? We sometimes unconsciously hide our insecurity behind an involvement in work, external pieties, or "maintaining the position of the Church." But the young today have an uncanny way of sniffing out such façades, especially when they approach us with one of life's real crises and ask where they can find God in this experience. It is then that our real colors come through, and the "appropriate theological answers" from the books have a ring of hollowness about them. Our questioners turn from us in surprise, amazed that such "unrealness" could actually have been the heart of our life-experience for so many years! If we do not personally live with Christ, is it any wonder that our words—whether pious, speculative, old manual, favorite spiritual author, kerygmatic, biblical, or what have you—do not beckon with an invitation to look further, to come closer, or at least to listen awhile longer?

Perhaps not only our pragmatic culture but also the very milieu of our years of preparation for apostolic work have toned our whole approach to reality. *We* have "made the grade," passed the scrutinizing eyes of myriad boards, committees, councils, and superiors and have been stamped for approval. *We* are acquiring the knowledge, *we* are getting the certificates, diplomas, and accreditation. *We* are responsible for the administration of the school or hospital, or for the teaching of this class. *We* have the background and the experience. *We* are the Sister, Brother, or priest who is the "professional religious" with our "uniform."

Is it really so strange that perhaps we have become dulled or almost lost our sense of wonder? And when we are continually approached "for the answers" and trained for years to acquire them and even to outdo our "secular" contemporaries in attaining competence in a specialty, is it, once again, not too surprising if many of us do not really know how to *listen?*

Openness, listening, and wonder have always been and still

are the most fundamental attitudes and spiritual qualities of a religious person of any faith or creed. This is so because these qualities are the expression of man's God-given spiritual nature, and as such are the clearest sign of his oneness as incarnate-spirit.

Perhaps we could best illustrate this attitude with a small example. How often do any of us approach our need for dialogue with God, at a time when we are anxious or fearful something may happen to hurt us, by going into the garden or the park, or even the local florist, just to look at a beautiful flower? Or better, if possible, to pick it and carry it home so as to touch it, smell it, and breathe in all the patterns of texture, design, balance and nuances of color and blend. How many of us can really pause to admire the flower's arrangement of petals, or its contrast against green foliage and against the background of a white cloud or the blue sky? How many of us are really capable, as human body-persons, of "looking at the wild lilies" of our field and personally trying to realize and know with all our being that "even Solomon in all his splendor was not arrayed like one of these"; and that "if God so clothes the grass of the field . . ." will he not much more take care of me? (Mt. 6:28–30.)

Some will object that this would be artificial and meaningless to them. And we would hasten to agree, respecting their feelings and not suggesting that they force any experience that repels them; but at the same time, we would recommend that they not prejudice themselves until they have tried many approaches, some of which might have surprising results, even for the most skeptical.

Everyone must search *his own inclinations* for those events, places, and moments that still elicit interest or excite a thrill of personal satisfaction. It matters little what they may be—whether it is the sense of accomplishment and mastery found in solving a math problem or hitting a home run; whether it is the smile of a beautiful child in the class, or witnessing the birth of a child; or even something so simple as feeling the warmth of the sun against our body on a crisp autumn morning. How many of us, when we want to talk to God, let our bodies search for Him as well as our hearts and our minds?

How often, for example, when we take a cool shower on a hot

day, or especially on those rare occasions when we can go swim-
ming, do we let the water on our whole body speak to us of the
sheer joy of this oneness, this unity that is my arms, legs, back,
and toes? How often do I allow myself to feel the freedom of
directed movement and consciously "possess myself" a little
more by choosing to relate with the wholeness of my body-person
expression in and with all of reality? What language does the
breath of a summer storm, the gusty wind of spring, or the humid
summer heat speak to me as I feel them against my face and body?

And so we could go on through the thousands of sights and
smells, touches, sounds, feelings and moods that make up most
of our daily lives. Yet how much of this is wasted in our dialogue
with God, in what could be a "body-person-alive-relatedness" to
the "everlasting love" of God's self-gift to us in all the marvels
of creation.

In our growth toward what we have been conditioned to believe is "maturity," our capacity for wonder has been most
neglected. We must once again be opened up to listen to our
whole "body-person-as-related" in order to discover the spiritual
dimension of our divinely created openness to all of reality, and
to reawaken our awareness of the mystery of man's human capacity to relate to the totality of being and grow in consciousness of
this relationship. In brief, we must seek to become aware of
ourselves as human.

Such a realization, lived out in my day-to-day encounters with
the world around me, is in fact a "way of the spirit." It can
become more consciously a "way of *The Spirit*" when the gift of
faith is received and responded to with love. This "natural way
of the spirit" within which Holy Scripture can reveal the divine,
creative presence of the living God, is one of the most important
"ways" in which God has chosen to give Himself to us through
our incarnate capacity for dialogue with and availability for
listening to all of reality. The very essence of man in his "becoming" is "to be open."

As body-persons situated in a material world whose physical
and social laws can bind, constrain, and even determine our
response, we must never lose the capacity for wonder. For wonder

stimulates sensitivity to ourselves as both spirit and matter, so that we may know our gift of incarnate-freedom as a whole body-person and thus consciously choose further to realize and personalize it. With the forfeiture of our sense of wonder goes a proportionate diminishing of that awareness and need to actualize the creative center of our emerging body-person—freedom.

The intimate relationship between cultivating and prizing the sense of wonder, and gradually resolving the tension between self-centeredness and other-centeredness can clearly be seen. For wonder truly calls me out of myself. Its invitation confronts me with myself as I truthfully am, as body-person, living in the world and not encapsulated within my own body as my *only* world of meaning. Living in relationship to more and more of the real world brings with it a deepening consciousness of my authentic self, my "real self" as incarnate-spirit, as body-person, and with this awareness comes the mature freedom that is man's as he grows into the wholeness of "becoming a person."

If, as we have said, while man is about this task of personal growth the Word of God should be preached to him, revealing the Spirit of Love at work within his daily struggle toward incarnate "personhood," then the energy of this drive toward authentic existence as a person can become for him the faith-filled experience of one who is led by the "Spirit of God." He does not live in constant fear of falling back into the "spirit of slavery," but cries "Abba, Father" in the spirit of sonship, rejoicing to be set free with " . . . the liberty and splendor of the children of God" (Rom. 8:14–21,NEB).

This liberty of God's children is the "gifted freedom" of their adopted sonship, which, in its turn, is the "gifted freedom" to be in dialogue with the Father, in the Spirit with the Son. This "gifted (or graced) freedom" is our reception of the Spirit, who "intercedes for us with signs too deep for words" (Rom. 8:26, RSV). Our dialogue with the Divine Persons, then, is really a "graced-dialogue" within our experience of interpersonal communication and development, which man is capable of entering in faith, if God should choose freely to communicate Himself in this way.

The important aspect that needs stressing today is not so much the gratuity of God's gift but rather that this very gift truly waits on man's free, creative, incarnate availability for dialogue. This openness to "be-with," to listen, and to respond in a personal self-gift, in spite of the very tension that man always experiences between isolation and community, between self-centeredness and other-centeredness, is not something we are born with as fully realized or actualized.

Instead, it is the result of a long, slow, developmental process in which the "real self," with its own growing capacity for self-gift, gradually emerges as a result of the self-gift of others. And, as we have already briefly noted, the "others" are those persons in my life-experience who are alive with the *agape*-life (selfless love) of the Whole Christ. This gradual discovery and integration of my "becoming" person, through the exercise of creative openness and freedom in my own unique response to life, is always accomplished through dialogue. Dialogue with "the others" and with all the world around me is the life-blood of my emerging "personhood." This co-creative discovery and integration of who I really am (my real self) into reality as it actually is, exhibits the self-realization of man's highest human values in authentic existence. It is the life of incarnate-spirit, struggling to achieve fullness through integration and wholeness.

The natural catalyst for each progressive step in this actualization is always a renewal in the sense of wonder. This, along with a kind of "availability," that is, the openness of spirit, allowing reality to reveal itself the way it truthfully is, makes it possible for man to personalize the true, human, spiritual values contained in his every response to life (existence) itself. This reverential listening, this existential obedience to the call of the authentic transcendent values in Being, colors the whole thrust of man's "becoming a person" that has now been "graced" by the Incarnation of Jesus Christ.

Our natural, human way of spiritual growth must always be a dynamic, creative, personalized, and *inspired* "becoming." We use the word *inspired* in order to describe what we mean by openness or availability. The original meaning of *in-spirare,* "to breathe in," aptly conveys this personal attitude that our "becoming" person should have toward all reality.

The "spiritual man," then, through the growing capacity for an authentic availability in his body-person presence, is really one who is open to "breathing in" the infinite "ground" and source of all reality—God-Incarnate. One who consciously sets about this task as a way of growth is, therefore, growing in the spirit. He has chosen to remain open, breathing in all of reality that comes to him. Such a person, people say, is "inspired," because he seems to see more and to possess a depth of insight that the ordinary person does not have. Those who have understood the intimate relationship between spiritual and personal growth have been grasped by the unity that is their own oneness as incarnate-spirit in the Whole Christ. Through their response to the selfless gift of *agape,* they are able to penetrate some of the opaqueness of their self-centeredness and truly discover the depths of their real self in their own capacity to transcend isolation through availability in openness and self-gift. As such, they have been "breathed into" by some of the "breadth and length and height and depth" of reality (the Whole Christ) that lies beyond the first primitive levels of ordinary cognition. Such men and women of the spirit must be today's Christian apostles.

When this basic direction of spiritual growth (which is really another way of saying "becoming a person") is the faith-response of "breathing in" the Spirit of Love, and when that which has been "breathed into" us is truly the *agape*-life of the Divine Persons dwelling in our innermost being, then the vast implications for developing an "active-contemplative" prayer-life relevant to all men and cultures, because it is grounded within the very "becoming" process toward authentic human existence, opens before us with an overwhelming impact. If we ourselves can develop such personalized dialogue with the Whole Christ, the relevance of the Good News of man's salvation in Jesus Christ can be preached with intelligibility and compelling eloquence by the very sacrament of our interpersonal life with one another in the family of man.

We could well afford to spend more time in exploring how

each of us must open himself to the wonder of created reality as a sacrament of the presence of the living God and a revelation of the divine self-gift. Such open listening and sensitive response with a faith-filled body-person involvement in the richness of human existence itself forms the foundation of any balanced Christian prayer-life. Since, however, we have limited our reflections in this book principally to our growing interpersonal relationship with the Whole Christ, it is along these lines that we now wish to discuss further something of the incomparable richness of the Whole Christ, the risen and glorified Lord as He is incarnationally expressed and present to me in His growing Body.

For the remainder of this section, we shall propose these thoughts to the reader as further reflections aimed at helping the development of an incarnational prayer, a contemplation that is truly caught up within man's experience of "becoming a person," so that our interpersonal relationships may become for each of us a conscious faith-response in "becoming a person in the Whole Christ."

MAN'S "BECOMING-PERSON" AND
ENCOUNTER WITH GOD

We have seen so far that man's human growth is capable of being "graced" by God because it is primarily a "becoming-person" development. Man's personal growth as incarnate-spirit is open to the Infinite and able to be raised to an I-Thou encounter with God Himself. Man's spiritual development is fundamentally the deepening awareness of the presence of the Infinite to his finite, created spirit. Growing in the spirit, therefore, includes the effort needed to extend one's self-consciousness as a created human being to the point where we realize that this very createdness encompasses a radical openness to the uncreated God.

Our body-person consciousness must contain an integrated awareness of the Infinite dimensions within our lives, communicated in our daily experiences with the world and especially with other people, so that a wholeness results in us. This growing wholeness is, of itself, ordered to God because its very existence is dependent on a conscious response to the infinite dimension within life.

We are, however incarnated into a visible history of time and space, with human laws of evolution and gradual development. God's loving care has not left our earthly lives estranged from His self-gift. In the Incarnate Word there is that perfect identification between Person and total self-gift, *agape*. Because of this, man's "becoming-person" is now his "gifted" growth toward more intimately sharing in the natural Sonship of Jesus Christ. This is accomplished through the gradual response of his human nature (total body-person) to the free gift of divine *agape* communicated to him through the Body of the Whole Christ.

It is through the Incarnation that the love-life of the Trinity communicates itself to the humanity of Christ and in and through this humanity to each one of us. Our personal response in faith to God's self-communication and our personal communion with the Trinity is grounded in our relationship to the Whole Christ. God gives Himself to us in the Incarnation, and we, in grateful response to the divine goodness, direct our personal I-Thou relationship toward the Continuing Incarnation of the Whole Christ in His Body. The true greatness of man is that he cannot be fullfilled apart from an I-Thou relationship to God.

Having been created with a vocation to become a person, each of us is then given the potential for an I-Thou relationship with God. If God's free self-communication (grace) presupposes this capacity in the incarnational economy of salvation, what actualizes it? We have said that it is God's own initiative to give us Himself, but that this self-gift is mediated through the Whole Christ, those men and women of our experience who gradually develop our human potential for I-Thou relatedness. We have said that in the normal course of personal growth, God's self-gift is given primarily through those persons who are able actually to love us with a *selfless* love, and that at some time in one's early life, this human expression of divine *agape* must have been constant and deep enough in order that the "becoming-person" might little by little risk the return of selfless love toward the Whole Christ. Every mother who selflessly loves her child is giving birth to the new life of his emerging person, as well as sustaining the physical life that she has already given him.

This new life unfolds within the historical, visible interpersonal relationships of each man's existential life-experience. The Christ whom each human being must be helped to risk believing in and loving is the incarnated Lord of his body-person experience, Who becomes sacramentally visible in the people in his life. *Our experience* of the Infinite in our lives, of God's self-gift, always remains creaturely because we, the recipients of this gift, are finite creatures.

"WE" CONSCIOUSNESS AND PERSONAL GROWTH

In a previous chapter, it was stated that the "We" encounter with our Lord is the level of personal relationship He extends to each of us. It is this form of interpersonal meeting that each of us must explore and make his own as he attempts to meet the Body of the Whole Christ in a "reflective-body-person-selfless-presence-to-others."

We have already discussed at some length the key theological truth that is at stake here, namely, the free gift of divine faith. But the question of our participation in the developing "We" encounter lies largely in the existential order of "how" and in "what way" do I live out my openness to the gift of faith as a human being? This, of course, involves the authenticity of my human life, and in particular its interpersonal levels of response to the call to faith within my entire growth toward personhood. It is this level of the "We" encounter with other men that calls me out of myself to transcend my own tendency toward selfish isolation and to risk a true faith-encounter involving my whole body-person in the commitment to another. This "We" consciousness, rooted in the social character of man's very nature, is the dynamic power that keeps any genuine love relationship alive.

Today many women, both lay and religious, suffer deeply from an inability to fulfill themselves through an "alive-we-relatedness" to someone. It has been the authors' experience that much of the restlessness of married women who wish to leave their homes and family for outside careers originates largely because of the absence of a consciously cultivated "We" relationship to their husband *within the ordinary* tasks of housekeeping. Without this awareness or sense of "we-ness" in all that they do, the personal sacrifices demanded by monotonous chores, emotional fatigue, and the need for constant availability to young children in the home can become heavy, unbearable, and "dehumanizing" burdens that are anything but personally fulfilling.

When any of us, men or women, religious or lay, cease to hear the "sounds" of a new creation being born—that "in-between," "we-ness," or "community that is happening" as a kind of thematic melody in the background of our daily work—then our lives and our tasks become empty. When we cease to see the "Diaphany," the face of our beloved gradually revealed more and more *within* the daily tasks and experiences that absorb our energies of mind and body, it is then that we become lost in matter and disoriented in our body-person grasp of reality.

We are incarnate-spirit, and our human spirituality seeks not to abandon or escape the material world of our experience but to discover a new and deeper intimacy within it. Our constant yearning is to discover the spiritual dimension of matter and to release in it what we sense is its incredible potential for new levels of personal meaning and relatedness. As we grow spiritually, we do not grow *out of this world* but *into it with a new life,* a new intimacy, and an ever-deepening interpersonal "We" involvement. We are summoned by the transcendent Lord *in our midst* through our parents, friends, children, spouses, and all those we meet. The circumstances of life in which we meet them are filled with the presence of God. The call to growth in the Spirit is really a call from *within,* a gentle invitation to hear with "spiritual ears" the totally "Other" speaking in our midst.

This "Other" has implanted Himself into every facet of human "becoming," and we must learn through nearness and commitment to our "becoming a person" to listen for His Voice and search Him out. Here in our "becoming" He dwells. Only in the measure that we enter into that "becoming" will we find Him and realize our personal fulfillment.

THE LANGUAGE OF THE WHOLE CHRIST: EFFECTIVE SACRAMENTAL SIGNS

We now wish to propose what we believe are some of the dimensions of human encounter that could deepen our prayerful "entering into" a personal relationship with the Whole Christ through others. As the reader goes through the following pages, the previous discussion on the sacramentality of signs should be integrated with these new ideas.

Let us begin by recalling that throughout the Old Testament God revealed Himself to man through the prophets—men chosen to disclose His Word by their preaching and actions. They were His chosen instruments. Then the Word become Flesh and God spoke Himself in Christ. "When in former times God spoke to our forefathers, he spoke in fragmentary and varied fashion through the prophets. But in this the final age he has spoken to us in the Son" (Heb. 1:1–2,NEB).

But the Christ of our experience today is the Whole Christ. The Father Himself now speaks *in us* because we are, through Christ's Spirit, members of the Body of the Whole Christ. The continuing redemptive process of Christ at work in each of us must necessarily come to light in and through His Body, which, in the existential order of each human being's life-chapter in Salvation History, is his own body-person and the body-persons of his life-experience. The salvific, redemptive love of God is, therefore, expressed through the sensible signs of man's body-person communication. These signs are not mere accidentals or external trappings to human salvation and our growth in the Whole Christ. Instead, when witnessed in faith, they are truly the signs of life in the Whole Christ, whose Body within the family of man struggles to be the expression of *agape* to the whole of humanity.

For material signs to be effective they must, in fact, actually contribute causally to what they signify, granted that we respond to them. Any interpersonal sign is only a sign, as such, *within human action*. Therefore it needs a human meaning, an interior disposition or intention in the one giving it, so that this intended meaning can be expressed exteriorly in symbol. Any authentic and effective sign is essentially related to what it signifies and what the person intends to convey.

For example, a mother expresses love for her little child through the warmth of an affectionate embrace. The intimacy of her gentle caress is both a material sign as well as *the actual cause* of what it signifies. It is the embrace that communicates love, that *is* love-incarnated for the child. In our rational distinctions between the "pure intention to love" and the actuality of the embrace, we sometimes forget that in the existential order we can experience intentions only when they are incarnated. I cannot experience someone's "intention" to love me; I can only experience love-incarnated. This is the *effective* material sign that sacramentally communicates. Thus the intention and the sign become one effective reality within the very act of signifying, of communicating. The sign-action conveys the sign-value that is contained therein, and these two elements become integrated at the level of communicated or "signed" meaning.

The material sign-action is not just an external manifestation of the interior intention. Father Rahner has some pertinent reflections on this important point when relating it to the question of the Incarnation:

> The Incarnation is not rightly apprehended if Christ's humanity is seen as the mere instrument—ultimately external, after all—through which an ever-invisible God makes himself known. It must be seen as precisely *what God himself becomes* when, whilst remaining God, he empties himself into the dimension of that which is other than himself, of the non-divine.[1] [Italics ours]

[1] Rahner and Vorgrimler, *op. cit.,* p. 27.

A sign, therefore, is a human, visible reality, incarnating the interior meaning of the communicator. We should also remember that any effective, concrete, material sign that we use in interpersonal relationships must have the capacity to bear the meaning we want to convey in and through it.

When speaking of the Christian as an effective sacramental sign, we must again recall that sacramental life is not only cultic. In fact, if we value the authentic reception of the seven sacraments, we need to live out the value of our non-cultic sacramental life as a necessary disposition for effective participation in the liturgical worship of the Church. The "extra"-cultic both enriches and ministers to the cultic, and vice versa, because there is only one life of *agape* but many modes of expression. All of creation is potentially sacramental and therefore capable of communicating God's own Being and life (*agape*) to mankind. For those who view it in faith, it has become both a sign and cause of what it signifies (cf. Ephesians and Colossians), so that men may be brought into dialogue with the Father in and through the Whole Christ.

The sacramental efficacy or redemptive value of any real sign of human love involves an act of faith, a "believing" in the person loved, and a truly selfless going out on the part of the lover. Such sacramentally effective signs are due to the operative power of Christ's *agape* in the lover, whether he knows of Christ or not. By this act of unselfish love such a person has freely chosen to assimilate himself to Christ's redeeming, sacrificial intention for all men. This operative power of *agape* is, of its nature, oriented to action, and therefore any human act of selfless love toward another is a sacramental entry into communion with Christ's salvific intention for that person. "Love one another as I have loved you" (Jn. 15:12,RSV). Any human being who really loves another acts out in an effective, "sacramentally-signed" manner his body-person relationship to the other.

The Christian who can, in faith, consciously open himself to the life of *agape* within his daily human encounters—whether as giver, receiver, or both—is provided with the experiences for a more mature entry into an intimate "We" relationship with the Whole Christ.

In brief summary, we might draw the following conclusions: First, in order for our signs of selfless interpersonal relatedness to be sacramentally effective, they must be authentic. That is, they must signify our true intention and disposition, which we presume is one of self-sacrificing love. Healing takes place only when the sign of selfless love is authentic. We should, then, keep in mind that the fundamental efficacy of our interpersonal, sacramental signs of genuine selfless love is due to the depth of our relationship to Christ's salvific action in His Continuing Incarnation, even though we may ourselves be unaware of the fact that we are acting with the power of Christ.

Secondly, since we are body-persons, there must be a certain degree of visibility, of body-person communication for the effectiveness of the sign.

Thirdly, the sacramental effectiveness of a sign of selfless love depends on the degree of faith-involvement of both giver and receiver with God. This is not a contradiction with our previous point above, because all men, as a result of the Incarnation, have a certain sacramental character in Christ. Those who respond in a human faith to both the goodness and the real human needs of others answer a call to faith, effectively and sacramentally (visibly and materially) signified in the human needs of Christ's Body. When men commit themselves to answering these needs, or open to receive the love that heals them, they are committed to the Body of the Whole Christ, whether they know and believe this or not.

However, if either giver or receiver are joined to the Body of the believing Christian community, if they believe with the divine gift of faith that these needs are those of Christ's Body and lovingly respond to God's call in and through these human needs, then the sacramental character of their human "sign-action" is consciously united by faith to the power of Christ's *agape*. Their interpersonal response in *agape* is one that "joins and knits together" the human and the divine in the building up of the Body of the Lord.

In his letters, St. Paul tries to explain the same effective sacramentality of interpersonal communication that we have been stressing. In the fourth chapter of Ephesians, we read the following text: " . . . let us speak the truth in *agape;* so shall we fully grow up into Christ. He is the head, and on him the whole body depends. Bonded and knit together by every constituent joint, the whole frame grows through the due activity of each part, and builds itself up in *agape"* (15–16,NEB).

In this remarkable passage, Paul is saying that by witnessing ("speaking") the truth of *agape,* we shall grow up "fully" (i.e., with our entire body-person) into the Whole Christ, whose Body is joined and knit together with *agape.* However, the important point to note here is that Christ's Body grows through what Paul calls in Greek *energeia,* or, as we say, using the English derivative, energy, or the "effectual working" translated above as "due activity" of each part of the Body. Let us examine this fascinating word *energeia* before returning to the text from Ephesians.

In the New Testament, this word is not used to describe any merely human force, but rather to portray the action of a power that is beyond the strength of man and the might of this world. It is most frequently used to describe the action of God Himself. A word such as this is extremely important for us, because through it we can learn something of the divine power in the actions of the Whole Christ. We might single out its use in certain scriptural passages that may help us better to appreciate the sacramental efficacy of our relationships with one another.

Energeia, in both pagan literature and the New Testament, is *not* used to describe a man's *potential* action, but rather to demonstrate clearly the idea of powerful, strong, *effective* action. It is often used to describe the interior character or intention that is effectively incarnated in the exterior deed. In the New Testament, the sacramental value of the Christian's relatedness to the Whole Christ is brought out by using *energia* (and its various grammatical forms) to describe the energy and effective power of God Himself working in and through us.

The remarkable point to be noted, in the examples that follow, is that the same word is used to describe the divine power that raised Jesus from the dead and worked in the miracles of His ministry, as well as effected the selfless actions of the Christian community.

For example, the form *energein* is used to describe the miraculous power that *effectively worked* in the miracles of Jesus (Mt. 14:2; Mk. 6:14); and in Ephesians 1:19, *energia* is used to describe the *effective working* of divine power that raised Christ from the dead (cf. also Col. 2:12). "I pray that your inward eyes may be illumined, so that you may know . . . how vast are the resources of his power to us who trust in him. They are measured by his strength and the might which he exerted in Christ when he raised him from the dead" (Eph. 1:18–20,NEB). In Galatians 3:5, *energein* is again used to describe that power which still *effectively works* in the miracles of the Church and the charisms and graces of Christian life.

Various usages of this word throughout the New Testament reiterate over and over again the effectiveness of the power of God. It is constantly at work within the experience of the Christian community. In his letter to the Colossians, Paul discusses his own ministry as he toils with God's *energeia* working effectively (*energein*) within him: "We admonish everyone without distinction, we instruct everyone in all the ways of wisdom, so as to present each one of you as a mature member of Christ's body. To this end I am toiling strenuously with all the *energy* and *power* of Christ at work in me" (1:28–29,NEB). (Italics ours.)

In the same letter, he speaks of Christians being buried with Christ in Baptism and raised to a new life through faith in the *energeia* (effective operation) of God, which raised Christ from the dead (2:12). In Ephesians 3:20, Paul speaks of the power that *effectively works* within Christian life, and in Galatians 5:6 of the *energizing power (energein)* of *agape* in the Christian who lives with faith. In Second Corinthians, *energeia* is used to describe the action of that death which *effectively works* in Paul so that the Corinthians may have life. "Wherever we go we carry death with us in our body, the death that Jesus died, that in this body also life may reveal itself, the life that Jesus lives. For continually, while still alive, we are being surrendered into the hands of death, for Jesus' sake, so that the life of Jesus also may be revealed in this mortal body of ours. Thus death *is at work in us,* and life in you" (4:10–12,NEB). (Italics ours.)

The form *energema* is used twice in First Corinthians, 12:6 and 10, in the course of a description of the various charisms given to those who make up the Body of Christ. These gifts are granted and set in motion by the *effective, working power* of God. In Philemon 6, *energes* is used with reference to a *fully effective faith.*

From these texts and other usages of the word in New Testament literature, it is evident, particularly in the Pauline Epistles, that God's power is effectively working *in the world;* and that this divine power is *effective from within,* not coercing man from the outside. As Ephesians 3:20 and Philippians point out, it is a power that floods man's being from inside: " . . . for it is God who *works in you,* inspiring both the will and the deed, for his own chosen purpose" (Phil. 2:13,NEB). (Italics ours.)

Lastly, we can ascertain from a careful reading of Scripture that there are certain signs of personal communication through which the *energeia* of God becomes *most* effective. These are: the reading or preaching of His Word; His *agape* (selfless love) witnessed to by the signs of sacrificial service to the Body (the *energeia* is both an in-dwelling and an out-going power); the effective sign given in the constancy of the Christian's hope; the effective sign of apostolic zeal in spreading the Good News; and lastly, God's *energeia* working effectively through the mutual contact between the Christian and God in prayer.

Let us now return to our textual example from Ephesians: 15–16. What St. Paul is trying to enunciate is the richness of the sacramental meaning of *energeia.* He is saying that the whole Body grows through the effective working (*energeia*) of the power of God in each part (in each one of us), and thus builds itself up in *agape. Agape* comes to the Body through the joints that knit it together, but these joints will function properly, uniting the Body in *agape,* only through the *energeia* (effectual working of divine power) in them. It is *through* proper function of the joints in the Body that divine power effects the growth. The word used to describe the "due activity of each part" is *energeia,* which, as the reader can see, has a much richer meaning than is conveyed by the English translation of this text.

It is important to note that the contact of the joints (sometimes translated as ligaments), the effective joining and knitting together of the parts, is done through the *energeia* (divine activity) within each member. This is the effective, Christian, sacramental communication of interpersonal relatedness—that "in-faith-reflective-body-person-selfless-presence-to-the-other" that binds the Body together in *agape*. Our body-person "signed-presence," whether in availability, "active listening," or any of the other effective *agape*-signs of selfless interpersonal communication (which we will discuss next), is the existential contact of joint to joint in which the binding power of the ligaments is the *energeia* of God at work in us. He it is who makes it possible for our human language of selfless interpersonal signs actually to heal and build up the Body as we "become persons in the Whole Christ."

Our Lord's constant concern was that the world know He was from the Father, and that His disciples sent into the world by Him would also be recognized as ultimately sent from the Father (Jn. 17:13). So He tells them, as well as ourselves, that when men witness the *signs* of Christian union in *agape* (like His own personal relationship to the Father), they will then believe that the Christian is truly sent by the Son, who is loved and was sent by the Father. In other words, the sacramental signs of *agape* in the Christian's interpersonal communication will effect (effectively produce) the life of *agape* among men.

10. Encountering the
Whole Christ through
"Open Listening" in Faith

CHRISTIAN PRAYER AS THE
EFFECTIVE SACRAMENTAL SIGN OF
OUR OPENNESS TO ALL OF
REALITY IN FAITH

WE HAVE ALWAYS KNOWN that a cultic sacrament, in its religious context, is a visible and therefore material sign of God's self-communication (grace). However, we have been slow to develop a spirituality that actually plumbs the depth of meaning in what we have always acknowledged follows upon the Incarnation; namely, that we too, as body-persons, are spoken into existence by God in order that we may be sacraments, signs of His self-gift. As members of the Whole Christ, *we* are the continued spoken Word of God in this moment of history that is the "now" of His on-going creation.

Somehow the basic vocation of "becoming a person," to which God calls us through human creation, and our particular "religious vocation," whether lay or clerical, have become separated. It is little wonder then that the profoundly *religious* task of growing into personhood, as well as growing in my dialogue with God, has not become the focal point of the Christian study of prayer that it deserves to be.

Just as the humanity of Jesus in His visible, "signed" presence marked the end of the period of the Old Law by bringing a

196

profound renewal and perfection to Israel's worship of God (her existential prayer life), so too, for us, intensified consciousness of the effective, sacramentally "signed" presence of the Whole Christ in our humanity will help foster that renewal in the Church today which the Second Vatican Council has so earnestly recommended.

Any lasting liturgical renewal must be grounded in an authentic Christian prayer-life, a life in which the Son of Man is met and loved in the common, human, interpersonal relationships of daily life. The ordinary life of God's people with its "growing pains" in need, love, struggle, failure, and success can be gathered up and given their true significance in a renewed liturgy only when all these facets of human life are lived as Christian, sacramental prayer. Then such Christians, gathered together in the Eucharistic Celebration, can truly be the effective, sacramental sign of what the Eucharist brings to our midst—the Whole Christ.

We must bring to liturgical worship an authentic human existence in the Whole Christ so that the interior worship of each Christian's daily prayer-life conforms to his community worship. Our sensitivity to Christ's presence, especially in our interpersonal relationships, will find its peak expression in prayer as we receive and join with one another in the Whole Christ at the Eucharistic Communion. When the experience of ourselves as "becoming-persons" becomes our prayerful encounter with the Whole Christ, we will be better disposed for more authentic religious participation in cultic worship around the altar.

In this book we have already explored a number of facets of what "becoming a person in the Whole Christ" really means. *All* of our "becoming a person" is the subject matter of our prayer when it is permeated with a faith-filled "We"-consciousness. We have tried to show that our Christian prayer-*life* is precisely that —a Christ-filled human existence, a conscious, Christ-permeated "becoming," a developing body-person *life* within the Whole Christ.

In the following pages, we hope to express in the language of human interpersonal experience an approach to prayer that builds on what we have already presented. It is an approach that seeks to foster our growth in Christ in such a way that we avoid those un-Christian tendencies in prayer to develop a spirituality of "getting away from ourselves."

In creating the many hyphenated phrases throughout these pages, we have attempted verbally to convey something of the incarnated richness that Christian prayer encompasses. The most important of these phrases was the expression of our prayer-life within the existential order of our body-personal relationships with one another as the "in-faith-reflective-body-person-selfless-presence-to-the-other."

We spoke of this rich, human, interpersonal expression as a sacramental form of communication with the Whole Christ. For each of us, our prayer can be realized only in the here-and-now "body-person-conditioned" dialogue with the Triune God in *my life*. And this life, although limited as a moment in history, is unlimited in its openness to the divine self-communication in all of reality. The Christian person must stand among men as a prayer that speaks, through his openness to all of reality, of the Infinite dimensions—the "breadth, length, height, and depth" of God's incarnated gift of Himself in Christ.

Christian prayer, then, is essentially our openness in faith to receive God within all of reality. This broad description has the capacity to embrace all of the more traditional divisions of the prayer of petition, thanksgiving, adoration, etc. But what we wish to point out in using this more generic description is that prayer must become *sacramentally effective within interpersonal relationships,* and that this is possible only when our prayerful response to the divine self-gift is characterized by certain signs that have the capacity to communicate to others this attitude of openness in faith.

We have selected certain of these signs, which we feel should be reflected upon and consciously integrated into the pattern of our human growth, as *effective* ways of becoming a person in the Whole Christ. The two interpersonal signs that we have chosen to illustrate the truly sacramental character of our prayer-life in the Whole Christ are: (1) "open listening," and (2) "unconditional acceptance." In our discussion of each of these signs, we will first emphasize the *interior* disposition or attitude to be cultivated if the sign is to be authentic, and then the *visible "signed" action* or actions in our ordinary interpersonal relationships in the Whole Christ. However, the reader must always keep in mind that these two requisites of any sacramentally effective action are interdependent and inter-related, and only artificially separated here in order to help us become more aware of their rich possibilities for developing a kind of body-person dialogue with the Whole Christ.

We would describe the first of these signs with the following generic phrase:

ENCOUNTERING THE WHOLE CHRIST THROUGH "OPEN LISTENING" IN FAITH

If we wish to deepen our understanding of how this particular sign is effective in its distinctively interpersonal context, we must examine the broader role of listening within human growth.

In the previous discussion of our growth as incarnate-spirit in history, we saw that each of us not only has the capacity to be open to all of reality, but also to be conscious of this openness and to reflect upon it if we so choose. We are capable of listening to the world and letting the things and people we contact tell us something about ourselves. Moreover, this listening is more than just a kind of sense feeling or "dumb" contact with an object that can move my organism to react only instinctively.

As a human being, I am capable of "reflective listening to myself" when I encounter realities outside of me, which not only tell me what they are but also something about myself. They speak to me of the same constant theme: that to be human is to be open and growing in the conscious awareness that I am somehow becoming more and more filled with the depth and breadth of reality. My daily contact with matter and the world of material signs repeats for me (like the endless reminder of the ocean's presence in the sound of the surf) the growing magnetism exerted by a sensitive listening to my completion, my human actualization, and my increasing oneness with all that is.

These reflections, whether or not I am fully conscious of them or able to articulate them, nevertheless form at least some basis for an experience of the spirituality of my body-person as in-carnate-spirit. My part, a truly creative role within the growing realization that "I am being created day by day," is to continue advancing in the direction of increased transparency and more perceptive listening. This is an extremely important human value that we must intelligently support, meditate upon, and constantly emphasize at all stages of religious formation. A young person's gradual experiential opening to more and more of reality (made possible by adult alertness to his capacity for wonder) becomes the ideal base upon which a more conscious reflective growth in later years may develop into the genuine religious attitude of listening, in faith, to the mystery of "becoming a person in the Whole Christ."

Christian prayer cannot be achieved apart from something so fundamental to human maturity as this most basic contemplative condition of the growing person. Man is "contemplative by nature," but we err in developing this natural capacity if we step outside of his nature as incarnate-spirit. He can pray and con-template only *as a man.*

UNION IN FAITH WITH THE
BODY-PERSON OF THE
WHOLE CHRIST

We are so accustomed to viewing Jesus of Nazareth through pious religious eyes that we sometimes fail to see certain obvious, historical truths that can be great aids to understanding our faith and our role as apostles. When we consider the historical figure of Jesus, we find that in the apostolate He was actually quite second- or even third-rate. He traveled far less than St. Paul and met with relatively few people. He converted only a handful, as compared with the staggering accomplishments of the great mis-sionary St. Francis Xavier. He mapped out and established no organization with the genius of a St. Benedict or a St. Ignatius of Loyola. His job was a failure by the efficiency standards of today. We must, then, ask ourselves what did He do?

He brought to a small group of men *a personal revelation of Himself.* Only a few apostles, holy women, and a handful of His contemporaries in the villages and synagogues of the Holy Land actually experienced the closeness of this personal revelation. But this was their legacy, their message to pass on to others. Their personal lives were to "bear the mark" of contact with Jesus. They were "Christed now" and revealed Him by their own "personal" intimacy with Him in love and friendship. This personal revelation was not of a Jesus who was gone, a man whose only legacy was a fond memory in the mind of a few faithful followers. They were to give witness to Him, to spread the Good News of His coming, to reveal to others Jesus Christ *in themselves,* living in them, working in them, sanctifying in and through them. They were to reveal Him by their own intimacy with Him in the love of friendship, showing men that "They were to seek God, and, it might be, touch and find him; though indeed he is not far from each one of us, for in him we live and move, in him we exist" (Acts 17:27,NEB).

Such, too, is the call of every Christian apostle today. But the vocation of revealing Christ to others presupposes the personal capacity for our own self-revelation to Him in an openness and mutual friendship that makes it possible for us to "put on the mind of Christ."

When the question is raised about the *person* with whom we must develop this capacity for self-revelation and open availability, the impact of the answer stuns us if we have come to realize the meaning of the Whole Christ. Our self-revelation, openness, and authenticity with *one another,* in faith, *is* our revelation to the Whole Christ. We are immersed in Christ and have our being together with one another in Him. We can live the *life* of Christ *together* in the Whole Christ only through, with, and in His Body. It is only when we have the capacity to be authentic with other men that we can truly be related to the person of the Whole Christ.

St. Paul's letters to the early Church abound with his intimate, warm, candid, and tender self-revelation to the Whole Christ. His exaggerated authenticity ("If I must boast, I will boast of the things that show my weakness" [2 Cor. 11:30,RSV]) and his total availability to the only Christ he knew, *the Christian community,* seem to be *surpassed* only by what we can surmise to be the depth of his personal faith in the Whole Christ.

As the reader should have come to realize, religious *life* is basically an open listening to God's gift of Himself to each of us. It is that growing sensitivity of our whole body-person to Emmanuel. This includes listening to all of our emotions, bodily senses, passions, faculties of mind and imagination, chemical and physiological cycles, interpersonal needs, transcendent yearnings, as well as our capacity and need for masculine or feminine complementarity. We must be open to reflect on the fact that everything which makes us human persons is to be joined to the Whole Christ in a continuing, truthful dialogue.

I must pray with my whole body-person because I am one, a unity. There is an intimate connection between my *aptitude* for authentic interpersonal converse with God and my *attitude* toward my own body, emotions, passions, etc. Prayer engages the material part of me no less than the spiritual. I do not commit myself to a personal relationship with Christ, the Father, or the Spirit in order to save my *soul,* but in order that this loving, open relationship may redeem *my entire body-person.*

Christian prayer is at one and the same time both the most demanding and yet the most humanizing activity to which men can freely commit themselves. No set of rules, no philosophy of life, no school of ethics, or humanitarian socio-economic system can demand so much of a man and yet personally fulfill him so completely as does an authentic life of Christian prayer.

At the root of all unselfish friendship, self-sacrificing commitment, and faith in human self-realization, man ultimately discovers an attitude of open listening to the Whole Christ (even though it may not be recognized as such). This kind of trustful listening makes for that presence to reality which characterizes what we commonly recognize as balance, maturity, and good mental health. It animates that magnetic quality of interpersonal presence which heals and promotes human growth wherever it is present among men. Physical presence, in the form of group activity, has often been substituted for this much deeper level of personal presence. The presence of which we are speaking is primarily a spiritual reality that, although communicated through material symbols and signs, is nevertheless at heart a whole body-person presence to all of reality in open listening.

If growth as a person is not fundamentally a kind of daily encounter with more and more of reality through increased listening and conscious awareness, together with a deepening capacity truthfully to accept what is encountered, then our physical presence to one another will be superficial and empty. Before we can communicate an authentic presence through meaningful signs as body-persons, we must consciously be encountering the very realities we symbolize in our words, gestures, and all the other modes of human social activity.

A person whose underlying approach to reality is one of careful selection, on the basis of what he has decided he can afford to be open to and accept, is hardly in any position to listen with open availability to God's self-gift in all of reality. An honest and enlightened unmasking of the innumerable forms of rationalization and self-deception, which we all contrive in order to cover our weaknesses, is an important experiential source of encounter with the divine person of the Holy Spirit.

Insofar as each of us is faced with the *opportunity* and the freedom to choose between an approach of open listening or one of "calculated risk" with protective barriers, we have only one choice if we are to develop a genuine relationship with the Whole Christ. If we choose to "make our own peace" and fabricate Christ according to our own myopic view of reality, then there is no need for faith and no truthful relationship with the Whole Christ.

Another reason why it is so important that we make every effort not to develop a habit of closing off any aspect of reality is that once we allow ourselves complacently to take this approach, there is a tendency to continue closing off more and more elements that we find unpleasant, threatening, or inconvenient. This further entrenches us in a life of isolation by cutting us off from the threatening circumstances which produce the very tension that *reveals* our self-centeredness, as well as the power of Christ *within* us. Only when we can consciously live with this tension will we be able to undergo the necessary death and resurrection dynamism of a genuine Christian life. In this way we are "weak" with St. Paul but discover within this weakness the strength of Christ.

The attitude of open listening is a state of mind that permeates my entire approach to life. It sets my relationships to others, and to everything outside of me, in a very definite way. It makes me vulnerable to them. It allows them entry into me. It is a reverential posture of humility in the face of the truth that listening discloses, rather than one of egotistical preoccupation with self. The thrust of such an open personality is outward, not in the commonly understood meaning of extroversion but rather in the sense that there gradually develops a spontaneous love for reality, for life, and for human existence with all its unfolding wonders. Forcing oneself on others, intruding, breaking into them by abruptness, coercion, by exercising one's authority, or by exaggerated extroversion has no place in the interpersonal relationships of one who seeks to encounter the Whole Christ in open listening.

Open listening is therefore a loving awareness of human existence in a world of unthreatening realities. Although there may be many things in this world that can actually hurt me, nonetheless I do not live my life in a state of suspicious anxiety and constant fear. An attitude of open listening is one of trust, of respect, and of reverence for all of reality. It prizes and rejoices at the opportunity to expose and mature the beauty of human transcendentality and reflexivity at each new meeting with some facet of the unfathomable mystery of life.

PRAYER AS A "BODY-PERSON" ACTIVITY

Prayer is primarily the conscious activity of my entire body-person in its search for God. It cannot, therefore, be a turning toward God as though He were someone at a distance from myself and my here-and-now world of experience and meaning. For many, praying has too often become an activity that has lost most of its relevant connection with daily human existence. It has become a kind of turning away to someone "outside of my world of meaning," a world that must of course be returned to when the praying is finished. Even the language of many prayer books suggests anything but that vital "alive-relatedness" of the whole body-person which is the essential dialogue of real prayer.

This "turning'" toward God is perhaps better called an "opening" or an "open listening" to Him, that allows His immanent presence to become so real a part of my life that I can then respond through interpersonal dialogue, faith, commitment, and self-gift within each tangible life-situation.

Open listening, in faith, creates the conditions for dialogue through the actual *sharing* of my existential world of meaning with the transcendent God immanently present within my experience. But God must be a *part* of my experience if I am to share it with Him. For example, when I see a good film with a friend, he is caught up in the same experience as I, and we participate in it together. Therefore, we can share the experience with each other. I cannot fully share the film with someone who has not seen it. I can describe it and communicate my own reactions, but the other can never really join in the experience because he is unrelated to it. The point that we are trying to stress here is that unless God is experienced as a part of my daily life, I cannot truly share it with Him.

This real experience *together with* the Other (God) who is a part of my world, who has emptied Himself into the family of man, who is truly present and sharing in my experience of relatedness to the created world around me—this shared experience is the *conversational subject matter,* as it were, of an authentic incarnational communication between myself and the Whole Christ. When this turning or opening involves my whole body-person, then the totality of my being is available to be changed and penetrated by Christ's *agape* in a mutual encounter.

Obviously, the value of this fundamental approach to meeting the Whole Christ is not quantitatively measured by the length of time spent living this way or by the frequency of our "acts" of encounter. Instead, it is a vocation to the continuous placing of my entire body-person at the disposal of the Whole Christ. It is the existential availability of my total being to the Father in the Whole Christ under the Spirit. It is a continual choosing of "alive-relatedness" to the Whole Christ within the daily experiences of life, a choice ratified again and again by consciously bringing my "whole self" to Him so that He may actually enter into the wholeness I present to Him, and into every aspect of the body-person I truthfully bring to the encounter.

Human life, if I am really present to it, willing to be open, listening to, and accepting it, becomes a creative relationship to all of reality in the Whole Christ. It is within this growing affirmation of my human existence that I open myself to unselfish *Agape,* so that my growth may be personalized. For it is only openness and continuing response to *agape* within my relationship to all of reality (especially other people) that develops in me a capacity for truly "other-centered" living.

Such interpersonal relatedness, when kept alive with constancy, fulfills my nature as a social being. This brings mutual peace and harmony into my life with others, allowing them to give themselves to me and complete me as I, in turn, open myself to them in self-gift. As this enrichment and realization of my human nature continues, it creates that quality of communication and sharing which ultimately forms a communion in love (*agape*).

This union of persons relating to each other in Christ's selfless *agape* is the earthly image of the Community of Trinitarian Love. Here we have the ultimate goal of man's "turning," of man's "open listening" to all of reality, that he may discover and be "gifted" with *agape* in *this life* as he engages himself in it now.

We do not wait for a God of the misty future. Eschatology is now beginning to be a realized fact. "Thy kingdom *come,* Thy Will be done *on earth* as it is in heaven" (Mt. 6:10,RSV). "But if it is by the Spirit of God that I drive out the devils, then be sure the *kingdom of God has already come upon you*" (Mt. 12:28,NEB). "The kingdom of God is *upon you*" (Mk. 1:15,NEB). "To you the secret of the kingdom of God has been given" (Mk. 4:11,NEB), for "In truth, in very truth I tell you, unless a man has been born over again, he cannot see the kingdom of God" (Jn. 3:3,NEB). "The Pharisees asked him, 'When will the Kingdom of God come?' He said, 'You cannot tell by observation when the kingdom of God comes. There will be no saying, "Look, here it is!" or "There it is!"; for in fact, the kingdom of God is *among* you'" (Lk. 17:20–21, NEB). (Italics ours.)

Father John L. McKenzie, S.J. has the following interesting comment on the theme of the "Kingdom" in the New Testament:

> In some passages the kingdom seems to be identified with the person of Jesus Himself, in whom the kingdom comes. In certain passages Jesus appears where the parallel passages speak of the kingdom (Mt 16:28; 19:29; 21:9; Mk 9:1; 10:29; 11:10; Lk 9:27; 18:29; 19:38; AA 8:12; 28:31; Apc 12:10). Where Jesus Himself proclaimed the kingdom, the apostolic Church proclaimed Jesus.[1]

For many Christians, prayer is unreal and haphazard not because they deliberately choose to turn their backs on Christ in rebellion but because they do not know how to become involved with the necessary tasks of life while at the same time deepening their conscious realization of His presence. Our training in prayer, which usually began with an effort to *concentrate,* to *"think"* about the historical Jesus, or about His teachings so that we could imitate Him, has left us with a painful conflict as we try to deepen our conscious relationship with Him and simultaneously involve ourselves with the needs of the apostolate. We discover this when we realize that we cannot give our undivided attention to two things at the same time—our apostolic duty, job, or study, as well as our reflection on the person of Jesus. However, we also realize that we need to cultivate some sort of a deliberate effort to live in the conscious realization of the presence of Christ every moment of each day.

Our typical, somewhat rationalistic approach toward solving

---

[1] John L. McKenzie, S.J., *Dictionary of the Bible,* Milwaukee, The Bruce Publishing Company, 1965, p. 481.

the problem is to begin by analyzing the human acts involved, and then to draw careful distinctions by creating various levels and degrees of "intentionality." For example, we create numerous divisions within intentionality that depend upon the conscious recalling of an intention in a relation of proximity to the act itself. Some intentions must be recalled each time we act; others can be made once and then forgotten.

Such an approach may be quite legitimate in the rational and logical order, but is most unrealistic in the order of life-experience itself. Man, in the entirety of his body-person, is hardly moved to deeper commitment, let alone fulfilled and realized as a human being, at the level of intentionality. Nor does the age-old practice of *withdrawal* from activity, in order to focus one's attention on Christ, adequately resolve this tension (although a balanced amount of such retirement still is *necessary* and *valuable*).

Another historical attempt to resolve this problem has been the use of pious aspirations. They represent a genuine effort to integrate an awareness of Christ's presence with conscious commitment to the work demanded by our apostolic labors. However, this still does not bring about the true integration we seek because it is frequently only an effort to "baptize" the apostolic work with a rational awareness of the fact that I am doing it for and with Christ. The use of aspirations *can* tend to root us in the mentality which thinks that we must go *outside* of the work itself in order to maintain our union with the person of Christ. We do not really discover His face and His presence in the work itself. In a way, the aspiration, if improperly understood, can really cut us off from the possibility of an effective union with the person of the Whole Christ *within* one's apostolate. This is, of course, not *necessarily* true. But each of us must carefully examine our own attitude when we use aspirations. Do they lead us to discover Christ *in* our apostolic involvement with His Body, or do we slip away to find Him outside of it?

The futility of ever resolving the dilemma posed by the need for this integration grows only more discouraging and disappointing with the increased demands on our time, bodily energy, and mental capacities. This problem in Christianity is as old as the

Church itself, and much has been written on the subject. But the answer to this problem is much more complex than some books on prayer would suggest, because today it involves a radical re-orientation of many of the theological, philosophical, and psychological presuppositions that we have naively taken for granted with regard to human growth and growth in the Spirit. The writing of this book was motivated largely by our conviction that a more synthetic attempt in this direction was needed.

For example, Christ said that He came so that "we might have life and have it *abundantly*" (Jn. 10:10,RSV). Yet how often this is immediately understood with reference to a life "out there" or life "hereafter," one that seems to have very little to do with the day-to-day experiences that engage us now. The "abundance of life" that Christ has come to give is a true fulfillment of man's natural openness to discover God's incarnated communication in all of reality. This natural openness in no way *forces* God to communicate. The supernatural is always a pure gift, but it is a gift given to us according to our capacity to receive it. God has freely chosen to allow His self-communication to be determined by our own incarnate way of knowing. However, an essential element within man's natural way of knowing as a body-person is his natural capacity to be open to the incarnated gift of God's self-revelation.

In attempting to live the fullness of a supernatural life in the Spirit, which is the enrichment of our natural endowment for living a truly religious life (i.e., our capacity to be open to mystery), we have frequently descended to the traditional practice of making religious observance an end in itself. We have often lost sight of our need to take positive steps to preserve our natural openness to reality as the very means of discerning and remaining open to the subtle incarnations of the Spirit. The sheer weight of religious prescriptions, of the Rule (if one is a religious), and of the obligatory times and places of prayer can often seem to make a mockery of that *"abundance* of life" which Christ has promised us. Somehow the *life* itself can too easily become lost in the myriad rules, regulations, and customs through which it must daily be refracted. Rules and law are obviously meant to *preserve* life—

but they can never beget it! This is the basic weakness of the law that St. Paul so brilliantly exposed. Life comes only in the freedom of response to the gift of the Spirit. It is toward His presence that we must (in freedom) cultivate our life of open response. If we have lost the natural capacity to be open to the Spirit of God, we will be unable to discern His incarnate self-revelation in the ordinary language of our daily human existence.

Yet even today how many spiritual directors, teachers, and pastors, when approached by one in anguish over the task of bearing this heavy burden of legal prescriptions, would instinctively help that person to first learn to be open and to listen to all of reality? Where, in our religious communities, in the education of our students, and in the training of catechists is the sensitivity and attempt to create and support the kind of environment that encourages this most fundamental characteristic of religious growth?

"UNLESS YOU BECOME AS LITTLE CHILDREN"

Our Lord Himself told us about this essential quality of a religious life when He said that "the kingdom of God is among you" (Lk. 17:21,NEB), and that "whoever does not receive the kingdom of God like a child shall not enter it" (Lk. 18:17,RSV). Christ does not speak of the possession of His kingdom as something "out there," but as an *immanent reality* within the present life of each Christian. It is a new life to be possessed here and now. It is at hand, if we are able to approach like a child.

Our preoccupation with obedience and submission has traditionally colored our interpretation of this text, as if it were a sort of treatise on docility. Yet, as any experienced teacher or parent knows, the normal young child is anything but docile. He may be submissive simply because he is helpless and weak in the face of superior strength, but this is hardly genuine docility or the characteristic Christ would have made reference to in this example. Instead, the quality that initially suffuses a child's response to life is his *openness* to all of reality.

Children, until they acquire the prejudices, fears, and sophistications of the adult world, are fascinated by everything around them. They are full of curiosity and are spontaneously moved by joy, sadness, beauty, and ugliness. In the child there is the purity of "open listening" to all of creation, in which the beauty of an incarnational spirituality shines through, providing welcome entry into the kingdom of heaven. "The kingdom of God belongs to such as these. I tell you that whoever does not accept the kingdom of God like a child will never enter it" (Lk. 18:16–17,NEB).

This is a curious statement, but full of insight because of the strange paradox that it contains. We usually think of religious maturity in terms of free, rational self-gift to God. Yet a moment's reflection on childhood brings to light the well-known fact that a child, by virtue of his youth, is very selfish. He is so preoccupied with himself that for many years he is incapable of what we adults consider to be the capacity for mature self-gift.

Yet Our Lord speaks of a child's ready welcome into the Kingdom of God. We must conclude that this is not merely because of the child's innocence but because of some quality he possesses, since Jesus asks us to be open to the Kingdom of God *like* a child.

This universal characteristic of childlike "openness" must, therefore, dispose one in a special way to receive the divine self-communication. When we observe it in children, we realize that they have simply not yet chosen to close off any aspects of reality, and that this disposes them not only to receive God's self-gift but to receive it *in and through* all the people and things around them. The child's way to God is sacramental. Rather than becoming an obstacle to penetrating the mysteries that surround him, the material world becomes the very vehicle that stimulates his fascination and wonder. He can live in and with the material while preserving a sensitivity into the mystery of the Kingdom of God.

The mystery of the Incarnation and of God's self-gift in all of creation are spoken to the child through the language of openness and wonder. It does not seem strange to the little one that he should discover another mystery (let us say of God's speaking to him about the mystery of Himself) within the very mysteries of life that surround him. In fact, it would seem quite logical to the child (if we may impose this later development upon him), because the "alive-relatedness" that absorbs his probing and curious outward thrust into creation is filled with mystery.

The little child has not lost his sense for "mystery." Many adults unfortunately tend to misplace this basic sensitivity when they feel that they can *define* a portion of reality. The person who has lost his sense of mystery tends to close off with the *rational definition* as a sort of definitive landmark in the conquest of "mystery." The definition signifies that now we have one more piece of reality under our conscious control. This is especially noticeable in the adolescent who has a tendency to think that he has life experience when he can capture it with a rational definition.

There is, however, also a very valid reason for his too hastily drawn conclusion. We can learn a great deal by reflecting, for a moment, upon our own development toward maturity. As we grew toward late adolescence and acquired our first taste for rational speculation, we tended for a while to lose ourselves in the dizzying and somewhat heady capacity that burst upon us. Young adults love to philosophize, to reason, to argue. This is the natural tendency of their age, and it is filled with much satisfaction for them. It is the sign of their discovery of a new capacity within themselves.

At adolescence, a young person's changing body, no longer the body of a child, and the fact that society expects adult behavior from him, destroys his childhood self-concept. The emergence of his capacity for speculative thought comes at the same time that the adolescent is still seeking to establish an adult identity. He can no longer identify himself as a child, and yet adult society expects him to think and act like an adult. As he begins to discover the newly awakened power for abstract reasoning growing within him, he might in his insecurity tend to build his self-identity almost exclusively upon it.

The task of transition that lies before him is really one of integration. But if the adult society toward which he is moving is not sensitive to the genuinely valuable qualities of the child's natural openness to all of reality, so that it can encourage the adolescent to preserve his natural sense for wonder, then he will tend to build his new identity more around his emerging capacity for rational speculation. He runs the risk of failing to integrate the genuine value of natural openness that is his legacy from childhood. He is unable to make the distinction between the value of *openness* as a way of life and the *unreflective openness* that characterized his childhood attitude toward reality. He fails to see that his present task is to penetrate the *unreflective* openness of the child with his newly emerging capacity for reflection, rather than jettisoning this unreflective openness in favor of rationality as a source of self-identity. He must, in other words, find a new self-identity in terms of the wholeness that is his as a rational body-person.

As young adults, we do not preserve the naive openness of the little child but rather must begin the somewhat arduous task of suffusing natural openness with our newly emerging capacity for conscious, reflective, rationality. This is an important point that we have stressed in this work when speaking of a "*reflective*-body-person-awareness." The natural openness of the adult is a *rational* openness. It is not merely the unreflective openness of the child. The intellect must penetrate this natural gift so that man can reflect upon his body-person presence to all of reality and to the God who continually reveals Himself in it.

This "integrated-reflective-openness" can then be caught up in a faith-experience when the Word of God is preached in such a way that man begins to realize that God speaks to him *within* his natural growth as a human person. This is the kind of *reflective* openness into which the gift of faith can strike deep and lasting roots.

The Church has always held that the faith-response of man to the Word of God is not just a *feeling*. There is a reflective element, a rational quality to the response. It is not a feeling without reflection. Instead, it is the *whole* man who ultimately responds to God. He is endowed with a natural capacity for openness to incarnate-Revelation as well as with the growing ability to reflect upon his response and the gift that is given to him.

The task of any genuinely human education (which, if it is truly human, *is* by that very fact religious) is to provide the growing child, adolescent, and young adult with an atmosphere in which he can exercise and develop his evolving rationality, while at the same time integrating it with his capacity for openness and wonder.

We should all occasionally allow ourselves the time to contemplate a child's somewhat naive, unreflective attitude of openness toward reality. As light, sound, physical movement and the brilliance of color pour into his vulnerable little presence to the world, they do not merely strike him as ordinary sense impressions. Instead, they come with all the depth of their capacity *to produce wonder* left intact. The child has not yet learned to sift out elements and close himself off to the deep-down mystery in creation. And so this mystery, which as we know is the incarnational expression of the self-gift of a loving God, remains open to him, despite the tremendous self-centeredness and unreflectiveness that are the hallmarks of the young child. This mystery, which an adult too often tends to consider in abstract, theological terms, is for the child inextricably tied to his here-and-now, concrete, tangible life-experience. It is not the universal or the speculative that he grasps as meaningful, since it will be many years before his capacity to think in the abstract unfolds. However, this simple fact of child development, which we are all aware of, is an important clue in our understanding of the kind of openness toward which our Lord seeks to direct our attention when He tells us to become like little children.

The child is naturally a contemplative in action—not, of course, in the sense of being gifted with a mature faith or understanding of Revelation, but in the sense that he is naturally disposed toward the reception of divine love *within* the Continuing Incarnation (in the Pauline sense of the first chapter of Colossians). Obviously, Christ does not mean to extol the child's limited rational capacities characteristic of his age, but rather to highlight for the adult that this openness of the child *is* the Father's *natural* gift to all men. It is His way of inviting us, within the structure of our created nature, to seek Him out in all of reality. This gift is revealed to us in its very operation. The young child has not yet learned to close himself off from the many sources of incarnation that God continually uses as the way of His Self-Revelation. His openness is a *gift* that must never be lost through a hardening of the heart that dulls our sensitivity to the mystery of divine presence. An attitude such as this closes the way into the Kingdom of Heaven *within man's body-person daily contact* with reality.

This child's openness and perception of creation, as alive with a "mystery-within," is obviously not the mature, adult response to the preached Word of God. But it is one of the most precious natural endowments God has given us to seek Him out. When it is joined with His free gift of faith and adoption into the Trinitarian Family, the "mystery-within" can unfold for us in our ordinary day-by-day contacts with reality as the true *musterion* of the Whole Christ.

One wonders, when reading the lives of the saints, whether some of the anguish they expressed with such phrases as "the darkness of the soul" was not their confrontation with this necessary return to "becoming like little children." Being open to all of reality, and therefore to the pain and frightening experience of one's own limitations and those of others as well as the quite realistic frustrations of cherished hopes and dreams, creates a paralyzing fear. When one is gripped with the realization that the very essence of his growth in the Spirit involves this total vulnerability and availability to the truth of reality, and that this must be a constant way of life, the impact can be shattering, especially if this has not been the direction of one's previous life. The fear is great when we must risk *consciously* living with the vulnerability of the child.

Consciously and *reflectively* to assume, *as a way of life,* not only the openness but the actual deepening of one's vulnerability to be hurt, rejected, or humiliated, so that reality can be contacted in truth and the self-gift of God discovered within it, is not a choice that is easily or painlessly made.

One must throw himself with total abandon, complete trust, and a living faith into the arms of the Whole Christ. Such an experience is all too vividly realized as the death knell to the neatly ordered world of existence that we all create to protect ourselves from the constant sacrifice of open listening to the daily needs of Christ's Body.

RELIGIOUS "DETACHMENT"

"How hard it is for those who have riches to enter the kingdom of God!" (Lk. 18:24,RSV). So often we think of material possessions as a hindrance in themselves to our entry into the Kingdom of God, whereas it is neither the quantity nor quality of goods that is the hindrance, but rather our possession of them without the openness and wonder at the mystery of their "alive-relatedness" to God. The created realities that block our entrance into the Kingdom of God are those that we have turned into idols. We have made them ultimate values in themselves. Because of this we relate to them in such a way that they dull our openness to the rest of reality and close us in on ourselves.

"Detachment" has been a common word in the vocabulary of Christian asceticism, although frequently it has been given many un-Christian interpretations. This word, if correctly understood within the basic religious posture of open listening, should never convey the connotation of cutting ourselves off from reality (whether in our feelings, likes, interests, dislikes, etc.) through any form of repression, suppression, or similar psychological defense mechanism. This is a type of schizoid activity and the cause of much anxiety as our human nature rebels against such abuse. As we have said so often, it is the awareness, acceptance, and encounter with reality *as it is* that forms the natural foundation upon which a deeper and richer spiritual life is built.

An *attached* person has lost the freedom to discover in faith the presence of the divine in all his relationships, when he closes off some aspect of reality, either within or outside of himself, that he does not want to see, hear, or experience. Such a person allows himself to acknowledge only what he wants to see, and by so doing is no longer open to the real world to discover the presence of the Holy Spirit in the choices and multiple circumstances of his life.

When creatures or certain portions of reality are viewed in isolation from God, they can exercise a tyranny over the attached person. His very selectivity, often under the guise of religiosity, ends by enslaving him to a myopic and unreal view of that "abundant life" that Christ brought to us in His Incarnation.

Fortunately, the days are behind us when that naive understanding of the "world" led some religious to flee into the tyranny of neurotic fears and repressed emotions. Too often they slipped into a kind of childish and slavish obedience to customs, rules, and superiors in which originality, creativity, responsibility, and spontaneous action were either relinquished in large measure or totally sacrificed. Religious life must always guard against the type of atmosphere that produces a self-centeredness which focuses one's attention on a preoccupation with the opinions of others, with one's *progress* in the "spiritual life," or a neurotic sensitivity to "how one is being accepted in the community." This kind of atmosphere fosters a self-absorption so pervasive that it takes a constant battle with one's environment to maintain a true sense of Christian detachment and an ability to go out of oneself toward the Whole Christ in His Body, the Church.

Religious growth, whether in the home or in the religious community, demands an environment that is humanly and therefore personally fulfilling. As body-persons, we need to be "conditioned" favorably if we are to be open to reality and remain open as a "way of life." This conditioning is the normal prerequisite and atmosphere in which we are able to "listen" to God's self-communication within our world of experience and meaning. We grow because others *openly* love us.

The religious life, in all its training, prayer, and community relationships, must always create an atmosphere within which its members are in constant contact with the dynamic, changing character of reality and with the uniqueness of each person's response to it. Only in such an atmosphere can the moment-by-moment, creative, and redemptive will of the Father in the ever-present Spirit of Love be ascertained.

Detachment can never be a flight from the created world nor a disinclination toward creatures. Neither is it a safe, noncommital attitude of noninvolvement with others. Instead, detachment is a daring openness to all of reality, a solicitous, tender, warmhearted, genuine, unselfish love for everything in God's creation—but most especially for His children, who grasp and involve us in a "faith-filled-body-person-selfless-presence-to-the-Whole-Christ."

A QUESTIONNAIRE FOR THE
CHRISTIAN APOSTLE

Christian apostles must be ready repeatedly and prayerfully to challenge themselves with such unnerving questions as:

1. Am I letting my fears, my own personal inadequacies, my lack of faith and insight into the reality of Christ's presence and His Continuing Incarnation blind me to much of the truth of reality in my life?

2. Am I really making an effort to discover Emmanuel in all the circumstances and people I encounter? Or do I close myself off from them, using some acceptable label like "worldly" to escape the responsibility of entering into this experience to discover the Whole Christ?

3. Is my faith in God's protective love for me so weak and my personal maturity so inadequate that I risk serving Christ only where most of the circumstances are so "preconditioned" that there is little danger of failure, of sordidness, of repulsiveness, of contact with evil? Can I serve Him and love Him only in the safe, antiseptic world of my own "spiritual ideals"? Can I face life as it is, enter fully into it as He did, and so incarnate myself in it and understand it that I can risk taking on the burden of its anguish and so bring His strength and Life to it?

4. When faced with some ugliness, either in myself or in another person or situation, do I retreat into a private spiritual dream world? Am I profoundly convinced that by escaping aspects of my real life-experience, through living in a kind of Peter Pan "never-never land," I will never really be present to the world in which I am to find the Whole Christ and to which I am to communicate this discovery? Moreover, do I realize that under such conditions, my sacramental presence will be ineffective and unreal?

Do I really work at not living my "spiritual life" in a sort of dream world of my own making, a world that provides little true self-knowledge and even less protection against self-sufficiency, stubbornness, self-complacency, and immunity from any criticism of my way of life?

5. Do I tend to confuse the really "worldly" people in my life with those who simply are realists and see life as it is—a mixture of both good and bad in which the sinful, ugly, and sordid can be a valuable teacher, if only one is open and humble enough to recognize how much they speak to me of the needs of the Whole Christ?

"When Jesus came to the place, he looked up and said, 'Zacchaeus, be quick and come down; I must come and stay with you today.' He climbed down as fast as he could and welcomed him gladly. At this there was a general murmur of disapproval. *'He has gone in,' 'to be the guest of a sinner' "* (Lk. 19:5–7,NEB). (Italics ours.)

"When Jesus was at table in his house, many bad characters—tax-gatherers and others—were seated with him and his disciples; for there were many who followed him. Some doctors of the law who were Pharisees noticed him eating in this bad company, and said to his disciples, 'He eats with tax-gatherers and sinners!' Jesus overheard and said to them, 'It is not the healthy that need a doctor, but the sick; I did not come to invite virtuous people, but sinners' " (Mk. 2:15–17,NEB).

These few preceding ideas will have to suffice as a description of our inner attitude as we grow toward encountering the Whole Christ in the effective sacramental sign of "open listening." Let us now emphasize the more visible outward aspects of a sacramentally effective life of prayer in the sign of open listening to the Whole Christ—what we have already referred to as the visible "signed" action.

11. The Sacramental Effects of "Open Listening" in Faith

THE VISIBLE SACRAMENTAL EFFECTS
OF "OPEN LISTENING" IN FAITH

IN THE *Pastoral Constitution on the Church in the Modern World* we read:

> Now, the Father wills that in all men we recognize Christ our brother and love Him *effectively* in *word* and in *deed*. By thus giving witness to the truth, we will share with others the mystery of the heavenly Father's love. [Italics ours.][1]

The reader should note that the Council Fathers wish to bring the sacramentality of our witness through the visible, material signs of "word" and "deed" to our attention. It is on this level of interpersonal communication that we "share with others" the mystery of *agape* in our lives. Moreover, we are told without qualification that it is the Father's will that we effectively communicate *agape* to the Body of the Whole Christ.

Why this strong statement? Simply because man's nature as incarnate-spirit demands the kind of sacramental authenticity in his interpersonal relationships that caused our Lord to speak with equal emphasis when He said: "Not everyone who calls me 'Lord, Lord' will enter the kingdom of Heaven" (Mt. 7:21,NEB). This entire body-person truthfulness and sincerity in interpersonal

---

[1] *The Documents of Vatican II*, p. 307.

communication is perhaps our most effective sacramental sign, because it sums up within itself all that we have reflected upon in this book and, of course, much more. It gives a visible witness not only to the strength of *agape* over our pull-inward into isolation but also speaks volumes about our attitude toward mankind. It tells of an openness in order that we may communicate Christ's *agape* to others *in the way that they can receive* this divine life, and in the way they call out for Him and need Him.

The communication of *agape* is determined by the needs and capacity of the receiver. It is a patient, prudent love that does not force its way beyond the needs of the present moment. It is a love that always listens first before seeking the appropriate level of incarnate interpersonal response. "*Agape* is patient; *agape* is kind and envies no one. *Agape* is never boastful, nor conceited, nor rude; never selfish, not quick to take offense. *Agape* . . . delights in the truth. There is nothing *agape* cannot face; there is no limit to its faith, its hope, and its endurance" (1 Cor. 13:4–8, NEB). *Agape* shows a delicate sensitivity to the other person's "ripeness," so to speak, for the effective experience of Christ's incarnated presence.

JESUS—A VISIBLE, EFFECTIVE INTERPERSONAL SIGN

There is a most profound clue to the effective interpersonal sacramentality of Jesus' humanity in a short introduction to one of St. Luke's Gospel parables: "At that time the tax-gatherers and sinners were drawing near Jesus to hear him. And the Pharisees and the scribes murmured saying: 'This man makes sinners welcome and dines with them' " (Lk. 15:1,C).

The text is then followed by the parable that usually occupies our attention rather than these preceding words. But there is clearly evident here a description of the remarkable, effective power of Christ's humanity. If we consider the scene for a moment, we realize the extraordinary circumstances of the event. As we know, the intimacy of a meal was a sacred ceremony for the Jews. It symbolized their deepest religious feelings of union, covenant, and awareness of being the Chosen People. For this reason it was preceded by ritual washings and was carefully restricted in its membership. We can well imagine the concern it must have caused the Pharisees to see Jesus sitting at table with public sinners.

Let us attempt to recapture the interpersonal experience of this moment. In the rigid and tradition-bound environment epitomized by pharisaic Judaism, with its consequent social pressures for conformity and well-known resentment for any violation of approved standards of behavior, this Jewish Rabbi's personal attitude of openness, acceptance, authentic concern, and interest in these public outcasts was so effectively communicated to them, that they could not only risk the indignation of the Jewish authorities (whose influence and power was substantial) but even feel comfortable enough to join Christ in the intimacy of a meal. Christ's whole body-person presence to these sinners so effectively "signed" His interior attitude toward them that the impact of His powerful, effective, sacramental relationship evoked the incredulous remark from the bystanders that, "he even makes sinners welcome." He did not merely tolerate them but so obviously encountered them with the visible interpersonal sign of "open listening," and with what we will later describe as "unconditional acceptance," that they must have felt at ease enough to breach the barriers of rigid social conformity and join Him at table. What a marvelous picture this scene gives us of the sacramentally effective power at work in the humanity of Christ!

St. Paul must have caught the full significance of this dynamic body-person existential communication of the Spirit, in all of its sacramental effectiveness, for he wrote: "To the Jews I became as a Jew, in order to win Jews; to those under the law I became as one under the law . . . that I might win those under the law. To those outside the law I became as one outside the law—not being without law toward God but under the law of Christ—that I might win those outside the law. To the weak I became weak . . . I have become all things to all men, that I might by all means save some. I do it all for the sake of the gospel, that I may share in its blessings" (1 Cor. 9:20–23,RSV).

THE SACRAMENTAL PRAYER-LIFE
OF MAN AS INCARNATE SPIRIT

When we consider St. Paul's prayer-life, in which his whole being was actively and consciously involved with the Whole Christ, the more traditional definition of prayer as "the raising of the mind and heart to God" seems to be rather inadequate. It can easily tend, once again, to focus attention on a split between body and soul, between matter and spirit. This definition conveys the notion that the emphasis of prayer is almost exclusively on its "spiritual content" and on the use of "spiritual" faculties, resulting in a kind of "spiritualistic" personal relatedness. However, a more sound Christian anthropology should help each of us to understand and speak of prayer in terms of our total body-person as related to the Divine Persons.

Why can we not consider prayer as the growing gift of my "I" to the "Thou" of the Whole Christ, of an existential "We" encounter that, from the standpoint of my psychological awareness of it, is an authentic "in-faith-reflective-body-person-selfless-presence-to-the-Whole-Christ"? I must perceive prayer as opening up the experience of my human life itself as a vast reservoir of rich interpersonal discovery of Christ, who waits for my "spiritual eyes" to find Him related to me as I grow "close to myself." This relatedness is not isolated from a simultaneous growth in faith, but it is the conscious "we-encounter," in faith with the Whole Christ, that has already been discussed.

This "closeness to myself" is another way of expressing an aspect of open listening that tries to focus attention on and stimulate a heightened consciousness of my *feelings* toward persons, events, circumstances, etc. The goal of this awakened perception is to grow accustomed to experiencing my feelings not in isolation and alone but *with another*. Through refining a sensitive closeness to my *feelings* (which is the area of my body-person relatedness where I live almost ninety per cent of the time, whether I like to admit it or not), I achieve a peaked and extended consciousness of my unity as a body-person.

It must be stressed that this "closeness to my feelings" is not merely a sensing or instinctive reaction, but emphasizes the distinctively human consciousness of an integrated reflective awareness, involving my choice as well. I grow close to this enhanced oneness and fullness of my humanity within the very relationships that stimulate and sharpen the whole gamut of my feeling responses, as well as my volitional and intellectual perception. This closeness to more of the "real me" within every concrete relationship describes something of the dynamics of open listening that we have referred to as "alive-relatedness." When Christian prayer becomes the increasing of this "alive-relatedness," as the moment-by-moment, continuing act of faith in searching out the Whole Christ, our body-person becomes the visible, effective, sacramental sign that it is intended to be.

Our body-person expression of listening through physical posture, facial mien, silence, and tone or shade of verbal response are all symbolic of an attitude in faith toward the Whole Christ. Their importance can be realized when we are conscious of the fundamentally religious response they express. What is even more important for us as we become persons and take on the task of human growth in personal relatedness is to realize that these signs *can teach us.* They can actually cause a change in ourselves as well as in those persons who are open to receive them, if on our part there is an honest attempt to make them authentic. There is a kind of "learning by doing" principle at work here.

An ever-present struggle on our part is therefore necessary to effect a genuine correspondence between the human body-person sign and the interior attitude that it is to convey. This life-long task is also the conversational subject matter of our prayer. For our human growth is seen as the sacramental realization of our religious potential in which religion is most radically a listening.

Thus, a more active listening involves my whole being in the task—my body, imagination, feelings, senses, emotions, intellect and will—all that makes up the unity of my body-person. But what distinguishes my specifically *human active listening* from that kind of body-awareness which any living animal has is the ability to *take* my whole person as incarnate-spirit *to the task* of listening, and to be *reflectively aware* of this very process and the levels of interpenetration, so to speak, that are effected by my contact with reality.

For example, as a human person, I am not limited in my listening only to the material sound waves that touch the delicate mechanisms of my ear or to the heat waves that I feel against my body. As these material forces touch my senses, they tell me something about themselves and about myself. There is certainly a level of listening involved here. But even the family dog is capable of listening to what the winter's cold tells his body and his instincts. He is, however, incapable of making this "listening" a personal, "alive-relatedness" that can turn in openness to be gifted with faith by God.

Perhaps we can further explain what we mean by that active listening which *communicates authenticity* if we retrace our steps to a previous chapter in which we spoke of the child's openness. There, the reader will remember, we stressed that this God-given openness is "unreflective." It is characterized in the child neither by a penetration with mature faith nor by its integration into the adult's powers of speculative reasoning, but simply by the way in which it peaks within *sense awareness*. This insight from developmental psychology has been noted by sensitive educators and incorporated into certain approaches to teaching young children.

However, we emphasize it here because it is the natural human endowment given by our Creator as the necessary cornerstone, so to speak, of the emerging person's growth into the Kingdom of God. It is the foundation upon which we, as body-persons, continue to develop our contact with all of reality and remain open to God's self-communication to us *within* this reality.

It follows that we must, therefore, always continue to use our senses throughout our entire lives, so that as body-persons we touch, taste, hear, smell, and see not only with reasoning and reflexivity but with "graced (faith-gifted)-body-person-reflective-awareness."

All of creation is sacramental in the Whole Christ, as we have already shown. Thus it is meant to be "God-communicating" to us, if we can only bring our sensing body-person into contact with material things in a faith-filled "alive-relatedness." Such listening puts us in touch with much more than just the "outside" of things. It enriches our sense life in a truly human body-person way, not merely preserving the natural openness to the mysteries of life but unfolding the true *musterion* of the Whole Christ, until every color and sound, each nuance of shape, texture, and design becomes an unfolding of the presence of God.

We do not mean to imply that one constantly attends to the divine "presence" in what we would call a "thinking" way, logically adverting to or figuring out all these relationships. But this conscious presence becomes an integral and intimate part of our entire body-person contact with the material things around us. It is an intangible but very real presence of "the Other" to me in all the actions and decisions of my day. Perhaps this might be somewhat easier to understand if we use the analogy of a mother who takes several young children into a busy and crowded store. Even in the midst of trying to get through the shopping list, her presence to reality constantly includes a feeling (by no means purely intellectual) for just where those children are *right now*. She is not alone with the list of groceries. In much the same way, our consciousness of the presence of the Whole Christ must be this same sort of body-person conscious living in an atmosphere that is permeated with the presence of "Another."

This "in-faith-reflective-sensing" is a vital, effective sacramental sign, for people instinctively know when we do not live alone. Our entire body-person way of acting symbolizes a life of union. This type of "in-faith-reflective-sensing" also witnesses to the preservation and continued actualization of our "body-way" of knowing. It is the concrete, visible expression of a vibrant and humanly relevant faith—an effective, sacramental prayer. Its efficacy has been solidly grounded in the existential truth that my body is the God-given means for contacting Him through reality, through the development of my self-image, through creative self-expression, through the communication of personal needs, and through the body-person signs of self-gift to Him in the Whole Christ.

As body-persons, we cannot find Christ outside this world, nor can we come in contact with the full reality of this world outside of Christ. The Incarnation has so radically changed the nature of the created universe and human growth that we can never come to understand ourselves as human apart from the Whole Christ.

St. Paul very graphically, and perhaps somewhat indelicately for modern ears, described an approach to prayer that involves a growing sensitivity and consciousness of one's body-person in dialogue with the Body of the Whole Christ. In his letter to the Romans we read: "But thanks be to God that you who were the slaves of sin have now obeyed from the heart that form of doctrine into which you have been delivered, and having been set free from sin, you have become the slaves of justice. Because of your weak human natuure, I am using quite human language. Just as formerly you presented your bodily organs to uncleanness and lawlessness as slaves for the doing of lawless deeds, present them now as slaves to justice so that you may become holy" (6:17–19,C).

Paul is concerned with the very problem that we have already discussed in earlier chapters. Those who do not understand the meaning of the Whole Christ are faced with a very real difficulty as they seek the experience of a personal relationship with Christ. "How does body-person relate to non-body-person?" was the way that we tried to spell out their problem. If they do not "know" the Body of the *Whole Christ* and, in faith, discover the Person of Christ in the "signed" actions of His Incarnate presence in the family of man, then they are forced into the perilous position of having to create His Body in order to meet Him according to their own way of knowing as incarnate-spirits.

Paul realized that the "whole man" meets the Lord. Our commitment is not exclusively intellectual. We do not merely commit ourselves to *truth* but to *a person who is Truth-Incarnate*. This we always do as a whole body-person.

In the first part of the above-quoted text from Romans, Paul clearly refers to the free and conscious faith-commitment of his hearers, made at the time of their adult conversion and baptism. In other words, Paul is saying: "You knew what you were doing and you freely consented 'from the heart' to become obedient to the teachings of Christ. You freely involved yourselves in a kind of 'slavery' to the righteousness that is the life of Jesus." We know from the early history of the Church that at this time the catechumens were not allowed into the Church until they had been instructed. They were shown what Christ offered and what He expected of them. Only then could they make their decision to enter into His Body. This was certainly not a haphazard or spur-of-the-moment commitment, made under the influence of only an emotional experience.

But the early Christians, as human beings, were no different from those of any subsequent age. Frequently they experienced their adult, rational commitment going in one direction while the desires of their bodies went in another. How was Paul to direct them in prayer so that they could integrate their more reflective, rational commitment to the person of Christ with a true, conscious commitment of their bodily organs as well? How could he help them to unite their entire body-person with the Body-Person of the Whole Christ?

This is really a problem of integration and clearly points up the "developmental" character of Christian life. There is a sense in which we can draw a true parallel between the task of integration which confronts the adolescent and that which faces the Christian as he *grows* into a deeper and more mature life in the Whole Christ. The adolescent reaches a point where he becomes sensitive to his newly emerging physical powers and is faced with the necessity of integrating these sense appetites with his rationality, so that he can enter into personal relationships in an unselfish way as an integrated human being. The Christian is in somewhat the same position. At some time in his life he reaches the point where he needs to integrate a body-commitment to Christ with his intellectual commitment, in order that he can relate as a whole body-person.

Paul wished to help the early Christians make this integration so that their adult, rational commitment to the truths of the faith and the person of Jesus could penetrate their body-response to the Body of the Whole Christ, and thus they could live the life of faith as whole body-persons. The adult converts had been *instructed* in the faith of Christian life, but they still needed direction about how they were to integrate their bodily feelings and emotions. They had formerly "presented their bodies to unclean-ness" and rationally committed themselves to a life of lust. Now they needed help to be shown, in an adult way, how to commit their bodily organs to "Justice" rationally, deliberately, and con-sciously. They needed more instruction.

It is interesting to see that St. Paul, in exhorting these Christians who had already been received into the Body of Christ, refers back to their original free, conscious commitment. He then goes on to tell them that their continuing reaffirmation of this commit-ment involves the same emphasis upon *conscious awareness,* but he concretely illustrates it "in very human language." Paul ex-plicitly describes for them a "body-person" approach to prayer and growth in holiness, telling them to "present their bodily organs" for the task. This presupposes a conscious, open listening to their bodies and an acceptance of their bodily feelings, needs, and appetites in a free, deliberate, integral body-person self-gift to what he calls a "slavery" to "justice." He even goes so far as to tell them very concretely to involve their bodily organs con-sciously in their personal commitment to holiness, which he describes in a later verse as a new slavery to "the free gift of God . . . eternal life in Christ Jesus our Lord" (Rom. 6:23). Paul has to remind them that they cannot just ride along on the original commitment that was made at the time of their baptism and first reception into the Body of Christ. They must work at integrating their whole body-person into this commitment. Thus, as we have said, there is a true development within the Christian life. It is a vocation value "to be lived out." It is a true "becoming."

When Paul asks the Roman Christians to involve their bodily organs in their personal commitment to the Body of the Whole Christ, he is asking them to enter into that "in-faith-reflective-body-person-selfless-presence-to-one-another" (and therefore to the Whole Christ) which is the effective, sacramental sign of Christ's *agape,* present and alive within their interpersonal rela-tionships. Moreover, in this text, the word translated as "holy" is the noun *hagiasmos,* sometimes translated as "sanctification," "holiness," or "making for a holy life." The latter phrase better conveys the dynamism involved in this form of the word. Greek nouns that end in -*asmos* describe not a completed state but a process. This helps us to grasp Paul's understanding of the Christian's relationship to the Body of Christ as a *growing* and *developing* bond of union in *agape*.

Pauline "spiritual direction" continually stresses the Christian's active involvement in this process of development. This is evident in his exhortations to take up the *responsibility* of "*presenting* their bodily organs," or in another text to "Acquire a new, a spiritual way of thinking" (Eph. 4:23,C). That is, "you assume your part of this responsibility."

He tries to draw the connection between his readers' deliberate, reflective commitment to the "doctrine" of Jesus and their reflective commitment of the bodily organs that they present as "slaves to justice" so that they might become holy. They must, therefore, penetrate their bodily feelings with a "reflective-faith-awareness" of their presence to the person of Christ in His Body.

These adult Christian converts had the deeply ingrained experience of their bodily organs that they had formerly *presented* to "uncleanness," and as human beings they continued to have the experience of normal, bodily appetites. Moreover, they also had a consciousness of their rational commitment in faith to Christ—their personal *presentation* to the Lord. Paul brings the two together for them by telling them that they must now "present their organs as slaves to justice." Note that he does not tell them to *deny* the fact that they have feelings or appetites. It is the *sensing* organism that must be presented to the Lord. If they deny their feelings, they cannot present them to Christ. Paul says nothing of repression and defenses. He deliberately tells them to take their awareness of their sensing organism into a rational, free commitment, in faith, "to justice." This is done in order that they may "*become* holy" and be ever more caught up in the process of sanctification (the transformation of the Total Adam into the Whole Christ). This is also our Christian vocation.

In the above-quoted text from Paul's Epistle to the Romans, the word *justice,* translated as "present . . . to justice," is often translated as "righteousness," or "to present to the service of righteousness." This latter translation better conveys the idea contained here. It is a service to the new life of *agape* in the Body, conferred on the Christian by Jesus. The Pauline sense of "righteousness" is filled with the implications of the Incarnation. In verse 23 Paul goes on to speak of this free gift as "eternal life in Christ Jesus our Lord."

But Christ's eternal life is the life of *agape*. We have already seen Paul's synonymous use of "in Christ" and "in *agape*," as well as St. John's understanding that God's conferring of His own life of total selfless love on us, *agape, is* His *self*-communication.

Therefore, a "*presenting* of one's bodily organs to the service of righteousness" (to Christ's own life of *agape)* is to give oneself to the person of Christ Himself. However, we must remember who Christ was for Paul, namely, the Whole Christ, present to him in his interpersonal contact with the Christian community.

Indeed, Father John McKenzie, S.J., in his *Dictionary of the Bible,* states that: ". . . we ourselves *are* the righteousness of God through Christ" (the italics are Father McKenzie's).[2]

It is well to emphasize, once again, that the early Christian community was Paul's *personal experience* of Christ and, as such, his attempt to describe the relationship of the Christian to Christ is going to involve a struggle to express the mystery of the Whole Christ being revealed to him. His experience far surpasses his ability to express it in words, as we so often sense in reading him. Moreover, his Old Testament vocabulary needed to be enlarged to fit the fullness of his insight into the mystery of Christ. Certainly his writings could not be expected to contain a modern personalist development, simply because the growth in sensitivity to these values had not yet evolved as it has in some segments of the family of man today. Nevertheless, we can legitimately conclude that "presenting their bodily organs to justice so that they may become holy" reveals important insights into Paul's direction of this Christian community toward developing their

[2] McKenzie, *op. cit.,* p. 743.

prayer-life as a growing body-interpersonal relationship to the Body of the Whole Christ.

"OPEN LISTENING" TO MY FEELINGS

We mentioned earlier in this book that by the time many of us grow to adulthood, we have forgotten how to listen to our feelings—how to become close to them and integrate them into a reflective awareness of ourselves as body-persons. The value for each of us in this open listening is not merely to become more sensitively aware of when we feel warmth and affection for someone, or when we are destructively angry with them. It is not simply a matter of recognizing that I am jealous and anxious or fearful in my relationship to another person, but at one and the same time to grow in my capacity *to accept these feelings as my own.* In other words, I must grow close enough both in awareness and in acceptance of my real feelings so that I can simply try to *be what I am* at each moment of my life. When I bring the genuine reality that is "me" into an encounter of open listening to the Whole Christ, then the "real me" can be gifted with faith and His life in an authentic *agape* relationship with others.

Open listening to my feelings helps me to discover many unknown parts of my "real self" and, as a result, hopefully I can come to accept what I truthfully am through this more extended and intensified experience of myself. I am gradually coming *to be* through a more authentic harmonizing of my real feelings and my conscious awareness and acceptance of these feelings. This becoming process, of listening to what is going on within myself, opens me to *all* of my feelings. Not only do I grow more sensitive to subtle levels of discouragement, fear, pain, and threat, but I also begin to note with greater sensitivity my own deeper feelings of courage, joy, warmth, and wonder. Gradually I become able to live more openly with these positive feelings than I was in the past, when an attitude of defensiveness predominated as my existential approach to reality.

There is a thrilling freshness to the moment-by-moment unfolding of each day's unique experience. The configuration of feelings, stimuli, and life circumstances, which make up the newly developing pattern in my listening response and which I am aware of at this present moment, has never existed before in just this unique fashion. Therefore, my "becoming-person" is truly being created within the present moment of my "open-listening" response to the people and world around me. A more "real self" can emerge from this experience if I can allow myself to remain open to reality as it is, without imposing upon it my preconceived concepts of what I think it should be or what I feel I need from it. Within this continuing process I effectively witness, through the "sign-actions" of my authentic personal response, to my availability and co-existence with reality. I give visible "signed" expression to my *open* listening.

At this point we might note parenthetically that it is the "harmonizing step" between *listening* to one's emotions and feelings and then *accepting* them as one's own that is the most frequent area of psychological disturbance. This is the juncture at which we draw up our defenses in response to what we either presently perceive or anticipate will be too threatening to admit to our conscious awareness, or to our conscious relationship with a particular person or situation. We render them harmless to us either by admitting them to our awareness as distorted (by refashioning them in a non-threatening manner), or simply by denying them any entry into our consciousness at all. We usually resort to such defenses when we cannot match our concept, or picture, of ourselves as related to the world with what we are experiencing in our feelings. If the defense mechanism involves some unresolved critical threat to our self-concept, then we quite literally do not see, hear, or feel what is at variance with the consciousness that we already possess. In such cases, one would most likely find it difficult to make increasingly freer choices toward the harmonizing of his real feelings with a conscious awareness and acceptance of them. Professional psychiatric or psychological care will be necessary when the debilitating character of the defenses seriously block an authentic commitment and consequent interpersonal relationship with the Whole Christ.

However, to return to the main development of our thought,

all of us tend to block our growth in Christ, because—with varying degrees of freedom—we allow insecurity, inferiority, self-
hatred, jealousy, and the like to develop or remain as barriers
between our feelings and our conscious awareness of them. Often
we do not allow ourselves to listen seriously to the feelings that
we have toward certain people. We are unable to face the spontaneous feelings in our bodies toward various circumstances in
life because if we did, we would be presented with a number of
difficult decisions. We would have to accept what they told us
about ourselves or about the circumstances and people to whom
we were related. This would most likely necessitate either a change
in our feelings toward others or the sacrifice of acting out a response to their disguised needs, which we might begin to perceive
more sensitively as we really listen to them. Thus it is often easier
to distort the picture and flee the need for risk and sacrifice
through a convenient kind of repression or effort at refashioning
the other person into some sort of a straw man, in order to justify
our failure to come to grips with the truth that is really there.

In all of this, we twist and warp not only reality but ourselves
as well. Considering the question from the vantage point of our
deeper Christian view of human growth, we can now see that
these defenses, whether they be little or great, actually separate us
from discovering our "real selves" *within* the Body of the Whole
Christ. In other words, we do not come to know Christ within an
authentic interpersonal relationship.

Not only authentic listening but faith and even trust are stifled
in this atmosphere of defensiveness. Within such an oppressive
environment, our prayer is disposed toward begging God to
change me, my life-situation, or my weaknesses. It is characterized
by an attitude that begs God to *remove* these feelings, frustrations, etc., rather than asking for the faith to discover and see
Him more clearly *within the experience* of these very feelings
themselves—which, significantly, happen to be part of the experience of my "real self" at this moment. Rather than believing
that Christ's presence, when discovered in faith and freely responded to in love, will transform weakness into the conscious
experience of *"our"* strength, the defensive person who cannot risk

open listening tones his prayer with "escape petitions" and pleas for strength to "endure" life. From the preceding discussion, it should become even more clear to the reader that the substance of open listening involves the question of faith as a personal commitment to another.

This now brings us to the point where we must enrich our understanding of the effective sacramental "signed action" of open listening by discussing what may already be an important question in the reader's mind.

Let us briefly state the question, and then go on to discuss what we feel is an approach to answering it. The reader may be asking at this point: "If I take on the risk of growing in my capacity for an increased authentic congruence between my real feelings and my conscious awareness of them by diminishing my defensiveness, what do I do with the destructive, hostile, aggressive, and selfish feelings that will inevitably become a very real part of me? In my attempt to be authentic, how do I *not act them out* in a destructive and selfish way toward others?"

The answer, stated very bluntly, is simply that one *cannot* live this way for any length of time without Christ's *agape*. Secondly, this level of human authenticity, together with the consequent deeper interpersonal relationship to Christ that can result, needs to be taken on as a lifetime task of prayerful study and personally lived experimentation. Without this "alive-in-faith-body-person-relatedness" (that St. Paul is getting at in the text from Romans we discussed) *within* the very openness of listening to my feelings, inclinations, etc., so that they are *experienced* and *known reflectively* "in Christ," then the effective power (*energeia*) of His Selfless love at work in me (*agape*) cannot transform and resurrect my body-personal signs of communication with others. They cannot be an effective, visible witness to the growing divine life that is my becoming a human person in the Whole Christ. Instead, my feelings will be acted out with a great deal of self-centeredness that will diminish their sacramental efficacy.

In short, if my actions are to be sacramentally efficacious, *there must be a congruence not only between my real human feelings and my conscious awareness and acceptance of them, but between*

this whole dynamic process and the theological truth of my rela-
tionship to the Whole Christ. I cannot risk feeling, let alone accepting, unless I have faith in and understanding of the Whole
Christ that is congruent with my level of "becoming a person."
The two must grow together, or I will neither take the risk nor
be able to achieve the full realization of my personhood.

Moreover, as a Christian, if I am to live an effective sacramental
prayer-life, there must now be added to "open listening to my
feelings," and to the congruence between these feelings and my
conscious awareness of them, the efficacious sign that this harmonizing process *is related* to *"God-with-us."*

St. Paul makes this idea clear to the Philippians when he tells
them: "Let your bearing towards one another arise out of your
life in Christ Jesus" (2:5,NEB). In other words, let your interpersonal relationships grow out of the conscious relationship you
have to the Whole Christ, that is, precisely *within* your personal
involvement with one another *as* your *"in-faith," conscious re-*
sponse to Christ.

A little further on Paul tells the Philippians: "You must work
out your own salvation in fear and trembling; for it is God who
works in you, inspiring both the will and the deed, for his own
chosen purpose" (2:13,NEB). Here Paul exhorts them consciously to take on the task and the responsibility not of saving
themselves apart from God but of opening themselves to listen to
the God "who works in you." This response, he tells them, must
become more and more human; God's self-communication within
them is directed toward their whole body-person response because
He "works in you, inspiring both the *will* and the *deed.*" In other
words, their task at hand in responding to God's Self-gift, *their*
part in "working out [their] own salvation" called for a response
that was more and more a sensitive, open listening with the entirety of their spiritual and bodily faculties, so that their whole
body-person could respond in "deed." In the language of a sacramental spirituality, we would speak of this kind of Christian
living as a visible and effective sacramental sign of the Continuing Incarnation.

Paul taught the Philippians that they must work at discerning the presence of God *within* their understanding of their choices and all that would affect their body-personal actions ("deeds"); and both verses 4 and 5 stress that this "working out of their salvation" is primarily within the *interpersonal* context: "Let your bearing *towards one another*"; "You must look to *each other's interest* and not merely to your own." (Italics ours.) In this last text we have a clear expression of one of the sacramental signs of open listening.

SOME VISIBLE, SACRAMENTAL "SIGN-EFFECTS" OF OPEN LISTENING

Before beginning our description of the visible, sacramentally "effective signs" of God's presence in open listening, we wish to make it clear that *of themselves* these natural human signs *do not* have the power to convey supernatural revelation, unless the one experiencing or witnessing them does so *with faith*. We are presuming an openness in faith that is dependent upon Revelation contained in Scripture and Tradition in order to interpret these interpersonal signs as being effective, sacramental signs of the presence of God. In order to recognize their source as supernatural, one is totally dependent upon the gift of faith as well as on a knowledge of the *revealed extent* of God's intimate personal Incarnation within the life of the family of man. With this important pre-note as the background for our discussion, let us now examine *some* of the visible, sacramental sign-effects of this Christ-filled congruence in the sign of open listening.

In the safety and growing freedom of the congruence between my experienced feelings, my conscious awareness of them, and my relatedness to the Body of Christ, I can afford to allow myself to be open to experience life fully and deeply. This freedom is visibly "signed" to all around me as I daily enter into the thousand and one experiences and situations which the ordinary observer might consider that I would have good reason to exclude as being too *threatening* or *demanding*.

Another of these effects would be a visible, deep reverence for one's own experience of life in all its varying dimensions. There would be an openness to let each encounter with reality speak for itself and reveal its own meaning, rather than trying to hold certain experiences within the mold of preconceived ideas or prestructured forms. Consequently, there would be an obvious caution and restraint in rushing in to manipulate people and circumstances, to fix things, and to shape others into one's own image. There would be a kind of comfortable discovery of one's "real self" within the experiences of life and a willingness to simply *be* that "*real* self" and to let others *be themselves.*

Again, there would also be the visible increase of an ability to live with much of the uncertainty, insecurity, and ambiguity that is part of life, rather than forcing reality into an artificial framework to meet one's personal needs. The Christian's "peace" lies much deeper than in the negative removal of *feelings* of frustration. It witnesses to the positive relatedness we have just discussed.

A fourth visible sacramental effect of this Christ-filled congruence would be the "signed" presence of an interior strength or power that increasingly allowed the individual to choose and to act from an inner freedom and capacity for responsible decision, rather than always depending upon an "exterior" force to compel his assent. The more these free, personal acts are selfless and obviously the sign of a "gifted energy" at work within his total body-interpersonal response, the greater the visible, sacramental effectiveness of each interpersonal encounter.

Another sign would be what we might call the "humility of becoming." Confronted with the constant necessity for change, adaptation, and renewal—in fact, the realization that life itself is a continuing process—we would not display the negative signs of balking and bitterness, of stubbornly standing still, or of discouragement in the face of this truth. Rather, the visible expression in one's "signed" encounters, especially with others (although at times the prospect might be frightening), would be that this truth provides a fascinating, challenging, and deeply meaningful context for faith and trust in the process itself, which is the growing Body of the Whole Christ. Such a person's adaptability in his creative and constructive living would give ample evidence of sensitive, open listening and deeply rooted confidence in his "becoming in Christ." Living of this kind is *openly* on the frontiers of human evolution.

The sixth of these signs would simply be the absence of rigidity, defensiveness, and the need to function behind masks or through an "over-structured" system in one's personal, social, and religious life. If a person can afford to be fully open to his experiences and to life as "a becoming," because it is actually perceived through the eyes of faith "in Christ" and consequently does not have to be distorted through defense mechanisms, then once again, there is a powerful, visibly effective sacramental sign of Emmanuel in this congruence (for those open to receive it in faith). But *for anyone,* believer or nonbeliever, who comes into contact with such wholeness, there is clear evidence that this person is an active participant in an exciting, deeply captivating mystery that has broken through the barriers of anxiety and fear and has grasped the entirety of his personal living.

A rather obvious but not so easily acquired effective sign among the many that "open listening" symbolizes, is that degree of self-acceptance that manifests itself in a willingness to *share oneself.* This aptitude reveals a level of interpersonal life in the Whole Christ wherein one's self-identity is so deeply rooted in the experience of being able to "be myself" without fear of rejection, that within the ordinary interpersonal relationships of daily contact with others, I can afford to share myself without fear of being lost in this gift or of being crushed by the rejection of another. Here the sacramental sign is not only effectively present within the interpersonal sharing, but in the fact that what is shared is simply *the truth of myself.* I accept my "real self" as all that God has given me to share with others.

However, my need to express authenticity is governed by a sensitive listening to the needs of others. I can be authentic *without necessarily acting out all that I listen to* and accept in myself because I experience my "real self" as shared with Christ who accepts me just as I am. Needless to say, the fact that this often genuinely expresses my weakness and needs is seen not as a threat but as an expression of my faith in the power of Christ's *healing agape effectively at work* in His Body.

Perhaps one of the most important of these signs for effective communication of our life in Christ is the capacity to be able to enter into the different "worlds of meaning" of others as a result of our discerning and sensitive listening to them. Through open listening we have come to realize that when we meet another human being, we encounter a living history in which are embedded the values, feelings, hopes, and fears that characterize this person's unique response to all the peculiar physical, emotional, and psychic factors that have shaped his life. This is his unique world of meaning that has especially been molded by the significant human relationships of his life.

Moreover, this person can be understood and effectively communicated with only by sincerely attempting, through sensitive listening, to enter into his personally lived and experienced world of meaning. A history still in the making, but largely shaped by what has already come before, is being acted out in a unique way before us in every person we meet. To encounter that person as he really is, we must enter into his world of meaning. The Christian whose prayerful relationship to the Whole Christ has grown to maturity, and whose congruence between his feelings and conscious awareness of them has been integrated into a secure identity within the living Body of Christ, can not only risk listening to another's differing and perhaps threatening world of meaning but actually enter into it in order to make Christ a more conscious part of this faith-filled interpersonal experience. We can bring Christ into the world of another and incarnate Him there only by entering into that world ourselves through opening ourselves to it, listening to it, and accepting it—just because it is the unique, personal world of another human being. When this is acted out and received in faith, we are truly present to the other person as an effective, sacramental sign of Christ's personal understanding and selfless love. Christ respects human freedom and comes to people as they are. Through daily living with an existential closeness to His Body, the Christian who is "praying always" is opened up to give visible expression to that quality of Christ's love that has called men to respond to their personal vocation since the time when His sacred person walked among

us, as the incarnate expression that "God [first] loved us . . .
[and] if God so loved us, we also ought to love one another"
(1 Jn. 4:10,RSV).

A further important sign of open listening might be described
as the emergence of a deepening appreciation of and need for
silence. Not only is silence the fundamental requisite for developing the art of listening, but both mutually complement and
support each other. An inner attitude of silence makes it possible
for us to listen to new worlds of meaning, new potentialities in
ourselves and others, and new dimensions of effective, interpersonal communication that are not limited to the verbal. Some
examples of these more subtle forms of dialogue might be presence, acceptance, loyalty, availability, thoughtfulness, respect,
reverence, sensitivity to other's moods through gesture, posture,
facial expressions, etc.

As we all know, silence can be quite threatening and anxiety-
producing, because insecurities and unknowns rise up within it.
But this well-known experience actually heightens the effective,
sacramental witness of one who not only lives with a balance of
external silence in his life but is also continually attentive to
others with a deep, interior disposition of silent, open listening.
Why is this? Because this silence, which truly comes to penetrate
the whole body-person, gives visible expression to that individual's
conscious life in an interpersonal atmosphere of acceptance and
love, of trust and faith. These latter conditions are absolute
prerequisites for developing silence as an integrated and humanly
fulfilling value in personal living. The silence of interpersonal
isolation or of self-centered or neurotic withdrawal usually gives
evidence of the absence of this atmosphere. The development of
a truly mature and thoroughly human appreciation for silence
grows only in those who want to listen with greater openness and
sensitivity to all of reality.

When the capacity for silence in order to "listen" appears in
a person's life, people are led to ask themselves about the *living
source* of this power. What enables the open person *to remain
this way* in the face of daily rebuff, and actually to choose this
rather painful sort of existence as a life vocation? If those who

witness this remarkable capacity in one who is close to God also
bring faith and a certain knowledge of the 'incarnate way' in
which God reveals Himself in interpersonal life to ᵗʰⁱˢ experience,
then their contact with this "holy" person becon   ᵉm, a
visible sign of God's presence in the world.

But external silence (the absence of noise and   ⱼₙ that
holds the attention of my spiritual facul ᵣₑs) is productive of
interior silence only when the above-mentioned atmosphere of
"alive-relatedness" to the Whole Christ (a "We" consciousness)
is brought to these daily periods of external silence and can
perdure through them. To be open to listening to oneself and
to all of reality, one must however at the same time *experience
being listened to by another.* One must experience this personal
and unique acceptance within the very stumbling and often
painful process of human growing itself.

Our sacramental, Christian prayer must be such that it realistically creates an interpersonal relationship with the Whole
Christ within which each of us can afford to penetrate and explore the mysteries and uniqueness of his own life and that of
others. We must be enabled to listen to our own needs as well
as those of others, and to integrate what we discover into a
meaningful pattern of existence within an atmosphere of silence
that gives effective witness to the depth of our personal "alive-
relatedness" in Christ. In a word, Christian silence must witness
not to *escape* but to *the security of being heard.*

What we have tried to show in this section is that in encountering the Whole Christ through open listening, we give visible
expression within our body-person living to many effective, sacramental signs of our prayerful and intimate personal relationship
with our Lord. When we consciously listen to and accept our
bodies, our feelings, and the growing congruence between them
as the very existential and experiential "ground" of our dialogue
with the Whole Christ, then this growth can also lead us to
listen to *other people.* Listening in faith, with greater openness,
easily extends over into the "in-between-life" of interpersonal
relationships. Interpersonal relatedness is not apart from God,
nor do any of the signs we have just discussed have meaning

when separated from my relationship in faith to the Body of the Whole Christ—the "others" of my experience.

This brings us to the last of these signs that witness to the living, authentic permeation of our entire body-person with the life of Christ's Body. It perhaps gives the most concrete and visible integration of Christ's presence in us as a vital and living force in our personal relationships with others. This important sign appears to be the basis for our Lord's own instruction in the kind of incarnational prayer we have been discussing. It summarizes many elements of an existential prayer-life that we have already touched upon, but makes its own contribution by focusing our attention on the ever-present reality of human needs. What we will call "the sign of open listening to human needs," must be clearly visible in any prayerful life that hopes to give effective, sacramental witness to the salvific, healing power of Christ. We have already integrated aspects of this idea into various chapters of the book. We would now like to relate what we have already developed regarding "listening to the needs of the Body of Christ" to our growing insight into incarnational prayer.

In his epistles, St. Paul speaks of Christian openness as characterized not only by a listening to all of reality, but by a *truthful* listening in which there can be a discernment of good and evil under the guidance of the Spirit. The Christian is a man of the Spirit not only because he can manifest an openness to the world around him but also because he can truthfully discern his own relationship to all of reality, for the: "Spirit of him who raised Jesus from the dead dwells within you, [and] the God who raised Christ Jesus from the dead will also give new life to your mortal bodies through his indwelling Spirit" (Rom. 8:11,NEB).

The new life in the Spirit is given *now,* and the Christian who lives in the Spirit approaches reality with a kind of transparency and an ability to listen to and accept himself as a "needer." This he does through the gift of himself *as "needer"* to the Whole Christ in the Spirit, so that a transformation can take place within him. He grows "close to himself," experiencing himself as "needer" in the Whole Christ under the direction of the Holy Spirit.

In fact, the Christian must discover, as Paul did, that because of his tendency to isolation and self-centeredness, *this very process* of growing close to himself as a "needer" is in itself a gift of the Spirit. By emptying Himself into our "needing" humanity in the person of Jesus, God has, paradoxically, through the "needing" Body of the Whole Christ, brought us the answer to our helplessness. Is this not really God's effort to help us believe in love because He Himself is love? Does not the lover always place himself, to a certain extent, in dependence upon the one he loves and by whom he seeks to be loved?

"Behold, I stand at the door and knock" (Ap. 3:20,RSV). If we are to love, we must first *be what we are*. But individually and collectively, we are the "needing" Body of Christ. When we can truly unite ourselves to Christ *as He is among us,* then we can burst through the "eye of the needle" into our authentic life here and now in the Kingdom of Heaven.

Living in the Body of Christ as a "needer" opens and disposes me to a life of faith in His Body. I am conditioned and kept in a receptive mood, so to speak, to discover in faith the existential reality of the living Body of the Lord. The transition to recognizing the common bond of "needing" that unites me with my neighbor is not too difficult a jump for that truth-filled openness that marks the listening of a Christian. When my needs are listened to, accepted, and loved *as the "needs" of the Whole Christ,* then the leap of love to the needs of my neighbor, who is one with me in the Body of the Lord, may follow. Our Lord Himself said that He is present to us in a special way in the needs of His Body; and that if we are to enter into a personal relationship with Him, we must listen to these needs and answer them: "Come, enter and possess the kingdom that has been ready for you since the world was made. For when I was hungry, you gave me food; when thirsty, you gave me drink; when I was a stranger you took me into your home, when naked you clothed me; when I was ill you came to my help, when in prison you visited me. Then the righteous will reply, 'Lord, when was it that we saw you hungry and fed you, or thirsty and gave you drink, a stranger and took you home, or naked and clothed you? When did we see you ill or in prison, and come to visit you?' And the king will answer, 'I tell you this: anything you did for one of my brothers here, however humble, you did for me'" (Mt. 25:34-40,NEB).

Moreover, when we do answer the needs of another, we effectively give witness to the presence of Christ's own life in us. St. John speaks this truth as a solemn warning in his First Epistle: "But if a man has enough to live on, and yet when he sees his brother in need shuts up his heart against him, how can it be said that the divine *agape* dwells in him?" (3:17,NEB.)

By joining all men to the Body of His Incarnate Son, God has made it possible for us to know and experience a love-relationship with Him that does not take place in a human psychological void. We can experience our love for the invisible God by our love for visible men. We are creatures of time and space, and if our love is genuine, in the sense that it has permeated our body-person, it will of necessity find expression in our body-person relationships with one another.

The problem is that most men do not fit *our* preconceived notions of what the invisible, infinite, omnipotent God should be like. The visible form that God's love has taken is found in the "needing" Body of the Whole Christ, and this shatters our neat categories that had conveniently captured the divine mystery. Jesus of Nazareth, born in an animal shelter and earning His living at a tradesman's bench, was also a far cry from the Jews' exalted conceptions of the mighty figure of the expected Messiah. And yet in the bewildering wisdom of God, mankind was called to salvation in the "needing" humanity of Jesus of Nazareth.

How often we see Jesus using human "needs" to open and condition those whom He met, inviting them to go deeper into the reality of His person as they responded to His request for a drink of water, a meal, or a place to lodge! And He, in turn, always responded to the receptive mood created by their great human needs to elicit an act of faith, to raise each person a little higher in understanding and love. Consider His description of the Good Samaritan's quality of openness and vulnerability to allow the needs of the wounded man to "get into him" and call him out of himself, or Luke's account of Christ's own reaction to the need of the widowed mother: "When the Lord saw her *his heart went out to her*" (7:13,NEB). (Italics ours.) The spontaneous, congruent body-person reaction to the needs of another has now become the divine way of expressing God's loving concern for us. This is the *new* way of the Incarnation, but it waits on man's openness to incarnate the healing life of *agape* into the potential capacity of human wholeness before it can be a visibly effective, sacramental sign.

Thus, at the experiential body-person level of communication, the transcendent, risen, glorified Lord is incarnationally expressed and revealed to me *within* my experience of *agape;* but paradoxically, this is "signed" within the "weakness-strength" mystery to which I must open myself in faith. Through open listening in faith, I can discover this paradox both in myself and in my relationships to others. By living an authentic existential congruence between my feelings (many of which are selfish, hostile, etc.) and my awareness and acceptance of them, but *always as related* (and *as my growth experience* in the Body of the Whole Christ), I communicate both the genuineness of the "real me" with my human weakness, and (if I am open to the needs of others) the fact that I am simultaneously concerned and present to *their* needs.

For example, I may feel tired, annoyed, and bored. But in an authentic existential prayer-life, I can listen to this and accept it while at the same time struggling in faith to be open to more than just *my* needs in the Body of Christ. When I believe in faith that the needs of others *are* the needs of the Body of Christ, then in faith and love I can listen to Christ's needs visibly expressed to me through others. They can call me out of myself. As such, they can become efficacious, sacramental signs of God's love for me. When I respond to them in faith, I am in dialogue with the Whole Christ and the power of *agape* is maturing my humanity for self-gift "in Christ." In faith and love I can come to identify the needs of others as truly *my own,* for their needs are joined and made one with my needs in the one Body of the Whole Christ. To become a person in the Whole Christ, I cannot separate myself from my "needing" brothers. "The eye cannot say to the hand, 'I do not need you'; nor the head to the feet, 'I do not need you.' Quite the contrary: these organs of the body which seem to be more frail than others are indispensable, and those parts of the body which we regard as less honorable are treated with special honor. To our unseemly parts is given a more than ordinary seemliness, whereas our seemly parts need no adorning. But God has combined the various parts of the body, giving special honor to the humbler parts, so that there might be no sense of division in the body, but that all its organs might feel the same concern for one another. If one organ suffers, they all suffer together. If one flourishes, they all rejoice together. Now you are Christ's body, and each of you a limb or organ of it" (1 Cor. 12:21–27,NEB).

An incarnational prayer-life discloses within the experience of ordinary interpersonal relationships the disguised language of God present in the needs of Christ's Body, which, however, may be revealed behind very selfish actions. "I did not come to invite virtuous people, but *sinners*" (Mt. 9:13; Mk. 2:17; Lk. 5:32, NEB).

Once again, faith is even more important, because the visible expression of *agape* is almost totally diminished. Yet, if my need is joined as one to the deep, personal needs of this person calling for help in this strange and painful way, he can become for me a sacramental sign of God's self-communication.

When I am conscious of myself as a "needer," and yet, through faith, available to the needs of the Whole Christ, I discover that I am also *healer*. There is a twofold awareness of myself: as giver and receiver, as healer and "needer"; and slowly the separation between myself and my brother disappears, because he too is both a "needer" and a healer in the same Body of the Lord. His very needs serve to heal me "in Christ," which, in turn, enables me to heal him in our mutual experience of the bond of *agape*. In faith, I gradually come to live out, as an "alive-relatedness" in Christ, the mysterious paradox that God is communicating Himself to me as much through the human needs of others as He is through the obvious signs of *agape* in their acts of selfless love.

We can never really experience the power of agape in our lives until we have openly listened to our own weaknesses and self-centeredness. We have no real need for God until we have done this, nor are we provided with the experiential "ground" of our selfishness against which we may contrast the selfless love of another. And in a contrary manner, it is through another's efficacious signs of selfless love, mediated to us in the Whole Christ, that we can come to see more clearly the "figure" of our own self-centeredness. But then we realize that they, sharing the same tendency to self-centeredness as ourselves, have nevertheless opened themselves to the power of selfless love and have freely extended this gift to us. This is the "lived-experience" of *agape* in our lives that moves our body-person to risk searching for it at ever-deeper levels within the not so clearly visible signs of the divine presence. It is in this lived-out polarity between the needs of the Body and selfless love—needs calling out of us a gift that we of ourselves do not have, needs calling for a healing strength far beyond our ability, and yet, our simultaneous experience of the growing capacity to answer these needs—it is in this "lived-polarity," that we most effectively "sign" the living presence of Christ and come to know Him as body-persons ourselves.

This gradual Diaphany of the Whole Christ is dependent upon an authentic congruence in our sacramental communication because it is a *personal* expression of ourselves. The sacramental sign of selfless love is an incarnate expression of Christ's self-gift and must therefore be the genuine, visible, body-person expression of the Continuing Incarnation. The exhilarating, exciting possibilities of Christian prayer must seize and hurl us onto the mountain top where our light can shine before the world. Men must be "salted" with the sign of our total self-gift to their needs before they will say "Our Father." *We* must be their body-person experience of the divine self-gift. It is the task of Christian prayer to incarnate an authenticity into our sacramental expression of God's self-gift to all men.

In the psychological order, this means that in giving myself to the needs of others (while often simultaneously experiencing contrary self-centered feelings and weaknesses), I must be aware of a personal, genuinely *human fulfillment*. In addition, the substance of an authentic Christian prayer-life demands that, some-how or other, the communication of Christ must be manifested in the very tension between my "real self" (with my needs and weaknesses) and a genuine concern for the needs of my neighbor. In brief, this very *struggle* with my own inadequacies, fears, etc., must be preserved within the totality of my "signed" communi-cation, if it is to manifest an "alive-relatedness" in faith to the person of Christ. Within another's experience of my open listen-ing and personal self-gift to his needs, the mystery of the Living God must be revealed. The total harmony between feelings, awareness, and communication in a faith-relationship to the Whole Christ effectively "signs" this mystery. Incarnational Christian prayer must break through the barriers of defenses. At one and the same time it must allow all the personal needs, weaknesses, inadequacies, and even hostile and aggressive feelings to be consciously present, while permeating the total body-personal response to the needs of others with the effective sacramental signs of *agape* that we have just discussed.

Let us illustrate this congruence with an example. When the small child, who is uninhibited by any defenses, feels anger or discomfort, his feelings and his conscious experience of them are one with his spontaneous communication. In one integral, though primitive, body-person act, he communicates *himself* when he has a crying tantrum. There is a total congruence that is visible to us mainly because, as a baby, he has no other way to express his "real self" at that moment. In using this example, we are not, of course, suggesting that we act out our every feeling in this primi-tive, self-centered way. There is, nevertheless, ground for a valid comparison. The child is certainly authentic, and there is a basic congruence between his self-centered needs and his expression of them in the temper tantrum. In fact, when the pre-reflective selfish-ness of the child becomes the reflective, consciously acted out selfishness of the adult sinner, we are faced with the authenticity of a son of Adam. But there is as well a kind of "Christian authenticity," that depends upon a congruence lived out *"in Christ"* as an adopted son of the Father. Let us reflect on this for a moment.

Authentic, mature congruence involves an openness and listening to *all* of reality and a capacity for reflexivity as well as the exercise of judgment and a level of personal integration that affords considerable freedom for responsible decisions. However, for this congruence to be truly an efficacious, sacramental sign of Christ's *agape* (presuming, of course, an openness in faith on the part of the receiver), the total complex of listening, awareness, and communication must be permeated with that "alive-related-ness" in faith to Christ of which we have spoken. Unlike the baby, I am alive not only to my own needs but also to the real human needs of others *as the needs of the Whole Christ*. There-fore, what I act out toward others is under the influence of a faith-response to Christ; and, presuming that my fundamental attitude is one of love and service of Christ, what I communicate to others is the personal authenticity of my congruence with the mystery of the Continuing Incarnation in the Whole Christ.

We must emphasize again that the Christian apostle does not lack "Christian authenticity" when, for example, he *"feels* jealous," but only when he *acts this out* in some selfish way toward the Body of Christ. When *acting* in this manner he denies his authentic identification with the Whole Christ. He destroys his Christian identity. He is *unauthentic.* The point we wish to stress is that there is no need for him to distort, repress, or suppress the selfish feelings of jealousy, anger, etc., that rise within him, but only to be *in faith* what he truthfully is at this moment *"in"* the Body of Christ. However, he can do this only if he is listening and growing to accept himself as he is, because *"he is not alone."* He must listen to his selfishness *"with* Christ." He must listen to his own needs as well as the needs of the Body of the Whole Christ. To some degree, the element of "other-centeredness" must always be present within any human development toward authentic per-sonal living, whether in the Christian context or not. Without it, this way of life runs the risk of warping man's personal growth in a monstrous egocentricity. There is always great risk in plumbing the depths of personal life and human self-realization without the balancing force and intimate presence of Christ's healing and life-giving power of *agape.*

The prayer-life we have described is obviously not for the

faint-hearted. For when the Christian can receive the needs of Christ's Body under the signs of self-centeredness "through a glass darkly," and return the gift of *agape* through the interpersonal dynamism of an "in-faith-body-person-selfless-presence-to-the-other," the efficacious sacramental sign of God's presence is manifested in the mystery of His incarnate love. "I did not come to invite virtuous people but sinners" (Mt. 9:13,NEB). "Love your enemies; do good to those who hate you; bless those who curse you; pray for those who treat you spitefully.... If you love only those who love you, what credit is that to you? Even sinners do as much.... But you must love your enemies and do good; and lend without expecting any return... and you will be sons of the Most High, because he himself is kind to the ungrateful and wicked" (Lk. 6:28–36,NEB).

When the Christian acts in this paradoxical manner, the power of *agape,* effectively signed, can begin its task of healing, which may (if it is responded to in faith) gradually bring the other to the point where he too can begin to risk penetrating deeper into the self-gift of God in *all* the signs of need within the Body of Christ. He too then begins effectively and consciously to mediate the Spirit in faith to the "needing" Body; and thus it is that we grow through, with, and in one another toward "becoming persons in the Whole Christ."

Each Christian today must take on the task of developing a prayer-life that is more attuned to human needs. My personal contacts with the needs of the Body of Christ in my neighbor must become those decisive moments in my history in which life itself is destroyed or created. When I have made a choice, the very direction of my existence is altered, and so too are the very depths of my being. My continuing search in the Body of Christ to experience, as a body-person, the truth of the Whole Christ is, in reality, my personal quest for self-identity. I open and listen to the world so that I may learn who I am. If I cannot read the "signs," my "person" remains hidden.

To stand in the poverty of need as a whole body-person before the Father is to stand in the strength of the Body of Christ. It is also to live, touched by a sense of reality in the flesh and blood, as well as the Spirit, that is the growing Body of the Whole Christ.

Christian prayer must deepen man's identity and oneness in human need and intensify his awareness of their nuances, because when he swerves away from the truth of himself as a "needer," he ultimately turns aside from God, from his brother, and from himself.

12. Encountering the Whole Christ through "Unconditional Acceptance" in Faith

IN THE PRECEDING PAGES we used the rather generic phrase "open listening," together with a reflection upon both the interior attitude and the "signed" action in order to describe some of the distinctive features of this potentially effective, interpersonal, sacramental sign. We now wish to set forth the second and last of the interpersonal signs that we have selected to illustrate the truly sacramental character of Christian prayer in the Whole Christ. "Unconditional acceptance" is the title we have chosen for this sign, which should extend and intensify the sacramentality of our encounter with the Whole Christ.

The reader will recall that, earlier in the book, we spoke of an evolving sensitivity to more subtle levels of interpersonal needs throughout many segments in the family of man today. This is especially true within those national and socio-economic groups that are considered to be more affluent.

What we would like to propose to the reader is that we must *first* develop *ourselves,* through realistic, incarnational Christian prayer, as the *effective personal signs* of the presence of divine life *before* we can be the effective, sacramental sign of Christ's presence to either the many deprived and impoverished peoples of the world or to those who are more economically and culturally

253

developed. This idea is, of course, nothing new. But the truth of
this way of thinking tends constantly to slip into the background.

The ultimate effectiveness of the "sign" we give is not so much
in terms of *what we do* but of *what we are.* It is not so dependent
upon the *institutions* of charity or education that we provide (for
these are frequently equalled or bettered by the secular humanists),
but upon the *level* of *interpersonal life* that is both alive within
them and effectively communicated to others. In a word, *we ourselves* must be the sacramental sign, not the accouterments of our
apostolate.

Therefore, any apostolic work as an efficacious sign of *agape,*
in which men's lives are truly transformed *from within,* is dependent upon the depth of the Christian apostle's own capacity for
interpersonal life in the Whole Christ. Moreover, we are convinced
that this is the key sacramental sign. When responded to in faith,
it effects that *metanoia,* or "turning to God," which is the true
conversion leading to personal human fulfillment *within* the Body
of the living God. Our whole body-person must sacramentally
"sign" the effective, personal integration of the power of *agape*
with our "knowledge" (in the biblical sense) of the Whole Christ.
In order to know the Whole Christ with that "depth of understanding" which St. Paul desired all Christians to possess, we
should profoundly penetrate into the *inter*-personal life of the
Christian communities in which we now live. These are both the
training ground and the continuing source of our capacity effectively to "sign" this "deeper understanding" and knowledge of the
Whole Christ to all men. "My prayer is that your fellowship with
us in our common faith may deepen the understanding of all the
blessings that our union with Christ bring us" (Phlm. 6,NEB).

In developing this truly sacramental character within our prayer-
life, we must keep in mind an important observation regarding
our response to the needs of others. Within the *immediate*
Christian communities where many of us live (whether as religious or laymen), the needs of our family, co-workers, social
companions, religious confreres, and often the students we teach
are not usually the needs of the destitute, the hungry, the medic-
ally neglected, or the culturally, educationally, and socially deprived. Instead, their needs will often be found at a much more

subtle level of human want, of human evolution, and of personal fulfillment. Theirs are the needs that are centered around that kind of personal affirmation, for example, which says, "you are worth something," or even better, "you are worth something *to me.*"

Theirs are the needs that call for our delicately "signed" re-affirmation of them, so that they can continue to believe in themselves in a very mechanized and impersonal world. Theirs is that elusive call for help to go deeper into the discovery of themselves, of their potential for personal life, and of their capacity for an unselfish gift of themselves to others, and ultimately to the service of the Body of Christ. This is the sensitive realm of "unconditional acceptance" within the interpersonal relationships of the immediate social environment of most of us. It is especially here that we must begin to refine and deepen the effective "sign-value" of our relationship to the Whole Christ, if we are convincingly to extend a true witness to the meaning of that "abundant personal life" which our Lord would have us communicate in our service to the needs of all men.

But even within the more destitute communities where some of us serve, we must not allow the obvious physical needs for medical attention, adequate housing, equal educational opportunities, and legislation for social betterment to blind us to the deeper aspirations of the human heart. It is true that these needs may not even be acknowledged by many of those whose attention is focused on their immediate physical requirements. Anyone who has ever allowed himself to be impressed by the "dignity" of the poor, however, realizes that even in the midst of squalor and deprivation there are sparks of human grandeur that cry out for respect and acknowledgement. Here also there are quiet demands of a most subtle nature, equally as refined as those of the most culturally advanced peoples.

The attitude of "unconditional acceptance" focuses the Christian apostle's attention more on the human need of another for self-worth, rather than on the capacity for "open listening" or "availability" on the part of the listener, although these latter qualities are among the most effective signs of our acceptance.

We know, of course, that as members of the human race we

are essentially the same. But there is a vast and complex variety of individual differences which mirror for us, in their awesomeness and seeming infinity, the finite expression of the rich possibilities of human relationships. Each of us loves, prays, learns, and works in his own unique way toward self-realization. Is it any wonder, then, that when we experience through a sacramental sign the unconditional acceptance of our own individuality (an expression so in tune with God's own continuing personal creation of each one of us) that it should be something of a "religious experience"? This is really our incarnational way of affirming the theological truth behind the humanly experienced sign. Acceptance of another, in a way that is anything less than personal, can never convey, according to our sacramental way of knowing, the true nature of God's unconditional acceptance of each of us in the total gift of Himself through the incarnation of Christ. Each of us *needs* to experience and to continue to experience that depth of acceptance which so re-affirms our own uniqueness that we can risk believing in the living presence of Christ discovered throughout the painful and faltering steps we take toward self-realization in His Body.

Very few of us realize how widespread the anxious feelings of alienation, personal worthlessness, or of a sort of hopeless inadequacy prevail among those with whom we live. So often their exterior manner of acting and accomplishments give quite the opposite impression. Their deep need to achieve a sense of personal worth, of belonging, and of experiencing as a whole body-person within the depths of their personality that "someone really cares about me," is often hidden beneath remarkable intellectual, social, and economic success.

There are many environmental factors of a social, cultural, or religious nature that may be singled out as reasons for the increased number of people who suffer terribly because of being cut off in varying degrees from meaningful communication with themselves and others. But the important factor of human growth itself must also be considered, since it may heighten a man's sensitivity for interpersonal life long before his social environment is capable of answering this growing need. The resulting tension may produce many of the characteristics of a neurotic generation (or generations) seen in a self-rejecting, insecure, and rather intolerant people. Neurosis may, in truth, be widespread; but we must restrain our readiness to judge and to prescribe that a return to the "good old ways" of the past will be the answer. It is quite possible that many people suffer neurotic symptoms because they are frustrated, and that they are frustrated largely because they need to grow *out of the past* and *into the future.*

We do not intend to convey the impression that the deep need we all have for unconditional acceptance is a neurotic need. Quite the contrary. But an increased awareness of the necessity for acceptance can cause this need to become the focal point of anxiety. The rapid environmental changes that we are all experiencing may even be intensifying this interpersonal need at the present stage in man's evolution toward a higher personal life.

As Christians, we must look upon all mature personal growth, and the corresponding needs that become evident within it, as opportunities to incarnate the "abundance" of Christ's personal life into the family of man, through our capacity to answer these personal needs with His own *agape.* We must penetrate deeply into the "non-belonging" of so many around us and incarnate their redemption through our effective, sacramental sign of unconditional acceptance. Wherever we find the inability of men to listen to themselves and others, and wherever this results in self-distrust and an unwillingness to accept themselves (because of a kind of disembodied hostility toward the human condition), it is here that we must "re-incarnate," so to speak, these persons into the living Body of the Whole Christ through our sacramental, personal entrance into their whole body-person. We must help them truly to *live* in the Body of Christ and in the humanly fulfilling, personal communion that our Lord's warm and loving "unconditional acceptance" of our humanity brought to us in the Incarnation.

Our sacramental, interpersonal life with one another has to be *real.* It must be real in the sense that *we* are the incarnated body-person whose visible, effective signs of "really caring about this person" communicate to him the reality of his value as a human

being, which "the Word made Flesh" has incarnated into each of
us for all eternity. When others can begin to feel and experience
the safety, the trust, and the experience of someone "really caring
about me" in their body-person experiences with us, then they
will be able to recognize and understand what it means to be
saved in the glory of the Son of God who dwells among us.

THE INTERIOR ATTITUDE OF "UNCONDITIONAL ACCEPTANCE" IN FAITH

Many of the characteristics that would make up the disposition
or attitude of "unconditional acceptance" have already been described within our treatment of "open listening." As we mentioned
there, the separation that we made between these two interpersonal
signs was largely artificial and was chosen by us only in order to
highlight some aspects of their richness, which might have been
missed if they were treated together. Our manner of presentation
is intended to bring out certain characteristics of both these attitudes, which may serve as focal points for each individual's
reflection and personal integration. We leave it to the reader's
own initiative to relate the particular emphasis that will be brought
out by the meaning of "unconditional acceptance" with the preceding development of ideas in this book.

Let us now attempt to describe several more of the interpersonal
qualities that one might consider to be contained within the
attitude of "unconditional acceptance."

What does it mean to be disposed toward others with an attitude of unconditional acceptance, and how does one become
opened to living this way? An attitude that is so deeply personal
as this is not something that we can simply turn on or off like
a faucet. The reader will realize that it is the result of a gradual,
maturing growth, together with an integration of everything that
we have spoken of in this book. In particular, it includes that
slow, painful process of listening to oneself in faith *as related* to
the Body of Christ. There must then follow the extension of this
open listening in faith, with all its existential and psychological

realism, into my daily relationships with others, until I begin to encounter them no longer as isolated objects but as the living, unique expression of the "incomparable richness" of the one Body of the Lord. They must really "matter to me" not just because I give my intellectual consent to the *truth* of the Mystical Body, but because their lives, feelings, hopes, dreams, and human needs have *become my own* and I cannot *be myself* any longer without them. I cannot live "in Christ" without living *"in them."* Somehow the self-love that has grown, as I have grown over the years to love my whole body-person in Christ, spills over into an emptying out of myself that can be as *"totally for the other"* as is my love for myself in Christ. The barriers and the walls of separation must begin to dissolve into the one Body of the Lord. Whereas before people and circumstances were judged and valued from the *outside* toward the center of my self, in terms of whether or not they bolstered by self-image, gave me satisfaction, or held to the same values and viewpoints as my own, now I must gradually begin to see them as "God-related-in-the-Whole-Christ-to-me" rather than as merely self-related. In fact, I must begin to realize that I prize other persons as valuable and loveable in themselves, in a kind of direct proportion to the degree that I value and love my own body-person life in the Whole Christ.

Such love is at the opposite pole from sentimentality. It is truly and intensely personal. It is not restricted to "an *act* of the *will*," nor is it identified solely with the *feelings* that accompany it. Instead, the love of unconditional acceptance of another is that love which is deeply grounded in real knowledge. It is a real knowledge that begins with the person who is "myself," in *my* unique personal relationship with the Whole Christ, and then extends through "open listening" and "acceptance" into the personal relationships I have with others.

The growing real knowledge about another person that an attitude of open listening and unconditional acceptance brings us invariably carries along with it the kind of intensely personal love that is the hallmark of God's own unique relationship to that person. God knows and loves this person in the very depths of that which is personal in him. And so it is not strange, then, that

as living sacraments of Christ's own *agape,* we should find that
after struggling to remain open and to accept all our feelings
toward this person *"in Christ"* (feelings, perhaps, of dislike,
threat, boredom, or the like), that in our attempt to accept and
listen more deeply to his needs, we have actually come to "really
care" for this person. We have come to be genuinely concerned
about him and to realize that not only can we accept him fully as
a person but that, indeed, he is *loveable.* The growth and expression of such intensely personal love for another has nothing in
common with the erotic and sentimental expression of affection
that so often characterizes the popular image of love. This image
should not be mistaken for the personal self-gift in love of which
we are speaking. Self-sacrificing love demands the highest kind
of conscious, human wholeness and integrity, which is kept alive
only by the dynamism of death and resurrection in the mystery
of the Whole Christ. Neither is this attitude of unconditional
acceptance a kind of "professional care," an aloofness or concern "at a safe distance," or a sincere care "toned" by fear of
involvement. None of these less-authentic attitudes can communicate the self-gift of a body-person. They convey only a holding
back and a certain hypocrisy (nearly always unintended), since
the "whole" person is not available in self-gift. Only in communication through the *wholeness* of one's body-person can another
grasp and believe that someone "really cares" about him as a
whole person. The effective sacramental sign of "unconditional
acceptance" demands that we authentically (unconditionally)
accept *all* of the other individual as a body-person. We must not
just select *certain* aspects of him that we are attracted to, agree
with, or are not threatened by, we must be open to this human
being as a uniquely *integral incarnate-spirit.*

To illustrate this point, studies in contemporary psychology
show us that subtle, *non-tactile* ways in which we can convey our
interior attitude of acceptance or rejection of another's body are
clearly "signed" to the other through many channels that we cannot conceal or disguise. This only emphasizes all the more the
urgency for Christian prayer to be the in-faith development of
our whole body-person in Christ, so that our "in-faith-reflective-

body-person-selfless-presence-to-the-other" may be truly an authentic, sacramental sign of Christ's unconditional acceptance.

We should make it clear at this point that "unconditional acceptance" is directed toward the *person,* his "world of meaning," and his freedom to be himself. What we are accepting is his personal freedom to choose his own response to life. This does not mean that we have to agree with, approve, or accept *as our own* his feelings, decisions, values, ways of acting, etc. Whether these are right or wrong, noble or base, harmful or helpful is beside the point in an attitude of "unconditional acceptance." I must learn to understand and accept them *as his* because they are a part of *his* world of meaning. I accept *him* as he is. Whether a person's feelings have any objective foundation or whether his values agree with my norms of belief or conduct is quite irrelevant to the attitude of unconditional acceptance as we are describing it here. What is relevant is that certain values, feelings, etc., *exist in this person* whose individuality is so valued by God that He waits upon his free response to enter into a personal relationship with Him. I must become secure enough in my own identity in Christ that I can give some finite expression to this healing kind of unconditional acceptance at that moment when it is most needed (which usually corresponds to the individual's most "unloveable" expression of himself).

To approach another with an attitude of unconditional acceptance is to be willing to invest one's energies and abilities in an authentic personal concern for his human growth. It is an attitude toward all men that regards them as *potential* friends, realizing that "my" own fulfillment as a human being lies in this kind of consecration to the needs and development of the one Body of the Lord. As my love for the Whole Christ grows, so too does my self-discipline increase with a view toward insuring the well-being and fulfillment of the Whole Body. An attitude of unconditional acceptance toward others forces the Christian to rethink and replan his goals in life, so that "the others" may find opportunity and realization within them. To be disposed toward the unconditional acceptance of others is to imply that I deeply care and feel responsible not only for their physical existence but also for the growth and development of all their human resources for personal life in the Whole Christ. It is, in fact, to center my own satisfaction and personal fulfillment in the creative growth of another through the fascinating and sometimes thrilling life of incarnational prayer in the Whole Christ.

Unconditional acceptance, as an approach toward all people and as a way of interpersonal encounter, demands a deep faith-involvement with the Whole Christ. It calls for such a radical death to some of our strongest tendencies that without the power of Christ's *agape,* we could never live it out with any constancy. Such acceptance takes an "alive-relatedness" in faith to the Whole Christ in order really to allow another person to feel hostility toward me, to genuinely accept his anger as a real part of him, or to accept his immaturity and self-centered actions without rejecting him in my attempt to handle my own feelings of threat. It takes the security of a fully "body-person conscious relationship to the Whole Christ" to permit those I work with, teach, socialize with, or meet only in casual conversation to feel, act, and think differently than I do, particularly on those issues or problems in which I have a considerable emotional investment. Yet, in the existential order of every-day, body-personal communication, how can I sacramentally and visibly "sign" my unconditional acceptance of others, unless I permit them to have their own feelings, beliefs, and unique personal responses as a real and vital part of themselves?

We have spoken from time to time about each individual's own world of meaning. But now the reader must ask himself a crucial question regarding the effective communication of his own personal relationship to the Whole Christ through unconditional acceptance. Is he willing to risk trying to enter into the personal meanings, feelings, viewpoints, etc., of others with such sensitive emptying of himself at that particular moment that not only does the other's world acquire such value that he does not judge or evaluate it, but that he also actually begins to *lose* the desire to *approach others in this judgmental manner?* Can he acquire the attitude that as wrong or strange as another's world may seem to him, there is still something very precious in it, and it should "feel" almost sacrilegious to tread on his meaning with a heavy foot?

This does not mean that there is no value to the "judgments" implicit in law and the demands of certain standards of social conduct, which every society needs to function in an orderly way to achieve its common goals. These norms are there in order to make personal life possible, to support and motivate personal growth, responsibility, and the interiority that ultimately contributes to a well-ordered society. But we can never legislate the free, personal response of charity. "Disapproval" can never beget love. The reason we must approach another person's unique world of meaning without a judgmental manner is simply because this "way" of acting can do no more than reveal to him that he is self-centered. While this may be a laudable step on the way toward Christian life, it is only the first primitive level—a sort of modern parallel to the time when God gave the Law to Moses on Sinai.

As the reader has already come to realize, the Christian apostle who is living an efficacious, sacramental prayer-life must be so deeply rooted in his own mature self-identity within the Whole Christ that he is strong enough to retain his freedom and "separateness" in the self-gift of himself to others. He must have grown to that level of mature congruence in Christ where his own feelings, needs, etc., are listened to, accepted, and integrated into his sacramental encounter with others in such a way that he retains his own personal identity and independence, as well as balanced emotions and good mental health. His own human maturity and inner security in Christ must give him the freedom to go selflessly, with considerable depth, into the lives of other people without losing himself.

Lastly, in examining our disposition for communicating the sacramental sign of unconditional acceptance, we might ask ourselves whether or not when we meet others we can really encounter them as "becoming-persons"? By this we mean that our interpersonal relationship with them reaffirms and gives unconditional value to their unique vocation "to become themselves," to grow into their personhood, to continue toward "becoming a person" no matter what their past or what their present state of immaturity, ignorance, or self-centeredness may be.

Do we have a deep respect for the unconditional self-worth of each human being, whose God-given vocation in human history is one that he must *grow into* within the Body of the Whole Christ? Such an attitude toward all men can come only from each Christian's deep convictions, grounded in his own faith-experience of body-personal growth in the Lord. From such a personally "lived-experience" of myself as a continual "needer" comes the attitude of unconditional acceptance of another's whole "becoming-person"—past, present, and what he may become— if only I can be so "totally for him" that the power of *agape* may energize his "becoming-person" into its fullness of maturity in the Whole Christ.

THE VISIBLE SACRAMENTAL EFFECTS
OF "UNCONDITIONAL ACCEPTANCE"
IN FAITH

There are several other aspects of unconditional acceptance whose importance merits closer examination in the next few pages. We must, however, again preface our remarks by saying that the following signs are, of themselves, incapable of conveying divine revelation to those who witness them unless the persons involved have openly responded to the free gift of faith, and bring it to these "incarnated moments" of God's self-communication.

The first of the visible effects, which is obviously at the very heart of "signing" our acceptance of another, is the communication of a sensitive, open listening. This sign is so vital, and yet so easily neglected, that we must constantly work at becoming better and more active listeners. Our aim in listening is to understand the world of meaning of the other as he himself understands it, and therefore our listening takes on a special, visible quality. We strive to listen intently by trying to grasp as much as we can of what it is like to feel, think, react from this other person's point of view; in a word, what it is like to *be* this person.

We can communicate this to the other by keeping our attention on *his point of view* rather than "sizing him up," thinking ahead to "what I want to say" (and thereby not really listening to him), prejudging him, playing a role, launching into a monologue "to set him straight," etc. Our whole exterior manner of facial ex--pression, tone of voice, posture, etc., should tell the person that we are truly interested and care about how *he* looks at life. We intend to let him share himself with us without standing over him in judgment. We can convey this, for example, by *not* telling him *how well we understand* what he feels about something, "since we ourselves went through or are going through the same thing." This may seem like a strange way to show respect for another's freedom and uniqueness, but it is an important sign that many people of good will neglect. Most of us may recognize the danger of being too quick with advice, but we easily forget that we can know the experience of another only by analogy with our own, and that each person's encounter with reality is a unique mystery that we can never fully understand.

Another manner in which we may sign our unconditional acceptance is by using great care not to put subtle forms of pressure on another's freedom. We sometimes unwittingly fail in this by letting others know, in a variety of elusive ways, the importance of our position as priest, teacher, well-educated person, or religious. We imply that this carries with it an authority and a dignity that "tones" our personal world of meaning (and its feelings, opinions, and reactions) with a veracity which, in reality, it does not possess.

In a similar manner, we must not naively allow our position and sincere concern to become the means whereby another surrenders the necessary risk involved in personal choice. Many people, fearing the threat of their own freedom, will gladly hand their will over to another, but at the expense of their continuing growth toward personal responsibility and maturity.

"Unconditional acceptance" is just another empty phrase until it is actually communicated through understanding. By understanding we do not mean the type of knowledge that either "pigeon-holes" people or is directed toward "figuring the person out" by using our own subjective experience as the norm for another's approach to life. We are speaking of a sensitive empathy that attempts to understand another *as he really is,* not as "I" would like him to be. I begin to understand a person and convey this to him only when I can permit myself to listen to him and accept what I hear, as it *really exists* in the other. This is why truly entering into the world of another is both a sign of open listening and an indication of that depth of understanding which conveys unconditional acceptance. To say to another person, either in word or action, that "I accept you" but, in fact, to know little or nothing of his "real self" because I cannot or will not try to view reality through his eyes is certainly a very shallow acceptance.

Moreover, it does not require the power of *agape,* and therefore cannot be an efficacious sign of an authentic unconditional acceptance. But if I can try to understand another by actually entering into his world of meaning, seeing how life appears to him, how he feels about things, why he reacts the way he does, and *still accept him,* then this provides a profound experience of selfless love. This experience can initiate the self-knowledge and self-acceptance by the otheor person of his *real* existential life, with all its conflicts, self-centeredness, selfishness, and weaknesses. This is his first step toward personal growth in the Whole Christ. One has only to recall the many Gospel scenes that manifest our Lord's effective understanding of those He met, such as the meal with the sinners and tax-collectors that we described earlier, or His meeting with Mary Magdalene, to realize the impact of the effective body-personal witness of His attitude of unconditional acceptance. The Gospel's narration of His interpersonal contacts with sinners shows that while clearly preserving His personal integrity and rejection of sin, He never once conveyed the slightest indication of an attitude of moral righteousness or smugness that would have "signed" his personal rejection of the sinner. Christ knew they needed His unconditional acceptance if they were to be able to accept themselves as sinners, and to turn for their salvation in loving thanks toward One who had accepted them as they were.

Real understanding, which is not a permissiveness, a softness, or an indulgence, is rather the human sacramental sign of God's own respect and continuing confirmation of each person's freedom mediated through the Whole Christ. It is God's incarnated, personal sign of encouragement, His loving call to each of us to assume the responsibility and not to fear the risk of taking on the vocation to which He calls us. It is the visible symbol of God's here-and-now belief in us so that we can respond in faith because we have experienced as body-persons the living, unconditional acceptance of Emmanuel.

Effectively communicating unconditional acceptance presents a very difficult problem within the kind of social structure in which most of us live. Nevertheless, we must try to create in the atmosphere within which we meet and contact others a climate that is not characterized by external evaluation. This is one of the most serious barriers to communicating unconditional acceptance that the "church-identified" person must continually break down.

Obviously we are not holding for a kind of total indifference to externals, nor for religious indifferentism. We are saying that in the area of effective, sacramental sign-communication we must do considerable rethinking and restructuring of the atmosphere in which we educate and orient our young people for apostolic work, as well as very honestly evaluating the sacramental sign-value of all that is connected with the apostolic works which now engage us.

It is a psychological truism that the more anyone is faced with an evaluating environment, whether in the form of a person, an institution, or just the social atmosphere within which he must live, the more need there is for an attitude of defensiveness. This brings with it a consequent lessening of freedom, the denying and repressing of personal experience, and the use of other mechanisms to handle the inevitable frustrations that have stifled growth in responsibility, self-knowledge, and creativity through personal response.

To approach others without an attitude of external evaluation does not mean that one relinquishes his own feelings, ideas, reactions, and the freedom to express them. Instead, it means that one's communication must be the authentic expression of what we have discussed as an attitude of unconditional acceptance,

without any of the overtones and subtle sanctions assigning a
goodness or badness to another's differing world of meaning,
thereby implying that his personal worth is included as well. If
we are to communicate that rather intangible but crucial personal
value of "really caring," which may open the window on God's
"Personal concern;" we must never see people as objects that in
some way stand outside or over against us. Instead, we should
try to view them *within* us, *within* the *common* personal life we
share in our struggle to open ourselves to the Whole Christ. We
must find an identity, a oneness, and a strength in the common
bond of "becoming" in the Whole Christ, a becoming into which
the very life of God Himself has been suffused, so that we may
trust, rejoice, and openly share with others the wonderful Good
News of our salvation *within the human condition itself.* As
Christians, this is the principle moral ideal and the tradition we
must uphold. Insofar as we lose sight of it, we slip into a tragic,
blind, and isolated self-regard that "signs" to other men our vision
of them as "objects-outside" who must respond to reality in *our
image* before we will accept them unconditionally as persons.

Nor must we ever "sign" to others that our acceptance of them
is conditioned by our intention (no matter how noble) of mani-
pulating and controlling them for what we consider their own
good. By such subtle means we sometimes tend to rationalize what
is not a genuine sacramental sign of unconditional acceptance, in
which a person's growth in self-respect is made possible and in
which he can come to see himself as a person worthy of the
confidence we have placed in him. Instead, we have effectively
"signed" our lack of trust and faith in him.

A profound difficulty arises when the sacramental and visible
sign that is communicated (whether by the individual Christian
or by the Christian group with which he is identified), is one that—
rightly or wrongly—conveys to those struggling to remain Christians or to those outside the organized structure of the Church a
feeling of their worthlessness or alienation because they do not
measure up to certain standards and predetermined expectations.
In such instances we can not witness to the meaning of our faith
in the Whole Christ. Every human being first needs to be helped
to believe in himself and in others. The last thing that a Christian

should communicate to anyone is a betrayal of this most basic human need, by seeming to "use" another person for the "cause of Christianity," for the betterment of the Church or religious community, let alone to compensate for any unfulfilled personal human needs like status or a languishing self-image. The "signed-action" of unconditional acceptance has to be characterized by the *clearest* kind of honesty, human integrity, and Christian, existential congruence in the Body of Christ, as we have already discussed it. This is not possible unless such "signed-actions" are accompanied and supported by the type of incarnational prayer of which we have been speaking. They are empty unless, in fact, they *are* the very incarnated expression of our dialogue with the Whole Christ. This kind of "transparency" makes it possible for others to "look into" the living heart of the Body of Christ *within* their world of meaning, and to be moved toward entering into this life with belief and love. Failure here speaks much too convincingly for high-sounding words ever to retract that we ourselves suffer from a faltering faith in the Whole Christ, and as such have not yet been made whole. "Your faith has made you whole" (Mk. 10:52,C). We ourselves are "needers." We ourselves must always come to the Body of the Whole Christ in faith, asking to be made whole.

Faith is always the crucial issue in any religious experience. So too is it the decisive point at stake in our "signing" of unconditional acceptance, for it speaks in the concrete and visible language of body-person communication of that depth of entry which we personally have made into the mystery of the Incarnation. The risk in faith that all of us must undertake throughout our lives is in listening and accepting the self-centeredness, selfishness, and frailty in ourselves and yet continuing to believe in the good that is also there. We do not, of course, find God in our selfishness, but when we experience someone really loving us through his unconditional acceptance of us *as selfish,* we can then risk the same listening and acceptance of that selfishness in ourselves without identifying totally with it. We can risk being present to the evil within us, accepting it and trying to search for the same "power of redemptive love" that made it possible for this other person to transcend his own self-centeredness in order to communicate unconditional acceptance to us. When people can risk getting "close to themselves" in this way, they can then begin openly to acknowledge their need for a power greater than themselves if they are to continue to live and grow at this new level of "redemption." They can look for Emmanuel within this new way of self-discovery and self-worth, and in the new faith and trust they can have in the "in-betweens" of interpersonal relationships with others.

The Christian apostle enters into the very redemption of others when he effectively communicates in his whole body-person the unconditional acceptance he has for them. And this redemption, made possible only in and through the *agape* of the Whole Christ, is often first revealed to the beneficiary through the human signs of his own increased wholeness. It is found, for example, in the gradual breaking down of defense mechanisms, the growing capacity to listen to more of reality, in a greater freedom to make decisions and to assume the responsibility for them, and above all, in the capacity to believe in oneself and to want to share oneself with others. Truly, our growth as persons is not apart from our growth in the Whole Christ! Our prayer must help us effectively to "sign" our unconditional acceptance of another by lovingly and willingly entering through body-person, sensitive listening and understanding into his very incarnate being —his body as well as his spirit, his animality as well as his rationality. Our understanding, penetrated with the power of *agape,* must be dynamically directed toward every level of the person's affectivity as well as his cognitive powers, so that slowly the mystery of his own unique person may unfold within this experience of incarnated love. He can then grow to appreciate and love the unique mystery of others, inviting them to join him in the glory of being human, as they mutually share "becoming a person" in the Body of the Lord.

No more beautiful and deeply moving sign of our faith in the Incarnation and of our understanding of its continuation in the Whole Christ could be better expressed than to help another "incarnate himself" in "becoming a person in the Whole Christ." Our redemption follows upon the Continuing Incarnation in the Body of the Whole Christ.

13. Final Reflections on Self-Identity

A REFLECTIVE BODY-PERSON MEDITATION

In order to help the reader organize and make more tangible some of the rather abstract ideas regarding prayer presented in previous pages, we will bring our discussion of effective, interpersonal, sacramental signs to a close with the following schematic reflection. We simply propose this outline as one of many possible ways of organizing a personal "reflective-body-person-meditation" on the material just presented.

I. I begin with an attempt to *listen more actively,* more sensitively to all of the things I come into contact with around me

A. by allowing myself to *know consciously* what my bodily senses feel; for example, heat, cold, fatigue, affection, headache, etc., and

B. by consciously trying really to listen to and accept my feelings; for example, discouragement from being criticized, the feeling of depression because of having done poorly in an assignment or important job, the hurt feeling that follows someone's unkind remark, the insecurity of not being able to cope with a job, the jealous resentment at another's success, that gnawing anxiety about tomorrow's possibility of failure, etc. (*Really to listen,* however, is a gradual process that takes time and much honest effort; to learn to match whatever I am feeling with my awareness of that feeling also takes practice.)

II. However, while I am working at this first step, I must, as
a Christian, simultaneously learn to be open to what these feelings, sensations, etc., tell me about myself as a body-person in
the Whole Christ.

A. *As a Body-Person:*

1. I must learn to recognize automatically that all of these
sensations, appetites, feelings, etc., tend (to a greater or
lesser degree, depending on their strength) to focus my
body-person consciousness on "myself." For example, the
more I feel bodily heat, exuberant joy, discomforting pain,
a sense of accomplishment or aggressive and resentful feelings, etc., the more these tend to occupy the *center* of my
attention and my experience of reality. My body, my feelings, or my needs become the focal point of my *conscious*
preocupation. This spontaneously happens to me whether
I choose to be conscious of it or not.

2. Therefore, I have to grow in the capacity to advert to
this fact immediately, as soon as I am consciously aware of
how I feel at the moment, I need to *close the gap* between the
appearance of my feelings and my reflective awareness of
them. But I must answer the question:

3. Why do I want to know how I feel about this person, or
this situation, or tomorrow's uncertain circumstances? Precisely because I recognize that all of these feelings to some
extent (and particularly when they are strongly felt) *close
me off from listening to the needs of others.*

4. Therefore, to know when I am closing off or have
closed off to aspects of reality around me, especially other
people, is of extreme importance to my personal development and interpersonal maturity. My spontaneous feelings
and my ability to advert to them consciously must become
as simultaneous and close as possible through a more active
and reflective listening to myself.

B. *As a Body-Person in the Whole Christ*

1. However, as a Christian I bring a certain "graced"
understanding and faith to all that I discover about myself
in this harmonizing process.

2. Since these feelings (of their very nature) tend to focus my attention and my sensitive listening in on myself and, therefore, to close me off to others, I need to discover some *consciously experienced strength* in the midst of all this if I am to turn outward and keep in contact with all of reality—especially to listen to and answer the needs of the Whole Christ.

3. However, I experience that the "theological *truth*" of the Whole Christ does not seem to move me as a body-person. Of itself, it is not sufficient to heal my felt-experience of being strongly pulled inward by my selfish feelings and desires, no matter how sincerely I may will to accept and believe this doctrine. The Christ of history, of obstract faith, is not enough. *I need to find the Whole Christ in my existential life right now, as I experience it as a body-person.*

III. *The Task of Existential, Incarnational Prayer*

A. I begin to realize that my prayer and my conscious relationship to Christ must be such that within the growing "prayerful atmosphere" of my daily life-experience, my attempt consciously to integrate my body-person into the Body of the Whole Christ must be like a constant theme, a background melody—not something that is always "thought about," but more of an atmosphere, a presence, an added dimension that tones and colors my every action. I must become a contemplative in my faith-response as I put together my body-person and the Body of the Whole Christ. But the "subject matter" of my contemplation includes my body-person responses to the "Needing Christ," the "Loving Christ" as He manifests Himself to me in His Body. I contemplate before, during, and after my every encounter. This does not necessarily mean "thinking" about God, it does mean being "*aware*" that I am in His presence.

B. Consequently, I must begin to become more sensitive to those "in-faith-body-person" experiences of the Whole Christ that are personal to me, that I can *feel* about, that are an existential part of my world of touch, taste, and sight. And as I become aware of those moments when I experience being called out of myself by the "needs" and "love" of His Body, then I must begin to let these experiences be brought to bear on my own feelings of selfishness. I *cannot balance* a *"feeling"* of selfishness with an *"idea"* about God. Feelings are *balanced* by feelings. "Thoughts" can be used to repress feelings, but if my "selfish-body-person-feelings" are to be healed, I must open myself as a body-person to an *experience* of the incarnate needs and love of the Whole Christ *in order to be healed by them.*

1. Thus, I must set about integrating what I become sensitive to in faith in the Body of the Whole Christ. As my interpersonal life and my daily experiences of the world, color, sound, music, pain, and joy become suffused with the "sense" of God, I must let this body-personal experience of the Body of Christ be the source of strength that heals my selfishness. It is a beautiful thing when, for example, the Christian wife can, in faith, approach her husband's needs as truly the incarnate needs of Christ's Body *that only she can answer* and that, in turn, save her because they call her out of herself. She is surrounded by God in her husband and her family if only she has "the eyes to see and the ears to hear."

2. The Christian must be prepared to say with the Psalmist: "My heart is ready, O God, my heart is ready!" (Ps. 108:1,RSV). Our encounter with the world and our reactions to it must begin with the prayer: "Lord, I feel and know my need in Your Body, to be open and listening to *all Your needs.* I truly need the needs of your Body to heal me! Where are these needs in my life? Help show me where your needs are *in my experience.*"

C. *When I am actively involved with others*

1. If I am conscious of my need for Christ's healing presence while I am actually involved with others (or am soon to be), I make a kind of plunge in faith and try *really to listen* to one of those persons around me. I listen in such a way that I hear the real *feelings* that are *behind* the words, the *"silent* words and sounds" of what the person is really

trying to say. Thus, I try to be sensitive not only to his words but to the *tone* of them, to listen deeply to *needs* that perhaps even this person cannot risk speaking about. I try to put myself *in touch* with more of the real person that I am in contact with not by prying, asking questions, or pushing myself on him but only by a more *selfless, active listening*.

2. *I try to listen to someone else in the same sensitive, active way I have learned to listen to myself.*

3. I then may go one step further. Just as I try to accept all that I listen to in myself, so now I can try to accept what I hear in the *other person.*

4. Moreover, just as I have realized that I frequently cannot accept the threatening, painful, and frightening aspects that I find in myself or my life if I am in isolation and alone, so too, if I hear these in another, I realize that this person needs me and my acceptance of him "the way he is" if he is to be able to listen to himself and accept what he hears. No man can hear and accept himself alone.

5. So now I am challenged with the delicate task of trying to resonate what I hear back to this other person, so that he can gradually realize that someone cares enough to understand, that someone is truly struggling to listen to his "real self."

6. However, at one and the same time that I am both listening and resonating, I realize that I must communicate the *genuine acceptance* which I have of him before he can feel comfortable enough to risk the listening and accepting of himself. I must "sign" this acceptance in a body-person way. So I must mature in my capacity to communicate acceptance through the signs that might convey this attitude as well as open listening to him.

7. Some of the signs

a. First of all, my active listening and my struggle to resonate accurately the *true* feelings of the other is an extremely effective sign of my interest and concern for this person *as he truly is*. It implies a genuine acceptance and value placed upon his "real self."

b. Other signs might be: to listen without judging or evaluating what I hear, conveying this to the other not only in words but in posture, facial expression, tone of voice, and the like; *not* jumping ahead of him in my listening, anticipating what he will say next, and already planning what I am going to say *while* he is talking; *not* trying to "figure him out"; *not* previously making up my mind what the other person is going to tell me; *not* listening in order to manipulate the other person; *not* playing the role of counselor, teacher, or psychologist in my sensitive listening; but simply being another human being who is *genuinely incomplete* as a person without the friendship of this individual; allowing this other person to be *different* from myself and to remain with dissimilar ideals, values, points of view, etc., until he freely chooses *to change himself;* appreciating and accepting the other's deep regard or gratitude toward me (if it should be extended) in an unthreatened and genuinely grateful manner.

D. *When I am not actively involved with others*

1. I might begin this way, and then let the Spirit guide me: using my memory, I focus my attention on recalling and seeing in my imagination a person or persons, an event or circumstance of the past day, of recent days, or perhaps in the *immediate* future (preferably dealing with someone or some situation that is regularly a part of my daily experience).

2. I do this in order to ask myself very concretely a question or questions: "Where has Christ's incarnate presence been most obvious in my day today, or where will He be tomorrow? In what person or events did He call out for me, will He call out for me? Who needs me within my world of meaning? Where does Christ wait for me to listen to His needs tomorrow, this afternoon, or this morning?"

3. With my powers of recall, my imagination, and memory of past body-person contacts with a particular person or event, I re-create the scene in a calm, reflective dialogue with Christ, asking Him to help me find His presence in-

carnated in this situation, person, or event. Or I can simply use my imagination more, and see myself talking, teaching, nursing, visiting, or whatever it is that has been or will be my active interpersonal contact with the persons in my life who are, for me, the sacramental sign of the presence of Christ.

4. The point of my *real* dialogue with Christ in the *re-created* situation of my imagination or memory is to call me out of myself within a world of experience that is truly *real for me,* although not actively participated in at the moment. However, if such a contemplation is grounded in my real-life experiences, it can better serve to catch hold of *my entire body-person at prayer.* I not only "think" about people but in a sense, let their body-person presence to me (filled with their needs or love) be very real to me (like the "presence" of lovers who are physically separated) and, in faith, become aware of this felt-presence that incarnates the "needs" and "love" of others as, in fact, the presence of the Whole Christ.

CONCLUSION

If this re-creating of my world of meaning is not done alone but with Christ, it can then serve to help me grow more sensitive to His needs. I will see "with Him" where I was closed to this person or persons, and I can try to "tone" my coming day with greater sensitivity and more "open listening." Or, in the event that I feel very strongly pulled inward or find myself slipping into an unreal world of my own selfishness or self-preoccupation, the conscious effort to bring the Whole Christ into contact with *my real existential world* of experience in this kind of contemplation not only helps pull me out from this closing-off process, but takes me as a "needer" in faith back into that active involvement with others, but now more attuned by His continuing presence and with a renewed openness, in faith, to the life of *agape* that heals my selfishness.

A point to be remembered is that whether I am alone or

actively involved with others, my more reflective or more contemplative prayer must always be aimed toward keeping Christ
in *"my world of meaning"* in as much of *my body-personal awareness* as I can consciously bring to Him, and in experiencing Him
as someone who is *truly present,* alive, and relevant *to me.*

SOME FINAL REFLECTIONS ON
SELF-IDENTITY

As we bring this book to a close, hopefully the reader will
have to come to realize that the "identity crisis" of which we
spoke in Part I is, in many ways, a searching for what we might
call "a faith confrontation with ourselves in the Whole Christ."
It is the quest for a self-identity truly rooted in Christ as He is
present within our search for ourselves.

There is a strange kind of Gnosticism that pervades the philo-
sophies of man in our contemporary world, which, although it
speaks loudly of human self-realization, often uproots man from
his very identity as incarnate-spirit because it refuses the risk of
faith. No man can afford to become a "body-person" without
faith. His efforts to unravel and know the secrets of himself and
the universe end by alienating him either from his body or his
spirit if he approaches the mystery of his oneness apart from faith.

But this oneness is a body-person unity in "becoming"; as such,
it must grow toward self-realization within a Body that strengthens
and supports the totality of the emerging person. Each of us
must discover that our "becoming-person" is somehow caught up
within "another Becoming-Person," and that the mystery of our
growing union and identity with one another as incarnate-spirits
is rooted in the depths of the gradual revelation within us of a
much deeper mystery: "We, though many, are one body in
Christ, *and individually members one of another"* (Rom. 12:5,
RSV). (Italics ours.)

Somehow each of us must risk the tension of being at the same
time one and many, body and spirit; we must plunge in faith into
the life-experience of gradual integration if we are to find our true
self-identity. We will discover our identity only when we can risk

living an openness in faith to breathing in *all* of reality. Such a struggle for body-person wholeness cannot help but bring us into contact with the wholeness and holiness of the Body of the Whole Christ. Trusting in the incomparable selfless love of God, we must open ourselves to be gifted with "the eyes to see and the ears to hear," in faith, that we are "becoming a person in the Whole Christ."

In His Body I must grow in oneness and in the resolution of the apparently insoluble tensions of my existence. In His Body I must find my true self and be reconciled with my very being. In His Body I must learn to believe in myself and to accept the frightening estrangement that from time to time wells up to challenge my faith. In His Body I must learn to love the emerging "real self" and to experience the affirmation and acceptance that silences the confusion and loneliness of those trying moments when I begin to lose myself as *really* being *"in Christ."* In His Body, I must come to know as a whole body-person, as did St. John, that "I am the disciple whom Jesus loves."

My Christian self-identity is a vocation, a goal, a mandate to be realized, to be gradually grown into and personally made my own. It was given to me in Baptism, but given to me *in* the Body of the Whole Christ. What I bring to this vocation is my own unique, human response to life. This life is my personal history, encompassing all the forces, circumstances, people, and environments within time and space that shape me and call out for my response. My self-identity in the Whole Christ is, therefore, immanently involved in my human growth and development. It is this unity of the human with the One Body of the Lord that must be the guiding principle directing our religious formation, education, and prayer so that our response to God's self-gift may be an integral and body-personal one.

This direction should then continue in greater personal depth and with increased integration and freedom within the vocational commitment we make to the Whole Christ—whether in marriage, the priesthood, single life, lay institute, or the religious life. The specific preparation, "formation," or education that we establish to help those who enter upon their vocation must mature and support this direction of personal development toward a firm self-identity in the Whole Christ, making it possible for authentic "in-faith-body-person-selfless-presence-to-others."

The "personal realization" of so much that goes into the entire process of human development is learned not only through study and reflection but by "atmosphere" and by the concrete, visible signs that form the experience of "becoming a human person." We learn most effectively and are influenced most deeply throughout life by our relationships to those aspects of reality that touch us as whole body-persons. This is just as true of our capacity for religious experience as well.

The whole area of knowledge about our human nature in its incarnate-spirit drive toward interpersonal realization has been largely overlooked in religious formation. Studies in the behavioral sciences have helped us realize more clearly that we come to know ourselves *in relationship* to the realities around us, especially to other human beings in our interpersonal dialogue with them. The growing self-image and consequent self-identity acquired in this environment is what we then take to all our relationships with others, including the Divine Persons.

However, the *intellectual grasp* of the psychological laws of human growth and sound mental health, accurate and insightful as they may be, are never enough to develop within a person the capacity for self-gift and mature, responsible love. What is needed is an *experiential* knowledge that can be grasped by the whole person, responded to in faith, and then lived out in the Spirit.

The real spelling-out of this on the horizontal level is the task of religious formation and education today. It is a challenge in which the struggle for human wholeness, human integration, and self-realization as body-persons is discovered in faith as our growing awareness and identification with the Whole Christ.

Conclusion

WHAT WE HAVE TRIED to develop in this book is an approach to active contemplation, solidly grounded in a philosophy of man that emphasizes his wholeness as incarnate-spirit in a "becoming" process made possible by the human, spiritual qualities of transcendentality and reflexivity. We have further incorporated these insights into an explanation of man's interpersonal growth by stressing a psychology that is developmental, evolutionary, and dynamic rather than normative. We have done this in order to avoid a stress that does not place enough emphasis on individual response and "readiness."

Moreover, we have accented a psychology of man that is cognitive rather than psychoanalytic. We feel that such an approach is more open to the philosophical, sociological, and theological synthesis that each of us must consciously make as we explore our potential openness to all of reality and take up the challenge of that basic vocation to which God has called us. That vocation is not only to become a human person but to become a human person in the Whole Christ.

Although the psychology used in this book depends for many of its insights on work done in the areas of abnormal, psychoanalytic, and experimental psychology, the development presented here represents our attempt to view man's psychological growth not from the standpoint of the curative or pathological but from a broader synthetic frame of reference. It is one that seeks to unlock and discover man's rich potentialities, especially his capacity for interpersonal relatedness, within the *normal* growth of his "becoming a person." Hopefully this has indicated something of the direction that "becoming a person in the Whole Christ" must take. Perhaps, too, some may be prevented from exhausting the wonderful gift of human life in those many futile attempts at self-actualization that frustrate the full flowering of the Father's call to "become a person in the Whole Christ." In this book we have not attempted to spell out these deviations or wounding experiences along the path of healthy self-realization in the Whole Christ (as necessary as they are to the complete picture of man). Instead, we have sought to concentrate our efforts on expressing to our readers what we believe are some clearer insights into the "way" of divine self-communication within the human evolution toward personal fulfillment. This is a gradually evolving synthesis that hopefully will be more clearly articulated as the years go on. But its already discernible presence today dares us to extend our vision and our personal living into the dynamic fringes of newborn life in the Whole Christ.

A man must first be a person before he can selflessly love; and our freedom to be a person is given to us by another, by one who loves us. Once we have known what it means to be loved and to be able to love, to be received by another and accepted for what we are, nothing can ever rob us of this strength, this inner freedom to live and to exist no matter what the external circumstances of our life may bring. We know what it means to exist in faith. We have experienced what it means to have someone believe in us. We know who we are because we have seen ourselves through the eyes of another, through the eyes of one who loves us; and we know our identity and our dignity.

Thus it is that a man possesses the strength to go out from himself and believe in others, to love and to give to those outside himself. He can now commit himself to love others because he can love the self he must give to them. He has experienced this self as loved by another. He knows he is lovable, and he can then want to give himself to another.

But finding ourselves as person is not something that suddenly happens. It is the lifelong task of man, for he was made in the image and likeness of the Three Persons in the One God, and the infinite complexity of man's person defies description, categories, and concepts. "Person" cannot be restricted to any of these, for it is incommunicable and unique, and its freedom and eternality ring with the immortal, the divine, and the infinite.

If God the Father is a person and Christ is a person and we are persons, is it no wonder then that even though the distance which may separate us is infinite, yet there is, nevertheless, something we share that makes it possible for both to be persons? Little wonder then if man is not born a person, if it does not suddenly happen at some stage of chronological maturity, but rather that his person must be called into existence by some mysterious degree of that which makes the Persons in the Trinity to be Persons—viz., their relationship in love to one another. For that which distinguishes the Persons in the Trinity is relationship, "relatedness" of one to the other—and this relationship is a love relationship. So man's coming into personhood must participate in at least some faint degree in the love relationship of the Trinity. Someone outside of him—another person—must call him out of himself to "be-in-relation," to be "love-related," to know himself to exist as love-related. No one becomes a person in isolation. And no Person can exist as Person in the Trinity in isolation. What makes the Father the Father and the Son the Son is their relationship to one another. And it is this relationship that makes them exist as Persons, distinct and incommunicable, loving and loved.

For man to become a person, then, is something that is given him, something to which he is called by another. He does not confer it upon himself, nor can he make it with his own creative powers and ingenuity. The process of becoming a person is a dynamic one, a slow and sometimes agonizing struggle to listen to the call of another and to respond. It is beset by all of the risks the complexity of man can contrive, by all the subtle nuances of personal confrontation from grossest exploitations to the ecstasies of profound openness and intimate union. There is a continual birth that struggles to take place, to open out of self into a world of love and communion, to climb toward integration and wholeness in encounter with the other, to discover and penetrate

the meaning of those mysterious forces within that cry out for
fulfillment and realization.

To carry forward this human task of becoming a person means
that after we have been called by another's love to discover who
we are, we then go on to share this discovery with others. We
accept the challenge of being loveable and turn this outward, not
inward onto self but we open ourselves to others, taking on the
risk of exploitation and approaching them in availability in order
that we may give.

But then suddenly within the very heart of love, at that moment
when we most deeply desire to love completely and openly with
the totality of self-gift, we discover that we can go no further.
We are helpless, for there is some deep-down, driving force within
that is trying to pull us back, trying to pull us to turn in on self
and away from the totality and perfection of gift to the other.
There is always some force that compels us to put up barriers to
protect ourselves from a kind of emptiness, a void, a break within
us that is not yet mended, an open wound that needs protection.

Even the most sublime of human loves, even the greatest and
highest expression of self-gift I can bring to offer another person,
even my most vivid and conscious awareness of his or her presence and the reality of our love—even all this has not the power
to call me out of myself for any but a flashing moment in the history of this love. I cannot sustain the gift of myself to the other
even though it is the deepest craving of my consciousness. Somehow I am still alone in the midst of my love. I am helpless to
control the forces that pull me inward and cause me to clasp
and pull my beloved into the web of my own ensnaring self. Once
again I must choose to go out and to believe. And so I reach
even further, risk even more the pain of opening myself as a
"needer," believing that Someone will grasp me if first I can
bear to extend my hand and touch.

Then slowly I begin to discover that I am being born once
again, that what I thought was finished has only just begun, that
now the pains of birth are even more severe than when it cost
me so much just to open myself to receive the love that made
me whole, that gave me the thrust forward which has brought me

into this new experience of birth and creative love. And I begin to realize that I have only just begun to live. For life is a gift, and I have just begun to give. Life is slowly beginning to course through the arteries that feed my emerging person in this new Body of love. Each day's confrontation with the Other who calls out more and more of gift from me brings new depth and growth, new energy and completion to the task of being a person. I am slowly becoming more a person through this mysterious communion with Another into which I have entered. I have found my "becoming-person" in the Body of the living God. I have found myself in the Whole Christ.

Only Christ can sustain me in love. Only Christ can open me to growth. Only Christ can love me so deeply that I can continue to call out to others to be, and to be in Christ. For without Him, at best I find I can only whisper this call like a dying echo. For my despair, my helplessness, my frustrations crush me deeper into myself with their growing weight if I move toward becoming a person outside of Christ. There is no hope outside of Christ. There is no life outside of Christ. There is no creative love outside of Christ—only fading glimpses like the colors in a sunset.

Appendix

A Meditation on the Christians Apostle's Becoming a Person in the Whole Christ

IN THE PAGES that follow we have attempted, in brief outline form, to provide certain material which is more immediately applicable to the apostolic work of those involved in Christian education, counseling, and other forms of pastoral activity. These schematic reflections are not a summary of the book, although they obviously build upon the insights discussed therein. The thoughts contained in the next few pages are presented in outline form in order that they may be more easily accessible to the reader either for personal meditation or as the basis for group discussion.

SOME PRELIMINARY REFLECTIONS

I. Most of us have had the experience of trying to communicate Christ to the modern generation and found that there are many other sensibly appealing attractions in their lives which compete with the more abstract truths of theology.

> Children: an interest in play
>
> Teen-ager: intense preoccupation with companionship, athletics, social life
>
> Collegian: concern with professional education, business career, marriage

286

II. If a young person's encounter with God is with the God of an adult world, then God seems quite irrelevant.

III. It is always the *God outside his experience* who is being imposed upon him.

IV. The evidence that most convinces today's youth that Christ is alive (and relevant) is their personal meeting with someone whose life is permeated with the implications of the Incarnation.

V. The object of faith is not a set of abstract truths but a Person; and the "truth" of a Person can only be witnessed in a truly "personal" life.

VI. The present stress on the value of "person" permeates the culture we live in as well as Church renewal.

A. *Positive value in the Church*

1. The growing stress on "person" in the documents of Vatican II. The basic emphasis throughout these documents is on the deep and delicate respect for the mysterious dignity and measureless value of each individual human person.

2. Scripture scholars stress the fact that the biblical understanding of "person" is important because God sees us only as persons, deals with us as persons, and wills us to become ever more the persons He made—saints. The documents of Vatican II have only one purpose: to glorify God by making total persons, or saints, of men.

B. *Positive value outside the Church*

1. Secular humanism and the value it places upon individual uniqueness and freedom.

2. The growing sense of solidarity within the family of man. Never before has there been such widespread sensitivity on the part of so many young people to their social responsibility for one another.

a. The Peace Corps, at home and abroad; Amigos Anonymous

b. The Civil Rights Movement

All of these programs are symbolic of the younger generation's struggle to find themselves as persons. They are concerned with other people as persons because they are searching for themselves as persons.

VII. All of this brings us to a more integrated approach to Christian formation in which we must emphasize our own personal growth in Christ as the source of effective catechesis.

A. The heart of this approach is a deeper discovery of Christ in our own lives, and as a consequence a more dynamic living faith that we can then share with those whom we encounter.

B. The "stuff" of my response in faith to Christ is found in answering God's call to me to become a person, in responding to this basic vocation which all men share.

C. It is in deeply penetrating, exploring, meditating upon, and accepting this vocation to become a person that I will discover the Person to whom I am to commit myself in faith; namely, the Incarnate-God who is fleshed in my very struggle to become other-centered as a way of life.

1. We truly apprehend the presence of God only when we become conscious of the transformations accomplished within us by His Presence.

2. Our most basic need as human beings is to become "persons." So it is within this struggle to become a person that Christ must become real for each of us. This is the point in our lives where we experience the "transformations" that are filled with the incarnated personal presence of God.

D. The first human, interpersonal phenomenon that we must become conscious of in this growth process is what we will call:

DIFFERING WORLDS OF MEANING

I. In His Incarnation, Christ presented us with the model for all effective communication of divine life to mankind. God comes to people to invite them *just as they are*. He communicates Himself on their "incarnate" terms.

II. We must bring Christ to others through their eyes and into their world of meaning.

III. This may seem obvious, but it is a point that is commonly overlooked and that requires tremendous maturity on our part because it demands:

A. a constant attitude of openness to another's way of looking at reality (which is usually quite different from my own)

B. a capacity for sacrifice and responsible love.

IV. If the Christian apostle is not to be removed from the experience of the one whom he encounters and not to seem unreal but rather to be capable of understanding his deepest needs —he must have a capacity for selflessness that enables him to discern in each individual whom he encounters, a deep yearning to respond to his vocation to become a person.

V. To be able to do this, each of us must develop the capacity for a kind of *special, deep listening* that involves the following sensitivities:

A. I must be able to listen to their needs, hopes, desires, and especially their disguised calls. In other words, I must be sensitive to everything about them that they bring to me *because* they are *human* beings—their whole world of meaning, precisely *because* it is theirs.

B. Entering into their world of meaning can be done only through the sacrifice involved in going out of my own. In other words, I must have the capacity really to listen to more than my own world of meaning.

C. The problem I soon confront as I listen to what people are trying to tell me about themselves is that they subtly express their genuine feelings through various masks that life has forced them to wear. If I am sensitive, I realize that these are the masks they *must* wear in order to protect themselves in various ways from those who cannot or will not try to understand and accept them as they really are.

D. But often, because of my own world of meaning and personal history, these masks are so repulsive that they threaten me and I close off in fear from the real person who desperately needs my authentic presence and understanding. Consequently

I require an entirely new power of life if I am to live with the pain and tension of this kind of daily threat. I need a new strength greater than my feelings of fear, insecurity, inadequacy, and inability to live with the pain of this kind of other-centered existence.

E. This obviously is where Christ must enter into our own growth as a person, in order that we may be able to risk entering the world of others, enduring the threat posed by their way of defending themselves and yet remaining open and authentic, strengthened by the love of Christ so that we may help them to become persons in Christ.

1. A natural problem arises here about entering another person's world of meaning. Does this mean that I must identify myself with the personal values of one who is childish, irresponsible, or selfish?

We must carefully distinguish between identifying with:

a. our shared need to become a person, and

b. different worlds of meaning and their values. I do *not* have to identify myself with their world of meaning, but I do have to try to *accept* and *understand* their world of meaning, precisely because it is theirs. I must respect their freedom and accept them as persons as they are here and now, just as God does.

F. *Conclusion:* My function as a Christian apostle is, first, to encounter other men *as a person myself* by entering into their world of meaning in order to reveal to them the mystery that is themselves—as persons. By encountering them in the openness of authentic acceptance, I enable them to find their deepest identity not in *extrinsic* cultural or environmental values, but rather in their potential capacity for selfless love and for personal gift of self to another.

1. When I, as a Christian apostle, encounter another, but without the capacity for entering their world, without the capacity for open listening and accepting them as they are, without the strength of this other-centered interpersonal life, I do not free them by this encounter to listen to and accept themselves as they really are. I do not reveal to them the

mystery that is themselves as person, by showing them their value through my acceptance.

2. I do not help another to be able to reflect on his own experience in his struggle to become a person, to be aware of the tension between other-centeredness and self-centeredness, and consequently to be opened up to the need for the power of an unselfish love greater than his own inability to transcend his isolation.

3. It is hopeless, barring some miracle, for anyone ever to experience the person of Christ in his own life if the one bringing the message of Christ is not himself a person.

THE BASIC EXPERIENCE IN THE WORLD OF MEANING OF ONE WHO IS STRUGGLING TO GROW IN PERSONAL LIFE—A DESCRIPTION

I. Let us now get inside ourselves and our own experience as one struggling to grow in personal life (i.e., one capable of leading an other-centered life with constancy in listening and responding to the real needs of others).

II. These next few points should be gone through as a reflective meditation in which the reader uses each succeeding point as a sort of springboard to his own experience. The statements point out what is common to all of us, but the reader must "personalize" each of the more generic statements by reflecting on his own life experience.

A. I experience the pain, or the rejection, or punishment caused by my lack of capacity to be social (e.g., the child who refuses to share his toys, or the conversation monopolizer who is shunned at a party).

B. I am aware of the frustration of continually living in this pain, of always being coerced to socially acceptable acts from outside by the laws, customs, and traditions of society.

C. I am aware of my helplessness in the face of this frustration. I experience my own self-centered needs as well as the punishment directed at me when I attempt to satisfy them. I find myself in a tension that I cannot resolve. I need help from some source other than myself and the law that coerces me if I am to resolve the tension in which I find myself.

D. I experience someone *"freely"* listening, available, open, and accepting me *just as I am* (*selfish and frustrated*). They do not impose conditions on their acceptance, implying that they will accept me only *if* I am good. They accept me the way I am.

E. This causes confusion in me and awareness of a mystery. What strength or power enables this other person to act unselfishly toward me without being coerced to their action from the outside? What is the source of this inner strength? I begin to realize that I need this same strength if I am to escape the tension in which I continually find myself. This is still a very self-centered attitude because I do not want this capacity in order to give myself to somebody, but only so that I will be able to escape punishment and rejection.

F. I realize that whatever I need is *not apart from* this other person relating to me. Somehow it comes to me *in* this person's free actions and attitudes toward me. Therefore, I need other people, and I cannot be fulfilled and happy without them, but . . .

G. As I come to know this other person better, I become aware that he has a capacity for free self-gift and other-centeredness as well as the same pull inward that I experience within myself.

H. I experience a certain ambivalence in his relationship to me and perceive that he needs help too. He has the same need for another's selfless love in order to be fulfilled, and especially to be fulfilled in giving of himself.

I. I come to realize that there are forces both within myself and from the outside that cause me to close off, to isolate myself in order to protect myself from the very people I need in order to grow in personal life.

J. I find myself listening only to my own needs and not to the needs of others, and living this selfish preoccupation out in varying degrees.

K. I come to realize that I am in a tension between self-centeredness and a call to other-centered life in a struggle to fulfill myself as a social being. I need to love selflessly in order to be a person, as well as being loved selflessly by others.

L. But I also realize that I cannot be coerced to love selflessly by the law. This interior power of a capacity freely to give myself to another is itself a *gift*. In other words, I come to realize that I can only love when I have *first been freely loved as I am*. This is the only way in which I can transcend my own selfishness.

A REFLECTION UPON MAN AS A SON OF ADAM

I. How does Scripture reveal to us that this human experience, which we have just described, is really our experience as descendants of Adam?

II. The Christian apostle makes God relevant precisely by showing that such a common human experience has been revealed by God to be the experience of man as a son of Adam.

III. When the Christian apostle enters into the world of another, he must be quick to sense the deeper personal life-experience of the other in order to reveal the Christian meaning of this human experience.

IV. With Scripture the Christian apostle shows them

A. Who God is.

B. Who they are (a son of Adam, in relation to God).

C. The Good News: not only are we sons of Adam (as we directly experience it), but also there is the possibility of experiencing that we are Sons of God as well.

V. We begin with our own human experience, not God's revelation in the abstract. We enter directly into their world of meaning in order to bring them the explanation that Scripture gives of their experience. (Example of St. Paul's speech in the Areopagus to the men of Athens regarding their altar to an unknown god [Acts 17:22–31]).

VI. How does St. Paul show that the experience of one who is struggling to grow in personal life, which we have just described, is really the experience of man as a son of Adam, awaiting a Redeemer? We must carefully read chapters 7 and 8 of his Epistle to the Romans:

A. We experience the pain and punishment caused by our lack of capacity to be social. Law as an external force (whether embodied in parents, customs, traditions, or civil legislation) reveals to man that he is self-centered. "In the absence of law, sin is a dead thing. There was a time when, in the absence of law, I was fully alive; but when the commandment came, sin sprang to life and I died" (Rom. 7:9,NEB). Apart from his painful conflict with the law, man does not realize that he is self-centered. The purpose of the law is to bring man's self-centeredness out into the open by placing it in conflict with a commandment to be other-centered.

B. We experience the frustration of living in this painful conflict. We acknowledge that acting according to the law and accepting our social responsibility is a value, but at the same time we find ourselves unable to do this because of another law (the law of self-centeredness which we discover within ourselves). "I do not even acknowledge my own actions as mine, for what I do is not what I want to do, but what I detest. . . . I discover this principle, then: that when I want to do the right, only the wrong is within my reach. In my inmost self I delight in the law of God, but I perceive that there is in my bodily members a different law, fighting against the law that my reason approves and making me a prisoner under the law that is in my members, the law of sin" (Rom. 7:15, 21–23, NEB).

C. Man acknowledges his helplessness in the face of this painful tension. He recognizes that the law itself, while valuable because it revealed his self-centeredness to him, is nonetheless unable to help him to do anything about it. "The commandment which should have led to life proved in my experience to lead to death, because sin found its opportunity in the commandment, seduced me, and through the commandment killed me. Therefore the law is in itself holy, and the commandment is holy and just and good. Are we to say then that this good thing was the death of me? By no means. It was sin that killed me, and thereby sin exposed its true character: it used a good thing to bring about my death, and so, through the commandment, sin became more sinful than ever" (Rom. 7:10–13, NEB).

D. Man acknowledges his need for help, his need for a Redeemer, someone who will freely enter into his frustrating struggle with the law of his members and the law of God that reveals his selfishness. Man can find no source of power either within the law of God or within his own members that will enable him to overcome the tension in which he lives. Paul summarizes the helpless frustration of this dilemma with the classic cry of the son of Adam: "Miserable creature that I am, who is there to rescue me out of this body doomed to death?" (Rom. 7:24, NEB).

E. Man experiences someone "freely" listening, available, open and accepting him *just as he is* (selfish and frustrated). Again it is Paul who breathes a sigh of relief: "God alone, through Jesus Christ our Lord! Thanks be to God!" (Rom. 7:25, NEB). Christ is the Redeemer who enters into Paul's agonizing struggle with his own self-centeredness. By becoming incarnated within the family of man, Christ brings a power into human history (the sending of His Spirit) that enables man to solve the tension from within.

F. Man acknowledges that the power which he needs is not apart from the person of Christ the Redeemer. Man cannot be fulfilled as a human person (one with a fairly constant capacity for other-centeredness) apart from Christ. "The conclusion of the matter is this: there is no condemnation for those who are united with Christ Jesus, because in Christ Jesus the life-giving law of the Spirit has set you free from the law of sin and death. What the law could never do, because our lower nature robbed it of all potency, God has done: by sending this own Son in a form like that of our own sinful nature, and as a sacrifice for sin, he has passed judgement against sin within that very nature, so that the commandment of the law may find fulfillment in us, whose conduct, no longer under the control of our lower nature, is directed by the Spirit" (Rom. 8:1–4,NEB).

G. We must finally place everything that we have discussed in the last two sets of reflections into the broader context of our development in the Whole Christ. Each man must open himself to the Whole Christ to be saved by the Whole Christ. His tension with the law is resolved when, in faith, he can accept the gift of self from another as the free acceptance of Christ. This is his experience of *agape* within the family of man that resolves his tension as a son of Adam, and through the gift of the Spirit enables him to repeat the joyous cry "Abba, Father" as a son of God.

HOW HAS GOD REVEALED TO US THAT CHRIST IS THE ANSWER TO THIS TENSION?

I. *The Old Testament:*

We must first recall that the primary vocation that God gives each of us in creating us as human beings is the vocation to become a "person." But first God had to reveal to man what it meant to be a person before man could become a person in Jesus Christ. Let us therefore briefly recall for a moment how God revealed this basic vocation to man in the Old Testament. What does man find out about himself from *the way God treats him* in the time of the Old Covenant? A few reflections on Yahweh's relation to Israel will give us a deeper insight into God's "personal" relationship to man, even at this more primitive stage of his "personal" evolution.

A. God's attitude toward man can be summed up in the following manner:

1. God *takes an interest* in man
2. God *freely* goes out to man
3. God *assumes the personal initiative* in inviting man into a Covenant relation with Himself
4. God, as other-centered, is *faithful* to man, even though man is self-centered and frequently unfaithful in his own relationship with God
5. God asks for a *free* response from man, and the Prophets continually underscore the need for a response from the heart.
6. God *shares His own life* with Israel (seen in the blood-sharing ceremony on Mt. Sinai).

B. Now let us attempt to get inside the Israelite, to see things from his world of meaning and consider this relationship that God has established. What does this relationship tell me about myself? Reflecting on this matter like an Israelite, I come to the following conclusions:

1. I have some intrinsic worth because God *freely* chooses to give Himself to me.
2. I know that I am not forcing God to do this, and neither is anyone else. Therefore, I must be of some value in the eyes of the person of God.
3. I know that a covenant union is a union of people capable of freely responding to another's gift.
4. This union shows me that I am free to respond, that God wants me to respond, and that the response is of person to Person.

C. Now, stepping outside of the more interior reflections of an Israelite, we can objectively consider the effects of God's relationship on the Hebrew people:

1. As God continued to reveal to the Israelites who they were, they began to realize that becoming a person involved individual responsibility to one another and to God. There is a profound evolution in Israel's sense of responsibility, manifested quite clearly in the Prophet Ezekiel. "The word of the Lord came to me again: 'What do you mean by re-

peating this proverb concerning the land of Israel, 'The fathers have eaten sour grapes, and the children's teeth are set on edge'? As I live, says the Lord God, this proverb shall no more be used by you in Israel. Behold, all souls are mine; the soul of the father as well as the soul of the son is mine: the soul that sins shall die. If a man is righteous and does what is lawful and right . . . he shall surely live, says the Lord God" (Ez. 18:1–9,RSV). The primitive Israelites had formerly thought that a son was punished for the sins of the father (the fathers eat sour grapes and their children's teeth are set on edge). Now God tells them that each man is responsible individually for his own observance of the law.

2. Finally, because God chose the husband-wife imagery to show His own union with Israel, this told the Hebrews something about the dignity and value of human love and interpersonal life, as well as about the intimacy of the relationship that they were called to live with God.

D. The presence of God to man in the Old Testament was seen primarily in the Law. But the Old Law was still only an external force in the lives of men. The perfection of interiority and new life in the Spirit, which was to come in Jesus Christ, had not yet been made manifest. Consequently, the tendency to stress God's presence mainly *through the Law and the exact observance of the Law* still left man with the frustration summed up in Paul's cry: "Miserable creature that I am, who is there to rescue me out of this body doomed to death?" (Rom. 7:24,NEB). It must be remembered that Paul himself had been a learned student and vigorous defender of the Law before his conversion: "As a pupil of Gamaliel I was thoroughly trained in every point of our ancestral law" (Acts 22:3,NEB). Yet even Paul felt the heavy burden of this observance. Without the interior power of the presence of Christ's Spirit, the Law was still helpless to free man.

II. *The New Testament:*

These few preliminary reflections on God's relationship to man in the Old Testament and the Old Law now bring us to the New Law, the law of love that frees man from this helplessness and frustration. It frees him to become a person within and because of the dynamic power of selfless love, *agape,* which has been loosed within him as the gift of God.

A. To live according to this New Law is a profoundly liberating experience for man because his whole growth process (his struggle to become a person) is now raised to God's own kind of interpersonal life—the life of *agape.* Man is now called to share in God's own divine capacity to love others with a personal, total gift of self.

B. Christian life, then, becomes not just a following of man's psychological potentialities for maturity and self-realization—for integration, human fulfillment, and actualization—but rather *the very transformation of these potentialities through, with, and in Christ as a member of His Body.*

C. The Christian can now act out in faith an increasingly free and deeper response to the presence of "this-Person-Christ" (the Whole Christ) in his own world of meaning, experience, and life history.

D. This brings him more and more into the personal, familial life of the Persons of the Trinity. It initiates him into a totally new world of personal encounter within his world of meaning.

E. Let us attempt to get inside this experience and make it more personal:

1. While my relationship to these Persons is not yet perfect open friendship, nevertheless the gift of faith that I have received from Christ enables me to struggle to commit myself more to discovering *His Presence* incarnated in my own world of struggle to become a person.

2. This lived-out faith: *that I am related to a personal God in Christ and that I will find Him related to me in my own world of meaning and experience* enables me to call Christ *my* Brother and Savior, to call God *my* Father, and to call the Spirit of Love the source of *my own personal love-life.*

3. This kind of dynamic faith becomes my answer to God; but it is *not* a response to "Someone far away" through a blind, inhuman, unknown, and unexperienced kind of effect. Instead, it is my whole human *body-person response* of emotion, senses, appetites, intellect, will—everything that makes for an integral, human psychological response—to the presence of the God who took on all of these human qualities as His own and "pitched His tent among us."

4. I commit myself to becoming a person, with all that this involves by way of self-awareness and acceptance of both myself and others, as I struggle to listen to their real needs and respond to them. I choose this now as a way of life because I believe that this very psychological, human process *is Christ's*. I believe that all things belong to Him, that everything is to be returned to the Father through Him, and that the Christ in whom ". . . everything in heaven and on earth was created . . . and in whom all things hold together . . ." (Col. 1:16–17,NEB) will reveal Himself to me in my life-chapter of Sacred History, as I struggle to respond to God's basic vocation for me—to become a person.

GROWTH AS PERSON—GROWTH IN CHRIST

I. Through the Incarnation, Christ has become so much a part of the process of personal growth, that to become a person and to grow in Christ have really become two aspects of the same reality. (They are in no way separable.)

A. We can grow as a human person only as we mature in our capacity for another-centered life. We become persons only by transcending our pull inward to selfishness (our heritage from Adam).

B. But the law is powerless to help us achieve this interior transformation. It is only through the free gift of *agape* and a gradual incorporation into the incarnate love-life of the Whole Christ that we gradually begin to be able to live with the inner life of the Spirit and transcend the "law within" which "leads us captive into sin."

II. To open ourselves in faith to the experience of growth as a person is to gain the possibility of access to an *experience* of Christ incarnated in our own personal life. The one does not exist without the other. This is the true meaning of "incorporation into Christ." We are "in-corporated," "em-bodied" within the incarnate love-life (*agape*) of the Whole Christ.

III. Scripture always tries to tell me something about my experience. It tries to tell me the truth about the deeper dimension and significance of my "person-life."

IV. We have these truths from revelation, but we have often so colored, interpreted, and reworked them in order to have them fit into preconceived needs or intellectual and ascetical traditions that *what we are, as revealed by God, frequently becomes clouded.*

V. Our personal history makes it difficult for us really to "hear" what God is telling us *about ourselves.* We are certain that He has spoken *to us,* but we do not realize the significance of what He says *about us.*

A. After 2000 years we still find it hard to believe the radical significance of the Incarnation. We believe that it happened. But we cannot believe that a transcendent God has become so much a part of us. We still want to draw lines and say: "The Incarnation touches me, but only in the way in which I interpret it, with my prejudices and background."

B. *We find it difficult to believe that He is really Emmanuel at the heart of our interpersonal experience.*

C. It is so easy to let our historical prejudices cut us off from true sources of holiness.

1. The Jews drew a line between themselves and the other nations and refused to believe that "... the salvation of God had been sent to the Gentiles" (Acts 28:28,RSV).

2. St. Peter could not believe that the dietary prescriptions

of Jewish law presented artificial barriers that, for those who lived in Christ, no longer existed: "About noon Peter went up on the roof to pray. He grew hungry and wanted something to eat. While they were getting it ready, he fell into a trance. He saw a rift in the sky, and a thing coming down that looked like a great sheet of sail-cloth. It was slung by the four corners, and was being lowered to the ground. In it he saw creatures of every kind, whatever walks or crawls or flies. Then there was a voice which said to him, 'up, Peter, kill and eat.' But Peter said, 'No, Lord, no: I have never eaten anything profane or unclean.' The voice came again a second time: *'It is not for you to call profane what God counts clean'* " (Acts 10:10–15,NEB). (Italics ours.)

3. St. Paul, the careful student of the Law, lent the full weight of his scholarly background to crumble those artificial barriers that men place to the sources of God's presence in the world when he broke with a central prescript of Jewish life—circumcision. "If we are in union with Christ Jesus circumcision makes no difference at all, nor does the want of it; the only thing that counts is faith active in love" (Gal. 5:6,NEB).

4. But even in the recent past, many Christians themselves have sought to restrict the presence of God's sanctifying power to the visible structure of the Roman Catholic Church. And it remained for the voice of another Paul to speak once more the Christian truth in union with the Fathers of the Second Vatican Council: "This Church, constituted and organized in the world as a society, subsists in the Catholic Church, which is governed by the successor of Peter and by the bishops in union with that successor, *although many elements of sanctification and of truth can be found outside of her visible structure."* (Italics ours.)[1]

D. Man has a tendency to view portions of reality, of his own body, and of his personal growth as though they existed in isolation from the Continuing Incarnation of Christ within the family of man.

---

[1] *The Documents of Vatican II,* p. 23.

E. The truth which each succeeding generation must continually re-learn is that the Incarnation has radically transformed *all* of creation: ". . . no single thing was created without him. All that came to be was alive with his life, and that life was the light of men. The light shines on in the dark, and the darkness has never quenched it" (Jn. 1:3–5,NEB).

F. No matter how men may try to isolate creation from its Creator, the light of His incarnated presence will continue to break through the darkness, until the scales fall from their eyes and they relearn the timeless truth that "the world *is* charged with the grandeur of God."

6. As I experience the growth of *agape* and the capacity for other-centered personal life in my daily experience, it is one more link in the ever-widening mystery of the revelation of the Glory of God, the mystery of the birth of the Whole Christ that Paul described as the plan for the fullness of time.

A REFLECTION ON MAN'S DAILY EXPERIENCE OF DEATH AND RESURRECTION IN THE WHOLE CHRIST:

I. Let us return to our last reflection on ourselves as sons of Adam, the experience of ourselves in a tension between self-centeredness and other-centeredness as we try to become persons. Here is the invitation to faith; here is the possible Christ-event in my life *if I will:*

A. Continue to accept my vocation to become a human person, and

B. Respond to the gift of faith by recommitting myself to the discovery of the Whole Christ in this call to growth.

II. This involves Christ revealing Himself to me *within my experience of myself as related to "all" of reality and as related to the pain of my trying to relate to others with responsible love.*

III. Spelled out from the "inside," this means developing an incarnational prayer or dialogue, existential in its ever-deepening, conscious awareness of the *union* of the psychological and theological realities in my life *as my experienced relationship to the living God.*

IV. We might describe these reflections as *my growing conscious experience of myself as redeemed in Christ.* Let us once again try to listen to our own experience and seek to become reflectively aware of the divine gift that is constantly being given to us.

A. We are aware of a "pull inward" that we share with all other human beings.

B. At some time in my life, if I have been so blessed, I experienced someone freely listening, available, open, and accepting me just as I was. I found them sharing with me and giving themselves to me to fill up my needs.

C. I became aware of a kind of resurrection within myself. The free gift of a new life was being born in me. I began to discover myself as loveable, valuable, and as wanted.

D. A peace, joy, and gratitude began to grow in me as a result of this experience. I also began to experience a need to return this same gift to "the other."

E. I then experienced a tension within myself as I attempted to "go out" to the other, to say "thank you," to listen to his needs more than my own, to risk entering into his world of meaning.

F. I began to discover that before I could live with the same selfless life as he, I had to die to my own selfish tendencies. Thus, a real existential death had to precede each act of resurrected "living-as-free-gift."

G. As time went on, I became aware of the deeper realization that the one who loved me selflessly nevertheless shared the same "pull-inward to selfishness" that I experienced within myself.

H. I gradually became aware of the fact that in our unselfish moments, we both lived with a power that did not have its ultimate source within either of us.

I. Thus I am confronted with a consciousness of the mystery of *agape*. It is the presence of the power of the Spirit of Love, the witness of Emmanuel (God-with-me in my own relationship to this other person) that reveals that Christ is truly living, although seen "through a glass darkly."

J. I accept this moment of mystery with faith, as a Christ-event, and I surrender myself to this experience of reality "in Christ," believing that He will reveal Himself to me in this experience of relatedness with another.

K. Perhaps I may also experience another moment of faith when I experience my ability to love unselfishly and actually transcend my own pull inward. In this experience, I am able to listen to and selflessly respond to the needs of another (even while I am acutely conscious of my own self-centered needs). It is in this moment of "weakness" that, with St. Paul, I discover the "strength" of Christ.

L. I grow stronger in my awareness of who I am, of my real identity, of an interior strength and feeling of self-worth as I grow more conscious that *"I am not alone."* I listen to my feelings, struggles, reactions *as related to the Whole Christ.* These human experiences have now become a *"We" experience.* Christ is not an object outside of my world of meaning, but a Subject—the "Thou" of my relatedness to the other(s) of my experiences in human interpersonal life. I am not afraid to live close to myself and accept myself as I really am in my relatedness to others, because this life is close to Christ, to the Whole Christ.

CONCLUSION

I. From the very beginning Yahweh made it clear to Israel that they could discover Him only when they were able to risk the terrors of an act of true faith. His "personal" presence could be discerned as they opened themselves to the forces of creation, believing that they were *His* forces. The thirty-eighth chapter of the Book of Job paints a magnificent picture of the God of Creation as he "laid the foundations of the earth" and fashioned the awesome powers of nature that terrified primitive man.

II. The God of Israel then spoke through the mouth of Isaiah the Prophet and commanded His People:

> "Fear not, for I have redeemed you;
> I have called you by name, you are mine.
> When you pass through the waters
> I will be with you;
> And through the rivers,
> They shall not overwhelm you;
> When you walk through fire
> You shall not be burned,
> And the flames shall not consume you . . .
> Fear not, for I am with you" (43:1–5,RSV).

Just as the primitive Israelites were to find God in the forces of water, wind, rain, flood, and fire, so modern man must risk meeting the person of God in the equally challenging mysteries of interpersonal life.

III. It should give all of us courage and hope to realize that the real barriers that keep us from communicating Christ to others are not age differences, varied backgrounds and education, different cultures, etc., but rather our inability really to listen to ourselves and others, and to accept ourselves in our struggle to become ever more a person in the Whole Christ. We must be able to listen to and accept this very struggle within the world of meaning of every person whom we contact. It is only when we are faithfully taking on this task that we can then invite others to listen and to look in faith for the presence of the incarnate God *in their own struggle* to find themselves as "person" in "the Word that *is Flesh* and dwells among us."